Magazine Writing That Sells

Magazine Writing That Sells

Don McKinney

WRITER'S DIGEST BOOKS
CINCINNATI, OHIO

Magazine Writing That Sells. Copyright © 1994 by Don McKinney. Printed and bound in the United States of America. All rights reserved. No part of this book may be reproduced in any form or by any electronic or mechanical means including information storage and retrieval systems without permission in writing from the publisher, except by a reviewer, who may quote brief passages in a review. Published by Writer's Digest Books, an imprint of F&W Publications, Inc., 1507 Dana Avenue, Cincinnati, Ohio, 45207. (800) 289-0963. First edition.

Other fine Writer's Digest Books are available at your local bookstore or direct from the publisher.

00   99   98   97   96   7   6   5   4   3

Library of Congress Cataloging-in-Publication Data

McKinney, Don
    Magazine writing that sells / by Don McKinney.
        p.   cm.
    Includes bibliographical references and index.
    ISBN 0-89879-642-3
    1. Authorship. 2. Authorship—Marketing. 3. Journalism—Authorship.
    I. Title.
PN147.M475   1994
070.5'2—dc20   94-753
                                                                     CIP

Edited by Jack Heffron
Designed by Sandy Conopeotis
Cover designed by Laura Kuhlman

The permissions on the following page constitute an extension of this copyright page.

PERMISSIONS

The author gratefully acknowledges the following for granting permission to reprint their work, work that appeared in their publications, or work by writers they represent.

The Atlantic Monthly, for the excerpt from the article by William Langewiesche.

Conde Nast Traveler, for the excerpt by Ron Hall.

Esquire, for the excerpts from the articles by Phillip Caputo and Robert Sam Anson.

McCall's, for the excerpts from the articles by Glenn Joyner, Rick Soll and Gene Mustain. They are reprinted with permission of *McCall's* magazine. Copyright by the New York Times Company.

The Liz Darhansoff Agency, for the excerpt from the article by William Kennedy.

The Robbins Office, for the excerpt from the article by Ron Rosenbaum.

Peter Boyer, for the excerpt from his article.

Terri Fields, for her query letter.

Vanessa Grimm, for her query letter.

Pete Hamill, for the excerpt from his article.

Barbara Grizzuti Harrison, for the excerpt from her article.

Tyler Norman, for the excerpt from her article.

Jeannie Ralston, for her query letter and for the excerpt from her article.

Maxine Rock, for the excerpt from her article.

To Mary

ABOUT THE AUTHOR

Don McKinney was a magazine editor for thirty-one years, serving for seven years as assistant managing editor of *TRUE, The Man's Magazine*, another seven as articles editor of the *Saturday Evening Post*, and the last seventeen as managing editor of *McCall's*. He left *McCall's* in 1986 to take over the magazine sequence at the University of South Carolina in Columbia, and he retired in 1990 to Hilton Head, South Carolina, where he still teaches magazine writing at a branch of the university. He has written dozens of magazine articles and short stories, and he is currently editor of *The Good Life*, a publication for seniors on Hilton Head. This is his first book.

ACKNOWLEDGMENTS

Like an actor clutching his newly won Oscar, I feel there are far too many people to thank for their help on this book to list them all.

I particularly want to thank the writers who gave their valuable time to answer my questions and talk about their writing lives: Jeannie Ralston, Maxine Rock, Dick Meryman, Barbara Raymond, Dalma Heyn, Anne Cassidy, Dianne Hales, Judith Stone, Bil Gilbert, Joan Barthel and, of course, Bill Zinsser.

I want to thank the editors who gave me so much of their time, so that I could include the latest information and advice on writing for their publications: Midge Richardson of *Seventeen*, Stephanie Stokes Oliver of *Essence*, Rona Cherry of *Fitness*, Eric Schrier of *Health*, Janet Chan of *Redbook*, Pamela Fiori of American Express Publishing Corporation, John Mack Carter of *Good Housekeeping*, Mary McLaughlin of *Working Mother*, Mary Ann O'Roark of *Guideposts*, Ron King and Jim Sexton of *Special Report*, Tim Foote of *Smithsonian*, Phil Osborne of *Reader's Digest*, and Peter Moore of *Playboy*.

I owe a great debt to the librarians who were kind enough to share with me their knowledge of modern research methods and to correct the errors in what I wrote: Susan Fifer Canby, director of the National Geographic Library; Carol Tobin, head research librarian of the Thomas Cooper Library at the University of South Carolina; Michael Bennett, research librarian for the Beaufort County Public Library in Hilton Head; and Jan Longest, head librarian for the University of South Carolina/Beaufort branch in Hilton Head. And a special thanks to Chris Welles of the Freedom Forum for letting me reprint her definitive list of reference works.

I also want to thank those writers who allowed me to reprint excerpts from their work, who even dug around in their files to find the excellent examples of queries, leads and endings I have included in this book. A special note of thanks goes to Sylvia Burack, editor of *The Writer*, who graciously allowed me to reprint portions of articles that appeared originally in her magazine.

I want to thank all of the writers and editors I have worked with over the past forty years, for all of the things I have learned from them and which I have now passed along. I am thinking particularly of Bob Stein and Lisel Eisenheimer of *McCall's*, Bill Emerson and Otto Friedrich of the old *Saturday Evening Post*, and Doug Kennedy and Charles Barnard of *True*. And there were a great many more.

And finally, I want to thank my students who helped me translate a lifetime of experience into something coherent. If I had never turned to teaching, I could never have written this book.

Don McKinney
April 1993

Having spent more than thirty years seeing the low level of material submitted to magazines, not to mention the low level of much of what is eventually published, I know that it doesn't take any genius to break into print. This is the message I began delivering when I started teaching seven years ago, and a good many of my students acted on my advice. Some of them did extremely well.

I remember one particular student, Rebecca Sox, who was turned on by a John McPhee article called "Travels in Georgia," in which the writer accompanied two young scientists on a survey of the state's wildlife. Among other things, they collected the bodies of animals recently killed on the highway, and frequently cooked and ate them. A queasy subject, admittedly, but it caught Becky's interest, and she began digging around to see if anyone else had written about it. She came upon a professor who had done a book on road-killed animals and proposed a short article to one of the magazines published by Whittle Communications in Knoxville, Tennessee. The idea was okayed, the subsequent article was accepted, and she began sending them more ideas. Before long Becky's name was being passed around among the other editors at the company, and she was being called regularly with new assignments. Within a year, she was earning over $10,000 a year from her magazine writing.

And this was just a spare-time occupation. She was married, with a new baby and a part-time job, and was working on her master's degree in journalism. The moral here, of course, is that if she could make $10,000 a year in her spare time, think what you could do if you devoted all of your energies to the task.

There is no magic formula for selling regularly to local and national publications. It doesn't take any special talent, or friends in high places, or an armload of clips. None of these things hurt, of course, but they aren't essential.

Some years ago, a well-known company built its entire advertising campaign around the idea that there was a secret ingredient in its product that was responsible for its success. It turned out, when you read the copy, the secret ingredient was not a gimmick or even a real ingredient but something far less tangible — it was, the ad explained, the honesty and integrity of its maker.

Honesty and integrity are essential attributes for a magazine writer, too, but they won't guarantee success if that's all you have to offer. Magazine writing is a craft that can be learned, and anyone who is willing to work hard and has a reasonable ability with words can sell regularly. The ingredients of success really aren't secret; all successful magazine writers know them and use them. There's no reason why you can't do the same.

I mentioned hard work, and I meant it. You can't simply come up with an idea and jot it down on paper and send it off to your favorite magazine. You may earn a sale or two that way, but nothing you can pay the rent with. You have to know your markets and develop your ideas with specific magazines in mind. You have to research ideas thoroughly before presenting them, putting a substantial amount of the time and energy into getting the story before you even approach the editor.

As I said, writing is a craft. It is a profession. And it is the professionals who make money at it. Anybody can learn the techniques professionals use. Editors really aren't looking for big names — there aren't many in this business, and the writers whose names appear in large type on magazine covers have usually earned their fame through a best-selling book or some other well-publicized feat. Editors are looking for ideas that suit their publications, and query letters that promise solid, usable manuscripts. The writer may have sold a hundred articles or none — the *idea* is the key ingredient.

I remember two newspapermen who approached us at *McCall's* with an idea for a story about a nurse who had befriended a young girl in a state hospital. The girl had been labeled retarded, but the nurse saw real potential in her. After fighting the indifference and even hostility of the institution, the nurse finally succeeded in having the child retested — and declared normal. The little girl was placed in a foster home, grew up, graduated from high school, married and had a child of her own. The writers wanted to not only tell this story, but also to describe the reunion, many years later, of the nurse and the girl she saved.

We didn't know the writers who proposed the story, but we did recognize that the story was filled with the kind of emotional impact that couldn't miss. Again, the idea was the key.

I don't want to make the selling of an idea sound too simple, but I do want to get across the fact that there is nothing mysterious about it either. Editors are always looking for new writers and will work hard to help inexperienced writers with good ideas develop those ideas into publishable articles. There are never enough competent writers, and no competent writer should ever be without an assignment. Talent can't be learned, but competence can. And writing competently and professionally is what you're going to learn from this book.

Okay, enough warm up. Let's get going.

CHAPTER ONE

The First Secret Ingredient: Ideas

The genius of this business is ideas," Bill Emerson used to say. Bill was articles editor of the old *Saturday Evening Post* when I went to work there, and I was with him for seven years, first as his assistant and later as articles editor after he was promoted to editor. Bill knew what all editors learn very quickly: If there are going to be enough articles to make up the magazine, editors are going to have to think up most of the ideas. For the sad fact is that most writers don't produce enough good ideas. If you can learn to be one of those who does, your future is guaranteed.

"But I never have any ideas," is a common cry from my magazine writing students. Nonsense. Everybody has ideas — the trick is to recognize them when you see them. We all hear about situations that could be developed into salable articles. The young couple down the block, for instance; she works and he stays home and takes care of their new baby ("My Life as a Househusband"). The retired business executive who took up painting a few years ago is beginning to sell with greater regularity and for higher prices, and has now been invited by a local museum to put on his first show ("How I Found My Second Career — at Age Sixty"). Or how about your friend's son who was a football star in college and has been drafted in the fifth round by the Pittsburgh Steelers? Maybe he'll make it and maybe he won't, but isn't this a good chance to tell the readers of a sports magazine what it's like to try out for a professional football team?

READING FOR IDEAS

Somebody once did a survey of freelance writers to find out where they got their ideas. Topping the list was reading. Writers read several newspapers a day; they read the kind of magazines they want to work for, as well as magazines like *Time* and *Newsweek* to keep themselves up on new trends and ideas.

One writer I know told me he always made it a practice to read the local paper in any town he was in. He was looking for the local story — the one that didn't make national news. He read the columnists, in particular, since they usually had a good eye for human interest stories. He hit pay dirt on more than one occasion, but one I remember in particular because it turned into a story for *McCall's*.

It involved a woman who was bedridden with multiple sclerosis. By chance, she got a look at a doctor's report that said her condition was terminal. Furious that she had not been told, she was determined to prove her doctors wrong. She began exercising her arms, then her legs, and began to take tentative steps. By the time the writer came upon the story, she had taken up running and was planning to enter a local marathon. He called her, got permission to interview her and report on the race, and fired off a query. The result was a marvelously inspirational and suspenseful story — one that would have remained just a local story if one writer hadn't taken the ball and run with it.

Far too few beginning writers even see the ball, let alone realize what they can do with it. Some years back I spotted an Associated Press story about a woman who had been flying alone with her husband in their private plane when he suddenly slumped unconscious over the controls. Unable to fly herself, she had the wit to call for help on the radio. A nearby pilot heard her distress call and eventually was able to locate her plane and tell her how to land it safely. We assigned a writer and got a marvelous story.

The point here is that nobody came to us with this story: no local writers, who must have known of it before it went out on the AP wires, and not even any writers from anywhere who could have seen the wire story as soon as we did. The first writer we assigned was not available so we had to assign a second, and it was several days before she was able to contact the woman. During that time, dozens of writers must have read that newspaper story, yet none of them picked up the ball.

You have to train yourself to read the newspaper in a different way. Sure, you read to find out what's going on in the Balkans and who won the ballgame, but you should also read each story with an eye to how it might be developed into an article for some magazine. Or maybe more than one magazine.

MANY SALES FROM ONE IDEA

You're pleased to see that a high school girl won the amateur golf championship in your state. Let's think about this for a minute. Golf magazines often do articles on up-and-coming players.

What brand of clubs does she use? Perhaps the manufacturer publishes a trade magazine that uses freelance material.

Are there any publications in her hometown? A Sunday supplement, maybe, or a local magazine? And how about a magazine aimed at teenage girls? Wouldn't they be interested in the stress involved in achieving success at such an early age?

Many of these markets pay very little, but once you've done the basic reporting, it's not hard to slant it in different ways for different publications. And once you add them all up, it could be worth several thousand dollars.

And reading goes beyond simply newspapers and magazines. Have you ever thought of letting your fingers walk through the Yellow Pages? One writer I know of did this, and was interested to discover a number of listings for Chimney Cleaners, including one who wore the old-fashioned top hat and frock coat made popular by the movie *Mary Poppins*. That intrigued her and she called a few, finding an Englishman who was actually inspired by the movie and wore a costume like Dick Van Dyke. It made a charming feature story (and a $200 fee) for the local Sunday paper.

Look through the telephone book for unusual occupations, services you didn't know existed. A veterinarian who specializes in large animals or unusual pets. An automobile repairman who specializes in antique cars. What kind of experiences has a local locksmith had? Or how about somebody who puts on gorilla suits to deliver birthday balloons? And why not drop by the offices of one of your local detective agencies? Wouldn't they have some stories to tell?

As many people have observed, people love to read about people. All of the magazines devoted to gossipy stories about celebrities, from *People* on down, attest to that. And what else are the Yellow Pages full of but people?

Don't ignore bulletin boards, either. Sure, there are plenty of notices about upcoming auctions and bake sales, but sometimes you'll come across something interesting. Perhaps there's a man who will train your dog to be a watchdog. How does he do it? What kind of experiences has he had? Could an interview produce an article that would tell dog owners how to train their own pets to guard their homes more effectively?

Read everything you come across. Some years ago a writer was idly reading the copy on a bottle of Tabasco sauce and discovered it was manufactured in a little town in Louisiana. He got in touch with the manufacturer, went down for a visit and ended up with a long article in *The New Yorker*. All because he was curious enough to read the label on a bottle.

Don't ignore old magazines and newspapers, either. The story about the nurse who had rescued the young girl from the mental hospital came out of the back files of a newspaper. The reporters had been leafing through in search of something else when they came upon a story about a young woman who had sued her parents for abandonment. They looked her up, she told them her story, and the result was a series in their paper and an article in *McCall's*.

GO PLACES

While you can find a lot of ideas in the books and magazines and newspapers that come to your home, or you can find in the library, you can also get ideas just by being out there where things are happening. Make it a point to watch your paper for notices of public meetings, awards ceremonies or speeches by visiting dignitaries.

A few years ago, I noted an item in *The State*, a newspaper published in Columbia, South Carolina, where we were then living, which told of a series of awards in the arts being given out that afternoon at the State Capitol. One of the awards turned out to be for a grade school in Charleston, which incorporated the arts into its regular curriculum. The building that housed the school was in a poor neighborhood and, in fact, had been condemned, but some enterprising people had sold the city on the idea of a creative arts school. While parents were originally fearful of sending their children, it now had a waiting list of over fifteen hundred, with some children being enrolled even before birth. It seemed obvious that in a time of trouble for our schools the Ashley River Creative Arts School must be doing something right. I talked to some of the teachers at the ceremony, arranged a visit to the school, sent a query off to *McCall's* and got an assignment.

ANNIVERSARIES

You should always be on the lookout for anniversaries of famous and highly publicized events, or for an update on a story a magazine might have covered ten or fifteen or twenty-five years before. Perhaps they did a story on some unusual event — the first woman elected to the Senate, the birth of quintuplets, the first ascent of a mountain, a special space mission, the introduction of the birth control pill. A follow-up might well make a nice feature.

And think about some obvious and not-so-obvious anniversaries — the bombing of Pearl Harbor, the assassination of a president, the first arrival of the Beatles in America. Magazines love to do anniversary pieces, and if you come up with the idea first and have some fresh angle to justify a new look, you could get the assignment.

Finally, when you're thinking about what to read for story ideas, don't forget professional publications. Medical journals, for instance, report on new developments in health before the news reaches the popular press, and could give you a line on a new treatment or medication months before it becomes common knowledge. The same thing applies to any number of professions, so seek out the publications and get to the idea first.

START A CLIP FILE

Before I leave this subject, a most important point. When you see an item in a newspaper or magazine that sparks your interest, but doesn't suggest an immediate story, clip it out and file it away. It may not be a story yet, or perhaps you just haven't figured out how to make it one, but future articles might provide the information that will flesh it out. In her interview later in this book, freelancer Jeannie Ralston tells of having a file drawer full of folders; one file is on gambling and another is on guns and women. She doesn't know what she wants to do with them yet, but, as she puts it, "the minute I throw them out I know I'll need them."

Some years ago there were a series of strange newspaper articles about unexplained animal deaths in the West. As the weeks went on, different experts offered explanations. More deaths were reported. A writer who had started saving these clips from the beginning would have had a solid file when he was ready to write a query.

Invest in some manila envelopes and save everything that piques your interest. Leaf through them from time to time; you never know when an unusual set of facts will suddenly blossom into an idea.

PERSONAL EXPERIENCE

If something has posed a problem for you, it's almost certain that it's caused problems for others. Have you had trouble choosing a summer camp or school for your child? Have you or a friend had to cope with an unusual illness or injury? Do you have trouble getting along with your in-laws? Does your dog have a bad flea problem? Do you find yourself forgetting simple things?

Surely you've had *some* problems, and the solutions you've found could help others — and make articles. If you haven't found solutions, so much the better. Now is the time to consult the experts, study the relevant books and journals, do informal surveys among your friends. You're probably not the first to have this difficulty, but you could be the first to query a magazine about it.

A LITTLE HELP FROM YOUR FRIENDS

Friends can be a good guide to new trends and ideas. What are they talking about? What games are they playing? What kind of complaints do you hear most often? Are there common problems that might point the way to an article idea? Writer Maxine Rock says she gets all her ideas this way; in her view, once an idea gets into the papers, other writers may be ahead of her.

And think of your friends as resources. Chances are you know some people who might be the source for some good "How-To" story ideas. A stockbroker who lives on your street might have some interesting thoughts on investment strategies, and could tell you where to dig out the other information you'd need. A banker could tell you the best ways to refinance a mortgage, secure a loan or save money. A doctor or dentist might know of new techniques that could save you money—and your health or your teeth. Talk to a mechanic about ways to prevent problems with your car. Ask a police officer about ways to protect your home or to avoid being mugged.

And don't ignore such routine ideas as mothers who work; how do they handle child care, meals, cleaning? Talk to a dozen or so of them, and perhaps aim toward something called "Ten Ways Working Moms Save Time—and Sanity."

MAKING LISTS

Editors not only like "How-To" stories; they like lists, too. Look through a few magazines and see how many stories begin with a number. In one issue of *McCall's* I found "Five Hairstyling Tricks the Pros Use;" a list of the ten safest and ten riskiest states based on crime rate; five tips you can pick up from TV stars to help you dress more effectively; nine "best buys for your clothing budget"; five rules to follow in decorating your home.

Family Circle offered "Ten Smart Ways to Lose Ten Pounds" and "Mom, I'm Bored: Forty-Five Fun Things to Do," while *Woman's Day* really hit the big numbers with "170 Penny Pinchers: Save on Utility Bills, Clothes, More" and "248 Easy Ideas for Summer."

But the Big, Big numbers were saved for the Christmas issue. For Christmas 1992 *Woman's Day* promised "630 Merry Ideas" while *Family Circle* topped them with "660 Glorious Ideas." The mind reels.

When you're developing an idea, see if it lends itself to the list format, either for the main piece or a sidebar. (And think how much easier a list format is to organize!)

LOOK IN THE MIRROR

What interests you? What would you like to know more about? What makes you react emotionally? Do you always waste time waiting for service people? Does your bank account never balance? Is the mail carrier always late? Do people seem a lot ruder than they used to? If you're a woman, are you patronized by car dealers?

Look within yourself; if it bugs you, it's probably bugged a lot of others, including some of the editors who will consider your query.

Sometimes ideas don't hit you right away. I must have driven past an amusement park/gift shop/restaurant/motel on the North Carolina/South Carolina border twenty times before it occurred to me that it might make a good piece for the state magazine, *Sandlapper*. The next time I was passing South of the Border, I went in, talked to a young woman who did their public relations, read through some old clips of stories written about it in years past, was given the tour and had everything I needed to send off a query. They took it immediately.

A LITTLE SERENDIPITY

I'm not suggesting that you can't read for enjoyment, but also read with an idea to spin off story ideas. Michael Crichton's *Jurassic Park*, in which dinosaurs are cloned from traces of their DNA, makes a terrific adventure/science fiction story, but it might also suggest an article on just what scientists might accomplish with some of their far-out research. Genetic research is already an issue. Farm animals can be cloned and scientists are experimenting with cloning human fetuses. What might this mean for us all in the years ahead?

A new book on the Civil War might suggest a visit to some of the lesser-known battlefields. A popular historical romance, such as *The Volcano Lover*, by Susan Sontag, might suggest a travel piece on Naples, where much of it took place. The anniversary of the first publication of *Huckleberry Finn* could inspire a trip down the Mississippi river of today.

IDEAS FOR ALL SEASONS

When you're struggling for ideas, think about the kind of seasonal issues magazines will be planning for in the months ahead. (In most cases, I'm talking about five to six months ahead, so think accordingly.) Christmas in obvious, yet many magazines devote their entire issue to the subject, and as a longtime editor, I know how hard it is to keep coming up with fresh subjects for the holiday season. We all love to stockpile material against future needs, and I can remember buying Christmas pieces in January.

But don't quit at Christmas. Think about Thanksgiving, New Year's Day, the Fourth of July, Mother's Day, Father's Day,

(God help us, Grandparent's Day), Valentine's Day, Easter, Passover and back-to-school time.

Magazines don't devote entire issues to these subjects, but they usually want a few pieces to mark the season, and your ideas could be very welcome.

WHAT'S BEEN DONE LATELY?

Before I leave this subject, remember that if you can come up with an idea, so can a lot of other writers. Before you start your query, stop to see what else has been done. Check *Reader's Guide to Periodical Literature* to see what's been printed recently, and check recent issues of the magazine you plan to approach. (And remember, *Reader's Guide* only lists about 250 magazines, so make sure the one you plan to write for is included.) If it's a field in which there are a number of similar magazines, check the competition.

A similar article needn't stop you from going ahead with your proposal, even at the same magazine, but read what's been done so you can explain why your idea will be different. And knowing what a magazine has published, along with what their competition has been doing, and letting the editor know you know it is a sure way to get across the impression that you're a professional. And isn't that what this is all about?

HOW TO ANALYZE A MAGAZINE

Before I move into the subject of writing a query, I'd like to talk a little about how to make sure you're not only sending your idea to the right publication, but that you're pitching it in the right way. Every magazine is unique, with its own specific focus, its own concept of who its readers are and what they want.

Thirty-five years ago there were a lot of very similar magazines on the market. One query might be sent to four or five of them without having to be rewritten at all. But television changed all that, and the magazines that survived did so because they published very specific information for very sharply defined audiences. Your job is to study every magazine you wish to write for carefully enough so that you can get inside the editor's head and try to determine just who he or she is appealing to and what that reader expects from the magazine.

But this is the final question you need to be able to answer.

First, you have to answer some easier questions.

What subjects does the magazine cover most often? Are there some subjects that appear so frequently that it seems obvious they're always looking for material in this area?

What is the general tone of the magazine? *Vanity Fair* and *The New Yorker*, for instance, are quite sophisticated. *Family Circle* is fairly straightforward, presenting its material simply and directly. Other magazines may strive for cleverness, may even have a little of the wise guy about them, or may be academic and even pedantic in style. It may also be that all articles don't have the same style, so you'll have to read enough issues to get a sense of the predominant style and approach they seem to prefer.

Do the articles seem to be developed in any particular way? Do they like a lot of anecdotes? Do they use a good many quotes? Or are pieces mostly straight exposition? And how long do they run?

Take a look at the letters page to see which recent pieces have aroused the most interest. Read the editor's column, if there is one, to get more clues as to how the editor views his or her readers. Study the masthead, particularly if they have contributing or staff writers, to see how much of the publication is written in-house.

And finally, take a look at the advertisements. Are they mostly soaps and household cleaners, or do they advertise expensive cars and European traveling? What do the models used in the ads look like? Young women, women with children, older couples? Advertisers know who reads that magazine, and the ads they run are specifically designed to reach that audience. Ads give you valuable clues as to who that audience is, too.

If you can become so familiar with the magazine that you begin to think like one of its editors, you're ready to send them some queries.

CHAPTER TWO

How to Get an Editor's Attention

The most important element in any magazine article sale is not the idea, or even the skill with which the article is written, but the query letter you send to the editor. It seems obvious, but I'll say it anyway: If you don't impress that first person to read your letter, you'll never get a chance to impress anyone else.

So who do you send this query to? And how do you know that anyone will even read it, let alone offer you any encouragement? To answer the second question first, magazines are hungry for good ideas, and they will encourage a strong and suitable query letter no matter what the background of the writer proposing it.

What is a good query letter? Very simply, it is one that catches an editor's attention, suggests an article that fits the magazine's format and gives enough information about both subject and writer to persuade him or her that you can produce a publishable piece.

But let's get back to my first question. To begin with, you don't send it to "The Editor" or even to the editor by name. Manuscripts sent to nobody in particular end up reaching nobody particular. They pile up in somebody's office, or maybe even an empty space next to the water cooler, where they are known as part of the "slush pile." Slush isn't something you want on your sidewalk and, for the most part, editors don't want it in their magazines, either.

Some magazines don't read unsolicited manuscripts at all and simply return them with a brief form letter to that effect. In most cases they pile up until somebody is embarrassed enough by the stack of dog-eared material to sit down and go through it, usually with little or no expectation that anything publishable will be found. Expecting nothing, they find nothing; the main goal is to get rid of the stuff before somebody complains. Sometimes "slush" pieces do sell; I've bought some myself. But the odds are not far from those of winning $5 million from Ed McMahon.

AVOIDING THE SLUSH PILE

So how do you avoid the dreaded slush pile? Simply pick a name off the masthead and write directly to them. Not the editor, who is too busy, or the managing editor or executive editor, and probably not even the articles editor, although that person would seem logical. Instead, I'd pick somebody lower down on the masthead, somebody whose job is to find new talent and who will win recognition by discovering a new writer. This person will probably be listed as an associate editor or perhaps assistant articles editor, and he or she will be ambitious, not pressed by daily deadlines, and would love to be on your side if you have something to offer. He or she will see that your query reaches the right people and will be your contact if the decision is made to encourage you to go further. You will have a live editor, a friend in court, and you will have avoided the slush pile forever.

WHAT IS A GOOD QUERY?

Let me start by saying that a query has two aims in life: (1) to convince an editor that you have a good idea and (2) to convince that editor that you can turn it into a publishable manuscript. To achieve these purposes, you have to provide a number of things, all of which should add up to no more than two double-spaced typewritten pages, less if possible.

I think of the elements that make up a good query as the seven *W*'s and an *L*. They are:

Lead
What about
Why now
Who from
What treatment
Who you
What length
When deliver

Lead

Some writers on writing suggest that the lead should be the same as the lead you plan for the finished article, and while that will sometimes work, it can present problems. The lead you plan for the article may be far too long for a two-page query. A query lead should be kept to one paragraph; two at most. Also, you may not know what your lead is going to be until you've finished your research, and maybe not even then.

Just keep in mind that your lead has to catch somebody's attention. It might be a brief anecdote that helps explain your idea. It might be a provocative quote ("I know there are American prisoners of war being held in China because I've been in regular touch with them," says W. Eugene South, a prominent . . .) It could begin with some startling statistics, or a straight statement. An Atlanta writer named Maxine Rock once began a query to *Nova* magazine: "It has been man's dream to talk to the animals. Here in Atlanta, that dream is reality."

If you were an editor, could you stop reading?

I will have more examples of good queries at the end of this chapter, but let me get on to my *W*'s.

What About

Your lead may explain some of this, but probably not as fully as will be necessary to ensure that the editors know exactly what you have in mind. Try to summarize the point of your article as simply as you can, ideally in one sentence, no more than one paragraph.

Why Now

It's not enough to propose a good topic; you also need to explain why this is the right time to publish an article on it. Perhaps there's an anniversary coming up; you might, for instance, be proposing an article on the proven effectiveness of the air bag on the whatever-it-is anniversary of its first use. There might be a new study that sheds light on something like aspirin, or sodium use or the value of aerobics. Perhaps a newspeg is coming up; you're proposing a major takeout on some city because it will be celebrating its bicentennial in five months, or on the current state of the abortion controversy because of an upcoming Supreme Court decision.

Perhaps this is simply a subject that is frequently in the news, like genetic engineering, and you are proposing a major story to tell readers what they need to know to understand the breaking news. Maybe you're suggesting a profile of a person — a teacher, say, who has had great success in an inner-city school and whose experience might point to some solutions for a national problem.

You don't have to say "This is a good time to do this story because . . . ," but you do have to give the editors a reason to decide that the timing is, indeed, right.

Who From

Very simply, where are you getting your information? Who are your sources and have they agreed to talk to you? If there have been surveys, studies or reports you plan to draw on, list them. If you plan to back up your article with quotes from other written sources, you might indicate you know of their existence. Editors want the assurance of knowing you know where to get the information you need.

What Treatment

Very simply, how do you plan to handle this story? Lots of anecdotes? Straight exposition? With plenty of interviews and, if so, with whom? With humor? And what is your point of view? I don't mean you have to take sides on a subject like, say, school busing to achieve integration, or a national health plan, but you do need to make clear what your approach will be. Will you be advocating one side or another, or will you simply be presenting both sides and allowing readers to reach their own decision?

This isn't necessarily something you need to address directly, but the general tone of the query should clearly indicate your point of view.

What Length

Just tell the editor what you have in mind ("I see this as an article of about fifteen hundred words . . ."), but don't sound rigid, as the editor may be looking for short pieces or extra-long ones and will be the ultimate judge of what length would be most suitable.

Who You

In short, what can you say that might encourage an editor to entrust this idea to you? If you have had numerous sales to major magazines, you probably don't need to say much more. But if you haven't, think about why you might be a good person to take on this assignment. Is there something in your background that makes you uniquely qualified to take this on? If it's about education, are you a teacher? If you want to write about children, are you a parent? If it deals with health, do you have firsthand knowledge of the field? Does your job or hobby or education give you some special insight?

Perhaps you've written on this subject for a local or regional publication. Think about what led you to suggest an article on this subject in the first place, and see if that doesn't suggest some reason why you'd be a good person to write it.

When Deliver

This doesn't have to be an ironclad promise, but it will give the editor an idea of when it might be available for scheduling purposes. It's also a good opportunity to remind the editor that this idea hasn't just popped into your head. "I've been looking into this for several weeks and have interviewed a number of the people I'd need to talk to. I've also checked out the material already published on the subject. For these reasons, I think I could have a finished manuscript within four weeks of your go-ahead . . ."

Some writers wind up their queries by saying they're "looking forward to your response," but I don't see a world of point in this. As an editor, I knew they were hoping for my approval or they wouldn't have written me in the first place. I'd recommend simply winding up on a businesslike note — perhaps a statement saying when a piece could be delivered — and then send it off and start work on another query. You can't have too many of them out there.

Then What?

The sad fact is that even though your proposal is only a page or two, it may take six weeks or longer to get an answer. That eager junior editor has to hustle it to a less junior editor, who will pass it along to the articles editor, and, if it is still alive, to the managing editor and probably the editor. All this is going to take time, and an attempt to hurry the process could result in somebody just sending it back to get rid of you.

So be patient and get something else—a lot of something elses—in the works. Successful writers usually have a half dozen or more ideas in circulation all the time. If that first query hasn't gotten a response in six weeks, I see no harm in a postcard asking if they've received it. Offer to send another copy in case the first one has gone astray.

Don't sound impatient; don't threaten to take your idea to another magazine. Threats will get you nowhere. That second inquiry ought to get results. If it doesn't, and you haven't heard anything in a few more weeks, I'd feel free to submit your idea somewhere else.

MULTIPLE SUBMISSIONS

So why not just do that in the first place? The answer is: Most editors don't like it. It may not be fair, and it may mean that it takes far too long to get an okay on your idea, but if the word gets around that you go in for multiple submissions, this may work against you.

Remember, the world of magazine editors is a fairly small one. They know each other, they meet and talk over their work, and word on writers—good or bad—gets around. Also, think of how you'd handle it if you got an okay from one magazine and then another one called up and asked for the piece. Even if you lie successfully, Editor No. 2 is going to see your piece in Magazine No. 1 and know what you did.

On the other hand, there may be times when your subject is so hot, so timely, that you need to make a quick sale before somebody else beats you to it. Maybe that POW who was being held in China has come back and you have a chance to interview him. Then, I think, you can send off a query to a number of magazines, providing you tell each one what you're doing. Just simply say that because of the timeliness of the story and your fear that another writer will get to it first, you're sending similar proposals to magazines X, Y and Z. You will be delighted to do the story for the magazine that contacts you first.

SOME QUERIES THAT WORKED

Okay, I've told you how to write a query; now let me show you a few that worked. Since this is my book, I'll start off with one of mine. This went to South Carolina's *Sandlapper* magazine, and since I know the managing editor, Dan Harmon, and the staff is pretty small, I wrote directly to him. Here's how it went:

> Dear Dan:
>
> You've driven past it a hundred times, but I'll bet you've never stopped. You've always thought of it as a place for pale-skinned tourists with orange shorts and black socks and sandals who pull in because they can't stand the kids yelling anymore.
>
> We've all seen the signs as we drive up to North Carolina, or come home from a visit up north. "You never sausage a place," one of them goes, "Everybody's a weiner at Pedro's." The puns on the rest of them—hundreds of them, leaping out at you in garish orange and yellow and black letters every few hundred yards—are equally bad, and after a few smiles you stop smiling and just drive along, wondering how bad they can get.
>
> But do the signs really reflect South of the Border? Can you get a good meal there, or an inexpensive night's sleep? Are there really things for the kids to do, or is it just a big rip-off? As one who has driven past it more times than I can remember, I'd like to find out. If you agree that this would make a nice light piece for *Sandlapper*, let me know. I could deliver in a few weeks, and will supply pictures.

That brought a prompt response, and it was published in the year-end issue of 1991.

Here's another query, sent to *McCall's* during the late summer, a time when magazines are beginning to worry about filling up their Christmas issues. Note that it is not written as a letter; in this instance, the writer did a straight query describing the story she had in mind and used a cover letter to tell who she was. There are differences of opinion on which approach is best. One editor I know feels that receiving a query without a cover letter is like having someone come up to him at a party and start talking before he even introduced himself. Others see nothing wrong with weaving the personal information into the query letter.

If you want to use a cover letter, it should be confined to who you are, what your writing background is, perhaps some reason why you would be particularly qualified to write the story, when you can deliver and so on. Then the query itself can be used solely to sell the idea. While I prefer to weave all the information into one letter, neither approach is wrong.

By the way, this query grew out of a writer's conference at which I spoke and delivered my usual message about the need for Christmas ideas. Terry Fields came up to me afterwards, described her idea, and I encouraged this query. I have seen many assignments come out of such conferences, and I recommend them to you if one is being held in your area.

Query   Christmas Is for Caring

It is very early Christmas morning in Phoenix, Arizona, and Santa's elves are busily at work. Thanks to their caring efforts, a thousand needy people will soon listen to Christmas carols and enjoy a traditional feast of turkey and all the trimmings. Though it may be that similar scenes are happening at charity dining rooms across the nation, what makes this one quite unusual is that "Santa's Elves" are all Jewish. In the spirit of brotherhood, over a hundred members of Temple Beth Israel have volunteered to be of service on the dining room's busiest day of the year. This enables the dining room's Christian staff to spend December 25th with their families. Though the food is cooked ahead of time for the Temple group, everything else is up to them. Decorating, serving, organizing all the gifts and giving them out, as well as clearing and cleaning up are tasks they happily take on while voices ring out in joyous song.

Bringing out the solicitude and warmth of this situation is part of what I plan to do in the round-up article, "Christmas Is for Caring." The piece will cite several different communities around the country who've shown the Christmas spirit in very unique ways. The following are thumbnail sketches of the places that will be included.

For five years, the child had wistfully watched while other kids lined up to sit on Santa's lap. She wished she could talk to him too, but what was the point if she couldn't hear what Santa said back? That was all before a shopping mall in Dayton, Ohio, decided that every child should be able to talk to Santa and yearly now hires a special Santa who knows sign language. He's available all season, and in addition, caring employees have arranged for a school for the hearing impaired to have a day with Santa including lunch. Why? Director Jennifer Bankert says, "You have only to look at the smiles on these kids' faces one time and the question is easily answered."

To a child opening gifts by the tree on Christmas morning, the day seems to fly by in a second. To an elderly person all alone in an apartment, the hours tick on infinitely slowly. "It feels," said one woman, "like the longest day of the year." Residents in Boston don't want that to happen, and so many of them are giving up a part of their own holiday to spend it with an elderly person who wouldn't otherwise see anyone on Christmas. They bring a hot meal and a gift, but most importantly, they stay a while and on this holiest of days they bring the gift of friendship.

Christmas can be a time of great fellowship and festivities, but it can also be a time of frustration and stress. That's why volunteers in Chicago, Illinois, man a hot line twenty-four hours a day for the eleven days before Christmas. Last year, those volunteers took close to three thousand phone calls during their eleven days. One of the best remembered was from a little boy who called on Christmas Eve. "I think there is no Christmas this year," he said forlornly. His mother was working all night, and he was home alone. The volunteer on the phone told him Christmas stories, and reassured the boy that there was still a Santa.

Lisel, I'm not sure how long you want this piece to be, but I also have another a vignette from a shelter for runaway/throwaway kids in New York.

I think people would find these stories heartwarming. Amid the electronics and commercialism of Christmastime, it's nice to know that the human link of man caring about his fellow man is still present.

While this query is a bit long, I like it for several reasons. First, of course, it seems to have just the right spirit for a Christmas issue. It sets up its thesis quickly and, most important, shows us that she has plenty of anecdotal examples to back up that thesis. Finally, she ends with a good reason to include such an article in a Christmas issue. And I can't stress often enough the value of strong Christmas ideas; no matter what time of year you read this, it's time to get your Christmas queries in the mail.

Maxine Rock is another excellent writer of queries; she wrote the following query to *Nova* magazine. For more on her, see the chapter entitled, "The Writer's Life."

Dear Editor:

It has been man's dream to talk to the animals. Here in Atlanta, that dream is a reality.

At the Yerkes Primate Center, a young female chimpanzee named Lana has been "talking" to scientists with the aid of a typewriter-like computer. Lana has been taught symbols which stand for objects; she now constructs her own sentences by punching the symbols in sequence, on her computer. So, she can express her needs ("Lana want apple, please"), her feelings ("Lana want paper, pencil, draw now, please").

Scientists plan to have Lana train baby chimps in the use of her language, dubbed "Yerkish," so that testing can be done on whether animals, like humans, can transmit symbolic information from one generation to the next.

I am a science writer and have been reporting on work at the Yerkes Center for several years. My latest article on ape behavior, "Gorilla Mothers Need Some Help From Their Friends," appeared in the July 1978 issue of *Smithsonian* magazine. I also write for *The New York Times, Travel Magazine, The National Parks and Conservation Journal, Atlanta Magazine,* and other local and national publications.

Now I'd like to write for *Nova*. You're new and exciting, and I think Lana's story would fit your style. I have excellent photographs and can make more. I work well with scientists and can tell their stories in clear, bold language.

May I try this story for you? I'll look forward to a reply.

There are a few things I would have done differently and, given the fact that she wrote this over fifteen years ago, some things Maxine might have done differently as well, but I think she did an excellent job of explaining a complicated story in a single-page query. I would have found out the name of the editor before I wrote, I don't think she needed to tell them they are "new and exciting," and I think the last sentence is unnecessary. But it did the job it set out to do, and did it well.

Here's another, submitted to *McCall's* several years ago by a freelancer for the Midwest named Nancy Eberle:

"Please Pass the Uh . . . the Uh . . . the Uh. . . ."
WHAT TO DO WHEN MEMORY FAILS

A proposal from Nancy Eberle

Anyone who has reached for an everyday word—or for that matter an everyday object ("It was right here just a minute ago!")— and found in its place absolutely, positively . . . *nothing* . . . knows how embarrassing it can be. And although we laugh or snap or alibi our way out of it ("Who could think straight in a zoo like this!") who among us does not hear a faint bell of alarm, and wonder what's going on?

What happens when the word on the tip of our tongue, or the phone number we know as well as our own or the place where we parked the car or the doorman's name disappear from memory? Does it have something to do with the complicated, many-track lives we lead today? Is it a symptom of fatigue, depression— or worse? Is it a sign of aging? And most important, is there anything we can do about it?—aerobics of the mind for fitness of memory?

This article will address the questions raised above, describing different types of memory lapses; the reasons for each; who, when or in what situation one is most susceptible; and, most important, what can be done about it. (What can be done about it is rather amazing—at Carnegie-Mellon University two college students of ordinary intelligence were able to increase their digit recall from seven to seventy-nine digits!)

For one of my sources I'd like to use Ulric Neisser of the Cornell University Psychology Dept., who is known as the father of cognitive psychology and who is the author of *Memory Observed: Remembering in Natural Contexts.* The book's title is indicative of Neisser's orientation—away from the lab and toward the everyday.

I'm enthusiastic about the piece because it deals with one of those subjects that everyone worries about but no one talks about, so that when something is finally done on it, there's that euphoric "You, too?—thank God!" reaction. As I see it there will be a nice blend of:

- solid information (did you know, for example, that unless new material has some special impact, it disappears from memory in 30 to 60 seconds?);

- human interest (feats of memory like that of the Rev. Dr. Phelps, who could remember the day of the week, the weather and what happened for each day of the past sixty years);
- plenty of anecdotes (my friend the restauranteur once described, in desperation, a revolving door as "that thing that goes round and round that you come out from");
- ideas to think about ("Every person is a prodigy to his neighbors, remembering so much that other people do not know");
- helpful hints on how to improve memory, and failing that, how to cope.

This query got off to a great start by relating the subject to every reader. We've all had these memory lapses, and she knows this approach will ring an immediate bell of recognition. Already we're saying, yes, that's happened to me, and I want to know why. She also promises insight into how memory can be improved, cites a good source, and gives examples of intriguing anecdotal and factual backup material. I also like the fact that it has a good title; if memory serves, it's the one we used on the final article.

If I had a criticism, it would be that she doesn't mention enough sources, leaving the impression that a lot of the piece will be coming out of her own head. You might think it has an abrupt ending, but she did write a cover letter.

By the way, I've used the words "query" and "proposal" and "idea" interchangeably. They all mean the same thing, although "query" is the word most often used.

Here is a proposal from a delightful young woman named Jeannie Ralston, whose story of her career as a freelance writer also appears in a later chapter. Jeannie told me that the editors liked the query so much they were prepared to just publish it, but she persuaded them to let her develop it into the fifteen-hundred word piece she envisioned.

Jeannie Ralston

A HIMALAYA HIGH

Why would anyone want to spend a vacation at a hotel where 80 percent of the guests complain of nausea, headaches or sleepless ness brought on by the altitude? Where the only item on the room service menu is oxygen and where 30 percent of the guests order it so they can sleep through the night? Where a pressure chamber is being built to help guests adjust to the altitude? Where around the fireplace it's not unusual to see pale-faced, purple-lipped people with "are we having fun yet?" looks on their faces and brand new Vasque hiking boots they don't have the energy to use on their feet?

And why, of all things, would anyone pay $160 per person per night for the opportunity to suffer so?

Why? Because the hotel is situated on a thirteen-thousand-feet-high ridge in the Himalayas of Nepal that looks out on the most famous peak on Earth: Mt. Everest. And because the aptly named Everest View Hotel, which is billed as the highest hotel in the world, is the only easy way to get a glimpse of the legendary mountain.

Guests at the Hotel Everest View fly up from Kathmandu in a seven-seater Pilatus that lands on a short grass airstrip squeezed in between two twenty thousand-feet-plus mountains (round trip $290). After a forty-five-minute climb (yaks are available for those who prefer to ride), guests arrive at the flat, glass-and-stone building that looks like a Frank Lloyd Wright gone wrong. The rooms have a cheesy, Motel Six feel to them, but they are the most luxurious spaces in the whole Everest region: real bathrooms with real toilets, beds with cotton sheets, sliding glass doors that lead to a wood deck from which Everest contemplating can be done.

The hotel was opened in October 1990 by a Japanese firm after being closed for ten years. (It had shut down because of bankruptcy and because the Nepalese government took away the use of the Pilatus.) Everest View now caters to Japanese, but the hotel is hoping to start attracting affluent Americans and other Westerners.

I would like to write a fifteen-hundred-word piece that would discuss the hotel's sometimes comic, often desperate attempts to be an oasis of civility and comfort in a harsh, remote environment—arguably the harshest in the world. I would include the hotel's troubled history and a humorous account of my own stay there. Since I visited the hotel after several weeks of trekking, I could put the hotel in context, emphasizing how different it is from anything else in the area and pointing out what guests gain and miss by taking this shortcut to the Everest region.

And finally, here is an excellent query letter from a former student, Vanessa Grimm. She starts it in an interesting way and shows that she can write with some humor and style. She tells when publication would be appropriate, explains who she is, and shows where her material will come from.

Islands
3886 State St.
Santa Barbara, CA 93105

ATTN: Deuey Schurman, Senior Editor

RE: Query

Dear Mr. Schurman,

It was one year ago that I decided to move from one small, but rather well developed, island to another of similar size but vast cultural differences. Though the island I left boasted all the conveniences of modern technology, the thrill of a new lifestyle was what my heart craved. So I quit my job at the publishing house, packed my bags, and left Manhattan for a new life upon the Caribbean island of St. Thomas, USVI.

The year I've spent here has been all I'd hoped for. My senses have been tantalized by the tastes of a culture that is a melding together of West Indian, European, and Middle Eastern experiences.

The festival of Carnival, held here on St. Thomas last month, was an excellent opportunity to see such a culture in action. From the steel pan bands and circus-like stilt walkers, to the native cuisine and closing fireworks, the event was not one to be missed.

St. John, the smallest U.S. Virgin Island, will be holding their Carnival between June 29 and July 4. I will be attending and would like to share my experience in an article, accompanied by photographs such as the enclosed, for *Islands'* Feature or Island Hopping sections.

I realize you will not be able to respond before this event begins, but I plan on gathering information regardless. In fact, but the time you respond the article should be well underway.

I hope this idea interests you and I look forward to your response to my proposal.

FOURTEEN THINGS NOT TO DO IN YOUR QUERY LETTER

1. Don't try any cute attention-getting devices, like marking the envelope "Personal." This also includes fancy stationery that lists every publication you've ever sold to, or "clever" slogans ("The Write Writer for You"). As Jack Webb used to say on *Dragnet*, "Just the facts, ma'am."

2. Don't talk about fees. If the fee you mention is too high, it will turn the editor off. If it's too low, he'll think you don't value your work.

3. Keep your opinions to yourself. If you're proposing an article on some public figure, for instance, your personal views are not relevant. Bear in mind that you're offering your services as a reporter, not the author of an editorial or personal opinion column.

4. Don't tell the editor what others you've shown the idea to think of it. ("Several of my friends have read this and think it's marvelous . . . ") is a certain sign of the amateur writer. The same goes for comments from other editors. Sometimes you'll hear from an editor who wanted to buy your idea, but was overruled, and that editor might say nice things about it and even offer the suggestion that "It might be just right for Magazine X." Don't pass that praise along. Let Magazine X decide for itself.

5. Don't name drop. Editors will not be impressed that you once babysat for the state governor or had dinner with Bill and Hillary. However, if you do know somebody who works for that magazine, or writes for it, or if you know an editor on another magazine who has bought your work and likes it, say so. Contacts are valuable; dropping names to show what a big deal you are isn't.

6. Don't try to soft soap the editor by telling him or her how great the magazine is, but I would definitely make it clear that you read it. You could say that you particularly enjoyed a certain article, to show that you're paying attention, but too much praise sounds phony.

7. Don't send in any unnecessary enclosures, such as a picture of yourself (or your prize-winning Labrador Retriever). Just send in material that will sell the idea, which is usually nothing more than the query itself.

8. Don't offer irrelevant information about yourself. Simply tell the editor what there might be in your background that qualifies you to write this story.

9. Don't offer such comments as "I never read your magazine, but this seems to be a natural . . . " or "I know you usually don't publish articles about mountain climbing, but . . . " Know the magazine, and send only those ideas that fit the format.

10. Don't ask for a meeting to discuss your idea further. If the editor feels this is necessary, he or she will suggest it.

11. Don't ask for advice, such as "If you don't think you can use this, could you suggest another magazine that could?" Or, "If you don't think this works as it is, do you have any suggestions for ways in which I could change it?" Editors are paid to evaluate ideas and to offer suggestions for revision; they'll do this without your prompting. What they won't do is offer extensive advice on pieces they don't want.

12. Don't offer to rewrite, as this implies you know it's not good enough as you have submitted it. Again, editors will ask for rewrites if necessary, and they usually are.

13. Don't make any threats, such as "If I don't hear from you within four weeks I'll submit it elsewhere." If the editor is dubious about the idea anyway, that takes away any reason to make a decision.

14. Don't include a multiple-choice reply card, letting the editor check a box to indicate whether he likes it or not. I never got one of those that accompanied an idea I wanted to encourage.

Okay, now we've covered what to do and what not to do, and your next query is going to come back with an enthusiastic approval. It's time to go to work, and that usually begins by asking questions. Here's how to make sure you get the answers you need.

CHAPTER THREE

The Subtle Art of Interviewing

The most important and most encouraging thought to keep in mind as you set out on an interview is: *People love to talk about themselves.*

There are exceptions, of course; some people have been interviewed too often, some have things they'd rather not be asked about and others are so busy they don't want to take the time. But for the most part, everybody's favorite subject is him- or herself.

This is true even of people who have suffered some tragic loss, or endured some painful or wrenching experience, and would seem to be the last people in the world who would want to talk to a reporter. I have been surprised over and over again, both as an editor making assignments and as a writer, by the fact that very few people will turn down a request for an interview.

So once your query letter has struck gold and you have an assignment in hand, make a list of the people you'd like to talk to, no matter how unlikely their cooperation might seem. You'll never know until you ask.

GIVE THEM SOME TIME

I would phone for your interview several days before you want to have it. There are two reasons for this. You're going to have to do your homework before you sit down with your subject, but equally important, this will give them a chance to get ready for you. The person being interviewed wants to be helpful, but also wants to look good. If you're going to ask things like: "What was the most frightening experience you had on your job?" or "Do you remember any stories about those days in Australia?" they may need a day or so to think about it. It's very easy for the mind to go blank when asked a question you weren't prepared for.

At the time you make your initial contact, tell them who you are, tell them who you're writing for and, most important, give them an idea of the topics you want to cover. You may even tell them some of the questions you'll be asking.

Obviously, you have to use your judgment here. You may have some questions they'll be reluctant to answer, and you'll want their first spontaneous reaction. But other questions, particularly those seeking anecdotes or asking for specific information, will elicit better answers if the interviewee knows they're coming.

Once the interview time has been set, learn all you can about the person. Read everything you can find that has been written about them or that they might have written themselves. Talk to people who know them, who work with them. Talk to family members. If the person is in politics, talk to their supporters as well as their opponents.

With that information in hand, it's time to start thinking about what you're going to ask them, and this involves writing out your questions in the rough order that you plan to ask them.

I don't mean for you to be a slave to these questions. They are there primarily to make sure you don't forget something you want to cover. You may not even write them down in question form at all, but simply make a list of subjects you would like to talk about.

But remember, the main object here is to get your interviewee talking. The questions or topics are there to keep the interview going if it seems to be running out of gas, or to change the subject if the interviewee is straying too far afield. And, of course, you want to make sure you touch all the bases. Some writers never look at the questions during the interview itself, only running through them later to make sure nothing was missed.

MANAGING THE INTERVIEW

There aren't any hard-and-fast rules for managing an interview once it gets started. I like to let the subject talk about whatever interests them, and only steer the conversation back to my main points when absolutely necessary.

While you don't want to run out of things to ask, don't put down any questions unless you feel the answers will be important to your article. (One exception to this is cited by Maxine Rock in her interview. "Sometimes I'll ask an extraneous question, something I don't care about the answer to. The reason is that I want the person to keep talking while I'm catching up and writing down what they said earlier.") You'll find that the interview takes on a life of its own and takes up time on matters you never thought of bringing up.

Another thought to keep in mind: Try to make your interview as much like a normal conversation as possible. Begin by trying to establish a relationship. Don't take out your notepad or turn on your tape recorder, but simply talk about some things you have in common. You've learned enough about the person to know that he's a baseball fan or she likes country music or has young children or whatever. Try to find some areas of common ground, shared interests, to make the person you're interviewing feel as comfortable as possible with you.

(Let me just interrupt briefly to say that all this buildup isn't necessary if you're simply going to ask a city councilman a few questions, or consult an expert about some phase of your story. In such cases, you should simply ask your questions, learn what you came to learn and get out.)

The relaxed approach is a helpful beginning for any interview, but particularly so if the subject is a painful one. In his marvelous book, *Writing the Modern Magazine Article*, Max Gunther tells of the time he was writing a piece on childhood suicide and needed to interview the parents of a six-year-old boy who had attempted twice to kill himself. Max wanted them to look on him not as a nosy reporter but as someone who also had children, and was concerned about them as a parent, not just somebody looking for a story. He also wanted them to tell their story in their own way, not simply answer a set of questions.

As he tells it, the first thing he did, his notebook and pencil still in his pocket, was ask them: "Before we begin, tell me just one thing. Is your boy all right now?"

From then on, Max says, he hardly asked another question. The father and mother simply told their story, talking for two hours, revealing far more than they might have revealed in answers to direct questions.

A TAPE RECORDER—OR NOT?

I mentioned a tape recorder earlier, and this is as good a time as any to deal with this. Personally, I feel a little lost without one.

I want to keep the conversation as normal as possible, and that involves looking at the person I'm talking to. It's hard to do that and take notes at the same time.

Most people will not object to a tape recorder, but you do have to ask permission. Point out that your ultimate goal is accuracy; you want to be sure you get your quotes and your facts exactly right. Then, assuming they agree, I'd put the machine in as inconspicuous place as possible. (But do test to make sure it's picking up both voices.) You're not exactly hiding it, but you're not constantly reminding them that everything they say is being preserved for eternity, which does tend to cause some people to freeze up.

SHOULD YOU SHOW THEM THE QUOTES?

Some people you are interviewing may ask to see their quotes before you publish them. Some may even ask to see the finished article in advance. My first advice is: Don't promise anything without talking to your editor. Some editors will agree, some won't, but they'll be angry, and rightly so, if you show an article to a subject, or anybody else, before you show it to them.

Sometimes showing quotes to a subject can be helpful. They may correct a mistake you made, or may add additional information they forgot at the time of the original interview. They may simply want to be sure you quoted them correctly. I remember one occasion in the mid-fifties when I'd assigned a writer to interview Katharine Hepburn for *McCall's*. She wasn't giving many interviews at the time, and I wasn't surprised when she asked to check the quotes. As that was a condition for granting the interview, I said okay.

When the article was finished, the writer typed up the direct quotes and took them over to Hepburn's apartment in New York. Then she waited nervously while Hepburn took them into another room and was gone for what seemed like hours. Finally the actress returned: "Well, I'm sorry I said some of those things," the writer quoted the actress as saying, "but I said 'em, so it's all right."

Some people you interview will not be the class act that Hepburn is and will want to delete or alter certain parts of your story. This will be less of a problem if you tell them in advance that you are showing them the quotes in the interest of accuracy, and you do not necessarily agree to make all the changes they want.

This is where the tape recorder is invaluable; if you can play back their quote, they can hardly deny saying it.

They may back down, or they may simply refuse to let you use any of their quotes unless you make the changes they ask for. At this point, I wouldn't make any hard-and-fast rules for what to do next. I would try to explain that they agreed to the interview in advance, knowing that you were a reporter and going to write an article. You have acted in good faith and expected them to do the same. You've shown the material to them as a courtesy, but you cannot give them the right to determine what goes in your article. If you can't smooth things out, I'd say that you have to refer this to your editor. Let him or her worry about it from then on.

GETTING ANECDOTES

Good anecdotes are essential to almost any article, and they're often hard to get. Most people don't talk in anecdotes; don't have little stories ready to illustrate the points they want to make. You're going to have to dig them out.

How? Well, let's imagine you're interviewing a beloved teacher who is retiring after fifty years. You're going to want to know how she feels about not going back to that classroom any more, and what she plans to do to fill her time, but you also want stories that illustrate the high points of her long career. And they're not going to come by simply asking for them, but by asking the right questions.

You might ask, for instance, about the first student who comes to mind when she thinks over all the students she's had. What was there about that student that made you think of them? Was there some incident that you remember when you think of them?

How many students have you had who later became very successful or even famous? Do they keep in touch? What do you remember about them from their school days? What is your most vivid memory of them?

If they start telling a story but are skimpy on details, prod them a little. Ask questions like: What did you do then? How did you feel when he did that? What exactly did he say that you remember? In other words, remember the reporter's basic W's: Who, What, When, Where, Why. Don't let your subject off with vague generalities, but ask enough specific questions to help them fill in the details.

Just remember, anecdotes don't come easily, and they don't necessarily come out whole. That is, you might be told part of what could make a good story, and a few good questions would help you fill it out.

You may also get good anecdotes from someone other than the person being interviewed; we don't always want to tell stories on ourselves, but others may not be as reluctant. Then you can take that anecdote back to your subject and ask him what he remembers about it. By the same token, an anecdote you get from the person you're interviewing might be considerably improved if you asked one of his friends about it. "Remember the time you and Harvey went camping and he went out at night and almost stepped on a copperhead?" could evoke more details than Harvey could remember, or wanted to share.

GETTING INTO SENSITIVE AREAS

If you have to ask questions that you think your subject won't want to answer, save them for the last. When I interviewed Valerie Sayre, a young novelist from Beaufort, South Carolina, now living in Brooklyn, New York, who has written a number of sharply observed and not always sympathetic books about her hometown, I saved talking about her relationship with the townspeople of Beaufort until we'd been talking for over an hour. I could sense from reading *Due East* and *Who Do You Love?* that she had probably ruffled more than a few feathers, and I wanted her to feel comfortable with me before we got into that.

As it turned out, her response became the lead of my piece. "It feels awkward every time I come back to Beaufort," she said, "but awkward and wonderful all at once. I spend a lot of time longing to be down here, and then when I'm here, it's a hard time in so many ways."

She went on to talk about her family, particularly her mother, who sometimes appears in her books, and not always in a way she might like. She became very open on the subject, and I suspect she might not have if I'd brought it up too early.

The thing to remember is that the person you're interviewing can terminate the interview at any time, and this is even more possible if you're interviewing them by telephone. So get the bulk of your questions out of the way before you ask them about drugs, child abuse and those accusations about a fondness for pornography.

Sometimes, if the subject you want to bring up is particularly sensitive, or accusations have been made against them, you might want to ease into the topic by asking permission. Simply ask if you can ask a personal question. Maybe even sound a little embarrassed about it: "I hate to ask you this, but I think it's important to get your response." But don't be so gentle that they'll feel they can simply turn you off. If it's important that such material be included in your piece, keep after them. If things get sticky you can drop it for a while, but you still have the obligation to get that question answered.

If you want to talk to somebody about their reputation as a martinet or a slave driver, you might ease into this by attributing charges against them to someone else. "Mr. Perot, some critics charge you with being a potential dictator. Former President Bush has said . . ." and let Perot get angry at them, not you.

The same approach could be used with a police chief accused of allowing his officers to use brutal treatment on their prisoners, a politician believed to be guilty of unethical conduct, or even someone—a business executive, say—who was suspected of illegal acts. Don't ask them if it's true that they've stolen money from the union pension fund; simply cite charges that have been made against them and ask for their comment.

If they refuse to cooperate, don't let them off the hook too easily. Make it clear that these charges have to be part of your article and that you want to give them an opportunity to respond. Tell them you would hate to print only one side of the story.

If you get an answer that seems less than complete, you might simply change the subject and return to it later, phrasing the question a bit differently. Some writers tell me that they will come back to a subject half a dozen times, until they get the response they want.

One caveat: It's important that you know as much as possible about the facts behind these charges before bringing them up, and also that you've talked to some of those making the charges so that the person you're interviewing can't push you off too easily. The more you know, the harder it will be for them to avoid dealing with the issue.

WINDING UP

As you approach the end of your interview, stall a little. Spend a minute or two reviewing your notes, or checking your list of questions, leaving a few moments of silence. Most people hate silence and may feel a need to fill in the dead time. Mike Wallace was quoted as saying, when talking about his early days as a TV interviewer, that he would deliberately stop asking questions, just letting the subject sit there, knowing they would often blurt out something revealing.

You might plan your last question to be: "Is there anything you wish I'd asked you?" This could well turn up some fascinating information you didn't know existed and the subject is dying to talk about.

Another technique, which is a little sneaky and may go against your grain, is to simply shut off the tape recorder, put your pen back in your pocket, and just "chat" for a while. Some years back Jimmy Carter was asked by *Playboy* if he'd ever had an affair with another woman, and he said no, but that he'd "lusted in his heart" after someone other than his wife. Carter said this after the interview was over, when he and the reporter were chatting at the door before the reporter left.

The fact is that unless the interviewee says it's off the record, you can use it. But you'd better be sure to write it down as soon as you leave.

The novelist Truman Capote once said that he'd trained his memory so he could do sensitive interviews without taking notes. He would have someone read him a lengthy passage and then he would sit down when they had finished and try to reproduce it exactly. He would do this over and over, and when he had achieved 95 percent accuracy, he felt he was ready to interview the two murderers who had provided most of the information for his classic true crime book, *In Cold Blood*. He knew they would freeze up if he recorded them or even took notes, so he trained his memory to record everything for him. So he said, anyway; some critics felt that Capote, who was also a fine novelist, had created some of the dialogue out of his own head, and that his memory training story was designed to cover his tracks.

Whether his version is true or not, it *is* possible to train your memory enough to retain important bits of dialogue long enough to record them as soon as you can. Lewis Lapham, now editor of *Harper's*, but then a writer for the *Saturday Evening Post*, had been assigned an article on the making of a Broadway show. The idea was that he would hang around during all stages of production, right up to opening night, and thus show readers how a big hit musical is put together. As time went on, and things began to go wrong, Lew began hearing things he was sure the producers and directors and writers and actors would not want to see in the finished article. And he suspected that if he continued to take notes, he would be asked to leave.

His solution was to be as unobtrusive as possible and to excuse himself every fifteen or twenty minutes and rush off to the men's room to write down everything he could remember. He was sure they suspected him of a kidney problem, but he got his story.

A FEW FINAL TIPS

• If anything the interviewee said is not clear, or seems incomplete, don't hesitate to ask that it be repeated. And if you feel a question wasn't really answered, rephrase it — but ask it again until it's answered or the subject flatly says he won't comment. John McPhee, one of the great reporters of our time, said once that he kept going back at a subject if he wasn't satisfied with the answer so many times that he suspected that some of the people he interviewed thought he might be a little simpleminded. Don't worry about what they think; just get what you need.

• Don't ever argue with the person you're interviewing. And don't debate with them, no matter how absurd you think they're being. Your job is to record what they say, not try and persuade them that they're wrong.

• They may suddenly tell you that something they have said is off the record. I think your response should be much like the one Maxine Rock describes in her interview later in this book. "I tell them that when you invited me over here, or said I could come, you knew I was a reporter working on a story. Everything that's been said I've taken down and will use. I tell the person before I come that they can trust me with off-the-record material, but not if they tell me something first and change their minds later to conceal information."

This may work, or it may cause them to stop the interview entirely. At this point, there are number of ways to go. Maybe you feel you have enough, and don't mind ending the session. If not, you can try to talk them into letting you use at least part of it. You can also ask to paraphrase what they said, possibly without attribution.

If you are unable to reach any agreement, you will have to let your conscience be your guide. The essential point is that if they agreed to see you, knowing you are a reporter on a story, you can ethically use anything they say unless they specifically tell you beforehand that it is off the record.

Some writers simply say that they don't want to hear anything they can't use. This may be too rigid. Off-the-record information may help you understand the situation better, and may give you an idea about where to get the same information from other sources. But if you are told something that has been announced as being off the record, the ethical course is not to use it.

• The interview does not consist only of what was said. Make notes on how the subject looked, what he or she did during the interview, any details that will help the reader see the subject as you saw him. Describe the place where you talked. If it's their home or office, tell how it was decorated, what pictures were on the wall, what objects were on the desk or table. Not every detail, but those that reveal the personality and character of the subject, or help re-create the occasion.

One of the best things I've ever read about the importance of detail came from an article by *Newsweek* editor Karl Fleming, which appeared in a 1967 story in a trade publication called *Word Business*. Fleming had been in New Orleans working on another story when a senior editor named Bill Emerson (later my editor at the *Saturday Evening Post*) called. According to Fleming: "The religious section, Emerson said, was doing a story on a confrontation between Archbishop Joseph Rummel and an excommunicated female parishioner named Mrs. Una Gaillot over the school desegregation question on the archbishop's lawn.

"A New Orleans reporter and part-time 'stringer' for *Newsweek* had sent in a perfectly adequate file on the story, Emerson said, but he (Emerson) was right on deadline, and he needed just two questions answered.

" 'Number one,' he said, 'What does the archbishop's house look like? Is it wood, or stone, or brick? Is it Victorian with ivy on the walls? What kind of day was it? Was it balmy and overcast, or hot and muggy? What does the archbishop look like? Is he old and bespectacled or what? How did he walk when he came out of the house? Did he stride angrily? Or did he walk haltingly, leaning on a cane? How was he dressed? What is the walkway like? Is it concrete, brick or gravel? What do the grounds look like? Are there oak trees and rose bushes, magnolias and poppies? Were birds singing in the bushes? What was going on in the street outside the grounds? Was an angry crowd assembled? Or was there the normal business traffic, passing by oblivious to the drama inside? What were Mrs. Gaillot and her friends wearing? Did they have on Sunday best or just casual clothes? What happened as the archbishop confronted Mrs. Gaillot? Was he stern and silent? Or did he rebuke her? What was the exact language she used?

" 'Now,' he said, 'question number two . . .' "

Fleming went on to tell how he did the reporting, filed it off to New York, and then reprints the first two paragraphs of the story as it appeared in the magazine: "It was a cloudless, languid spring morning last week when Archbishop Joseph Francis Rummel emerged from his two-story, red-brick residence in uptown New Orleans and unknowingly moved toward a uniquely dramatic confrontation. Dressed in a long, black cassock topped by a velvet-lined cape, carrying a black cane in his left hand, the thirty-five-year-old prelate walked haltingly toward a tall white statue of Our Lady of Fatima. There, fifteen neatly dressed ladies, on an annual pilgrimage to the shrine, awaited his greeting.

"The gray-haired archbishop had just finished welcoming the group when Mrs. Gaillot, excommunicated by Rummel the day before for her attempts to block desegregation of the area's Catholic schools, came stalking past fifteen pickets who were protesting the desegregation outside the archbishop's garden. Marching onto the lawn, Mrs. Gaillot threw herself on her knees in front of him . . ." Now that's detail. And every item is there for a purpose, and every one helps to re-create that dramatic scene and makes the story as vivid and alive as any television clip.

HOW TO USE WHAT YOU'VE GOT

As soon as you get back to your home or office you need to get your interview on paper. If you're working from notes, type them up in as much detail as possible. Type them up while the interview is still fresh in your mind; by the next day you may have begun to forget important details.

If I've tape recorded the interview, I sit down and play it back, taking notes as if I was listening to the interview itself. I type up those notes, then go back and listen to it again, to pick up anything I missed. You may want to listen to your tape several times before you are satisfied that you've gotten all you can out of it.

If you're using a word processor, re-create the interview as well as you can and then print out a hard copy. Once you're sure you have it all, you're ready to go on to the next stage in your research.

CHAPTER FOUR

How to Find What You Need

The fact is that most of the material you will need for any article, and sometimes all of the material, will grow out of the reporting and interviewing you do yourself. You will talk to the people involved; you will go to the city hall or the water commission or the Bureau of Motor Vehicles and dig out the information you need to flesh out and substantiate your story.

And this kind of reporting is not only highly valued, but the ability and willingness to report well is rarer than you might think. I was talking recently with Janet Smith, a young woman who was then editing a local publication, *The Hilton Head Monthly*, and she told me that her biggest problem was in finding people who would report. I've been told the same thing by most of the editors I interviewed. "It's easy enough to find people who will give me their opinions," Janet told me, "but hard to find writers who will go out and talk to people, dig up facts, do the hard work needed to get a good story."

This is not an ability that requires unique talent or specialized training; what it involves for the most part is simple hard work.

Let's imagine that you have been assigned to do a feature story on the future availability of fresh water in, for example, the area where I live, Hilton Head Island, South Carolina. Newspaper stories have reported that saltwater is invading our chief water source, the Upper Floridian Aquifer. By sometime in the early twenty-first century, it may be too saline to drink. A South Carolina state magazine like *Sandlapper* might be interested, or perhaps some regional publication. Perhaps a magazine devoted to nature and natural resources. Or maybe a business magazine concerned about future development on this resort island. In any event, you have the assignment.

By going through the files of your local newspaper, *The Island Packet*, you learn that two government agencies discovered the future threat to the island's drinking water. They were the South Carolina Water Resources Commission and the United States Geological Survey, Water Resources Division, which is part of the Department of the Interior. A few phone calls reveal that the people to talk to are the executive director of the Water Resources Commission, Freddie Vang, and the chief hydrologist, Camille Ransom. A call to the USGS Water Resources Division tells you that the chief of that division is Glenn Patterson.

Interviews with them will obviously give you the background you need. Now you have to find out what's being done about it. A visit to town hall reveals more sources of information, beginning with the town engineer, Jack O'Hanlon, who maintains a full library of the various studies and reports that have been made. While you're in the building you'll want to call on the town manager, the mayor and members of the Town Council and of the Town Water Commission. You will also want to talk to the general managers of the several water utilities on the island. Each of them may tell you of others who should be interviewed.

By this time you'll have discovered that there are two main alternatives being investigated. One is to dig even deeper into an aquifer far below the level where the sea water is creeping in. A primary advocate of this approach is the chairman of the Town Water Commission, Leonard Tinnan. Tinnan will tell you to talk to the project manager for the town's new test well, to the hydrogeologic consultant who designed the well, and to the people who where hired to do the engineering studies before the well was dug.

You will also want to talk with those Town Council members who favor building a pipeline to obtain water from the Savannah River. Say "Savannah River" to many people on the island and they think of the Savannah River Nuclear Facility and imagine radioactive water gushing into their homes. Others will tell you that residents of nearby communities have been drinking it for years, with no ill effects.

You will note that through all of this long litany of information sources, you have not had to consult a single database, or even go to the library. For many articles, the information is there for the taking, and one source usually points the way to the next. But there are obviously stories in which all of the information is not tidily contained in one small area, or in which the historical background is not readily available. That's where real research comes in.

THE LIBRARY

Most of what you want, if not all, can be found in any large library. In fact, if you simply go to the reference librarian and ask for assistance, the librarian will help you navigate through the possible sources. If you're not near a large library, talk to your local librarian about the reference and journal collection and how interlibrary loan document delivery and computer searches might be arranged.

Before you start, you might want to take a look at the *New York Times Guide to Reference Materials*, by reference librarian Mona McCormick. It discusses search strategies, using reference materials, searching by computer, as well as listing reference books by type and subject area.

Several familiar library references such as *Library of Congress Subject Headings, Reader's Guide to Periodical Literature, Books in Print* and a library catalog will help you broaden or narrow your search. Do you want information on caves? Does that mean ice and marine caves? Does it include stalactites, stalagmites, cave animals, dwellings? You need to figure out all of the possible terms you want to focus on, as well as to decide what you aren't interested in, such as information more than five years old, printed in a foreign language and so on.

To see what the general interest magazines have said about your topic, *Reader's Guide to Periodical Literature* is a good place to start. Updated every month, with quarterly and annual cumulations, it indexes 250 of the most popular magazines. If your library has it on CD-ROM (more about this in a moment) or via an on-line service, it will be more up to date, but there may be a fee for this. Decide how current your information needs to be before spending money on a search.

Next turn to specialized reference works that are published in virtually every field. To see which ones are appropriate for your subject, check Eugene P. Sheehy's *Guide to Reference Books.* One excellent list of source books is the Fundamental Fifteen, which was compiled by Chris Wells, formerly Director of Library Services for Gannett newspapers and now Vice President of International Operations of the Freedom Forum. If you can't find what you need in one of these volumes, you will at least get some ideas about where it can be found.

1. *Almanac of American Politics* (National Journal)
2. Almanacs (*Information Please* or *World Almanac*)
3. *Chase's Annual Events* (Contemporary Books)
4. *Contemporary Authors* (Gale Research)
5. *Current Biography* (H.W. Wilson)
6. *Editor and Publisher International Yearbook* (Editor and Publisher)
7. *Encyclopedia of Associations* (Gale Research)
8. *Facts on File: A Weekly World News Digest* (Facts on File)
9. *Physicians' Desk Reference* (Medical Economics)
10. *Standard and Poor's Register of Corporations, Directors and Executives* (Standard and Poor's)
11. *Standard Directory of Advertisers* (National Register Publishing)
12. *Standard Periodical Directory* (Oxbridge Communications)
13. *Statistical Abstract of the U.S.* (Government Printing Office)
14. *United States Government Manual* (Government Printing Office)
15. *Who's Who* (regional, subject, international — Marquis)

Be sure to ask about all of the various *Who's Who* volumes; they include women, finance and industry, the arts, science and even fictional characters (*Imaginary People: A Who's Who of Modern Fictional Characters*).

If you're seeking information on something that has been in the news, *The New York Times Index* is in most major libraries, either on paper or accessible by computer. If your library provides access to a CD-ROM system for newspapers and magazines, you can search one source for as many as fifteen hundred journals to find abstracts of articles or sometimes even the full text. For example, about twenty-five thousand libraries around the country are now equipped with a database called Social Issues

Resources Series (SIRS). It contains about ten thousand articles, most full text, and covers more than forty major subject areas for over 850 journals and newspapers. SIRS covers subjects from acid rain to zero gravity, including along the way such things as black holes, circadian rhythms, embryo transplants, hurricanes, mummy DNA, quarks and quasars, tornadoes and even unidentified flying objects. And it's only one of about forty-three hundred databases available.

Another outstanding index to world news is *Facts on File, The World News Digest With Index.* Updated weekly, it contains brief summaries of news from seventy English-language newspapers and magazines. It also includes a world atlas, containing such interesting items as the fact that the population of Argentina is 32,860,000 and the population of Antarctica (minus penguins) is zero.

If you plan to search in depth on your subject, Lee Ash's *Subject Collections* is a guide to whole collections on specialized topics in the U.S., arranged by subject. Another referral gem is *Biography and Genealogy Master Index.* This superlative bloodhound is a consolidated index to over eight hundred current and retrospective biographical dictionaries, which means that it does not contain the actual biographical information but tells what sources do, sparing you from searching out each *Who's Who* separately. Among the other sources indexed by this tome are *American Men and Women of Science, Biography Index, Contemporary Authors, Current Biography* and *Who's Who.*

COMPUTER SEARCHES

Computer databases are only about thirty years old and are generally limited to ten to fifteen years of data. Still, they can be a tremendously fast way to access material, and writers should learn what's available from them.

Begin with *The Directory of Online Databases,* which is just what it sounds like — a list of available databases. Computer vendors, such as DIALOG, NEXIS, LEXIS, WILSONLINE, BURRELLE's and DATATIMES index, abstract and provide full-text magazines, newspapers, radio and broadcast news, newswires, press releases, books, dissertations, conferences and conference papers, business reports and more. Databases have grown like kudzu—as noted, there are now over forty-three hundred of them.

Some cover only the popular literature (*Time, Smithsonian, Natural History*); others are highly specialized, such as *Nuclear Science Abstracts* or *Zoological Record*. On-line searches can provide you with anything from a profile of the mayor of Miami to information on reipedia, a new species; it can provide a list of works by Archibald MacLeish, the magazine in which an article called "Caribou Year" appeared, a comprehensive bibliography on pain, Japanese newspaper articles on Japanese women, producers and distributors of videos in the Los Angeles area, and a great deal more.

It's important to note again that in on-line searching, you must have the subject defined as narrowly as possible. Librarians who do searches are trained to help you and will not only help refine the search, but help you control costs, which could run to a hundred dollars or more. Most searches, though, run no more than fifteen minutes and will cost between ten and twenty-five dollars. Still, it's wise to search the more conventional print (or CD-ROM) reference sources before going on-line.

Some names to remember in on-line databases are the previously mentioned NEXIS, which covers the *New York Times* and other newspapers and magazines; LEXIS, which covers federal court cases and case law for the U.S., France and Britain; NEWSNET, which provides the full text of 175 newsletters; and PR NEWSWIRE, which includes press releases from seventy-five hundred companies, going back ten years. And if you want to avoid looking something up in the *Statistical Abstract of the U.S.*, DATAMAP contains thirteen thousand tables of statistical data.

CD-ROM

CD-ROM, which stands for Compact Disc/Read-Only Memory, is a single information source on one or more discs, much as you might use to access a symphony or rock concert, and is a quick-and-easy way to search out any but the very latest information.

I recently turned to CD-ROM in search of background information on rollerblading, which has almost replaced golf and tennis as the national sport of Hilton Head. After a computer catalog told me the proper term was "in-line skates," I was referred to articles in *American Health, Library Journal, Current Health,*

Ski, (they say that in-line skating compares favorably to snow skiing in both excitement and camaraderie) and *Women's Sports and Fitness.* A further check pointed me to product reviews in *Consumer Reports,* and *Runners World,* and a news story in *Business Week* relating to the ski boot maker Nordica's recent purchase of half of the Rollerblade Company. By consulting other sources I found articles in *New Statesman, Maclean's, Better Homes and Gardens* and *Aspen,* not to mention *Sunset, Cross Country Skier* and even *Popular Mechanics.* It wasn't surprising that *Consumer Reports* had said that "In-line skates, nicknamed rollerblades, are the hottest skates around." A writer planning an article on the history, impact and future of in-line skating clearly had a good start on his story.

In addition to everything else it pays for, the U.S. government also uses some of your tax money to print thousands of documents containing all manner of information. Libraries list some of these, but to be safe, examine the *Monthly Catalog of U.S. Government Publications.* This handy guide lists subject, author and title of every publication the government puts out.

The Congressional Information Service's (CIS) *Index to Publications* includes all manner of committee reports and hearings, and *Index to U.S. Government Periodicals* lists all periodicals the government has published. *The Monthly Checklist of State Publications* does the same for individual states.

Finally, while we're on the subject, let us not forget the Library of Congress, which is, as Saddam Hussein might say, the mother of all libraries. While it does not contain every book ever published, as many people think, it does contain eighty-five million items, although due to a shortage of funds in recent years, not all have been indexed and filed. While anyone is welcome to visit, this is not a lending library, and you won't be able to use it effectively unless you are able to visit Washington, DC.

It is possible to get some of their material through the public library system, however, and this is, once again, a place to ask your librarian for help. This chapter was only designed to give you a rough idea of the different information sources that are out there. To reach many of them, you may need the help of a trained librarian, who can open up a myriad of information sources that most of us have never dreamed of.

CHAPTER FIVE

A Lead Is to Lead

She is sitting alone in the crumb-strewn kitchen, clutching a yellow coffee cup in her quivering hands and thinking of ways to kill her husband."

As article leads go, this one is almost as much of a grabber as " 'Take your hand off my knee,' cried the duchess," the classic example of a successful way to catch the reader's attention. I have no idea where the account of the duchess's experiences was published, if anywhere, but the first quote was used to begin an article in *Atlanta* magazine about an abused wife, written by Atlanta freelance writer Maxine Rock. Rock showed the clip to me at *McCall's*, along with some queries. It caught our attention, we gave her an assignment and she has gone on to write a number of successful pieces for *McCall's*, as well as a great many other magazines.

There is, of course, no *right* lead. By that I mean there is no lead that is the perfect, unquestionably correct way to begin any given article. There are as many different types of leads as there are different types of writers, and there may be a half dozen good ways to begin any piece you write. But the one element all good leads have in common is: *They get your attention.*

I will give several examples of different ways to get your piece going, but first, one caveat: *Don't get hung up on the lead.*

By that I mean, don't spend days struggling to hit just the right note; when you're ready to write, start writing. You may do an entire draft before you figure out the best lead, and there's nothing wrong with that. The important thing is to get going. All writers don't agree with this, as you'll find when you read the interviews at the end of this book. Some simply cannot begin until they've found their lead. I think that what they're doing as they search for a lead is really to search for a tone, a point of view, a theme, even an overall structure for the article. Searching for the lead may be their way of getting ready to write, and if it works for them, it certainly isn't wrong. I just think that for most of us, it's better to start those words coming.

To jump start your mind, you might ask yourself a few questions: Why am I telling the reader this? What is the single most interesting or surprising aspect of or incident in my story? What is going to capture the reader's attention, make him or her stop there and not turn the page?

If you're still stuck for an opener, start with the sections of the article you feel most comfortable with. I've known of writers who felt they couldn't do their pieces until they know how they ended, so they wrote the ending first. Whatever works for you is the right way to do it.

In a short piece of a thousand words or less, however, I do think it's important to get the beginning right before you can go on. I do a lot of book reviews, and I find that I need to work out the first sentence before I can begin writing. If the piece is only a few hundred words, the first sentence establishes the theme and leads into everything that follows. I began a review of a Frederick Forsythe book, *The Deceiver*, this way: "One of the casualties of the Cold War's end is the spy-thriller writer, who, for more that forty years, has used the seemingly endless struggle of East and West as the backdrop for his tales of intrigue and adventure." I went on to explain the new antagonists Forsythe had found to replace the Evil Empire, and then into how well he had succeeded.

I began another review, of a book I liked considerably less, this way: "Reading this novel is like being at a party with a group of people you've just met, who are intermittently entertaining but whom you'd just as soon never meet again." For me, this established the tone and point of view I needed to write the review.

But most pieces you write won't be short essays or reviews, and if you're doing a longer, more complex article, and you're hung up on the lead, I think it's important to at least get some of your piece on paper. I'll be talking about structure and organization later in the book, so I won't get into that now. Let's talk about leads.

A lead has four basic functions. First, it has to command attention. The reader is leafing through a magazine, trying to decide which piece to read or whether to even take the time to read one at all, and your lead has to make him stop leafing and start reading. (Before that, of course, and even more important, the lead has to catch the editor's attention. The editor also has a lot of reading to do and may never get past a weak lead to discover all the good stuff that follows it.)

The second function is to establish the subject and general theme of the article, to point the way to what is to follow. You've got the reader's interest, but he wants to know what it's going to be about, and this is not something you can withhold for long.

Third, the lead should establish the tone of the article. Will it be satiric or humorous, a piece of hard-hitting journalism, a straightforward description of how to build something or a thoughtful essay? Again, it's only fair to the reader to make this clear from the start. And never *mis-lead*. That is, write a lead that promises one kind of article and then delivers another. Don't start funny on a serious piece, or begin with a lively anecdote and then follow it with straight exposition.

And, more important, don't write a lead that promises more than it delivers. Somebody had better be reaching for the duchess's knee, and he had better mean business.

TYPES OF LEADS

There are a great many effective ways to begin an article, and if you added up all the different types defined by different writers on the subject, you'd probably have fifty or more. I'm going to break them into four types, with some subcategories in each one.

Before I begin, let me say something I'll probably say several times: There are no hard-and-fast rules about magazine writing. No rule could have covered Tom Wolfe's lead on a piece on Las Vegas in which he repeated the word "hernia" fifty-seven times. It was supposed to replicate the sound of a busy casino, and when you read it carefully, I guess it does. So while I'm going to give you some suggestions for leads that work, you may well come up with others that work even better. I hope you do.

Anecdotal, Narrative and Action

This is probably the most common type of lead, and for a good reason—everybody loves a story. As I was writing this chapter, I picked up a copy of one of the best-written magazines around, *Vanity Fair*, and discovered, not to my surprise, that nearly every major article started with an anecdote. To take one example, here's how Peter Boyer began his profile of the rabidly conservative talk show commentator, Rush Limbaugh:

> For Peggy Noonan, the awakening came on a dinner date at Manhattan's "21." Noonan, the best-selling political-memorist and speechwriter to troubled presidents, is experienced in power dining, but she was unprepared for what happened that evening.
>
> She and her escort were greeted by the maître d', the captain, and two waiters, all of whom followed the couple to their booth, intent on conversation with Noonan's date. Soon she noticed the stares of other patrons and heard the furtively whispered query, "That's him, who's she?"

She went on to describe the crowd that gathered around their table and ended her anecdote this way: "I have gone to restaurants with Dan Rather when he was No. 1, right? I've gone to restaurants with George Bush when he was running for president. And I have never, *ever* seen anybody get the response Rush Limbaugh does."

I like this lead because it promises to tell me a story. We start out with a hook — Peggy Noonan "was unprepared for what happened." Then we follow her into the restaurant, and we wonder who she's with and why he's attracting so much attention. And then we get the payoff; this is Rush Limbaugh, and he draws more interest than top TV newsmen or even presidents. This tells us that we should be interested in this man, too, and so we read on to find out why.

You can find the anecdotal lead in most magazines.

I opened one issue of *Reader's Digest*, for instance, and found:

> The aroma of barbecued chicken filled the air inside the bright, open room. Laughter floated from the groups of people who had sacrificed precious earnings to join in this neighborhood feast. It was February 15, 1992, a summer day in the Peruvian shanty-town of El Salvador . . .

This was the beginning of an article on Peru's Marxist guerilla terrorists, and the first seven paragraphs consisted of this long anecdote dramatizing the brutal tactics of the guerrillas.

An equally grim anecdote began Tyler Norman's piece in *Savannah* magazine on the tragic death of an architect who taught at the Savannah College of Art and Design.

> On the morning of October 30, Juan Bertotto fixed himself a cup of coffee and, like any other day, cut the crossword puzzle out of the newspaper and completed it with ease. Coffee drunk, puzzle finished, he walked up the stairs to open the drawer where all of his insurance papers lay, then went outside into the pretty, enclosed courtyard behind his Victorian home on Huntingdon Street and set to a task he must have been thinking about for some time: he soaked piles of rags and towels in gasoline, placed them in a far corner of the courtyard, doused himself, put the can near the house to prevent an explosion, and sat down on the rags.
>
> All it took was one match.

After this shocking beginning, she goes into the mysteries of his life, beginning with his arrival in Savannah and leading up to his tragic end. But with this lead, she has captured our attention, and we are forced to read on to find out what kind of man could do such a thing, and why he was driven to such a desperate decision.

A good example of the narrative lead is this piece by PBS newscaster Jim Lehrer, from *Reader's Digest*:

> At four that December morning I woke up with a dry tightness in my chest. My wife, Kate, and I had been to a Mexican restaurant near our home in Washington, DC, and sometimes the enchiladas and beans exact a price . . . "Let's call a doctor," said Kate.
>
> "No, no," said I. "I'll be fine in a minute."
>
> I got back into bed. The tightness did not disappear . . .

The story was called "What a Heart Attack Taught Me," and it continued in this narrative vein, so that the lead extended almost seamlessly into the body of the article.

Another good example of the action lead was written by William H. Meyers for an article in a special business section of *The New York Times Magazine*. Even though Meyers was writing a financial story about the struggle to buy New York's Plaza Hotel, he did not settle for a routine financial page lead. By opening with an action scene, he tells us right away that this will be no dry analysis of balance sheets and financial maneuverings; this is a story that is going to *move*.

> Donald Trump charges up a staircase, kicks open a fire door and greets the blinding summer sun. Surrounded by heavyset bodyguards wearing goldplated "T's" in their lapels, he stands eighteen stories above Fifth Avenue on the roof of the Plaza Hotel. Trump is on a flying inspection tour of his latest acquisition . . .

And we are plunged headlong into the story of how he pulled it off.

A splendid narrative lead that grabs the attention from the first sentence was used by Phillip Capute in a December 1989 issue of *Esquire*. The article was about a man who had committed a single horrible act of mass murder, and the author set out to re-create the day it happened in an effort to answer the question that is always asked at such a time: "Why?"

> He wakes up late on what he knows will be the last day of his life. Late rising has been his pattern for the past three weeks. His neighbors at the El Rancho Motel have seen him only at night, coming and going on foot or in his car, a restless young man with an intense and heatless light in his blue eyes. Possibly he's been suffering from the insomnia that has plagued him for years. Possibly, by prowling around till all hours, he's been trying to avoid his recurrent nightmare. Possibly he has been going over his plans. Who can say? Dave Goodman, who lives in the room next door, thinks he acts like a speed freak. He has been an alcoholic and addict since fourteen—plenty of pills, booze and reefer—but he's stayed clean this time. He needs a clear head for what he is about to do.

While Capute's narrative began at the beginning, a narrative doesn't have to. One story we ran in *McCall's* a few years ago dealt with a mother who had been reunited, after fifteen years, with a son she had not seen since he was two years old. The article did not begin with the father's abduction of the boy, because that was not what the story was about; it began instead with his grandmother's discovery of a newspaper article that she thought might reveal where the boy could be found. From there the lead took us into the narrative, flashing back to explain who these people were and what had happened to them, bringing them to the moment when the story opened and then on to the happy conclusion.

Similarly, the story of a treasure discovery might begin as the divers sight the coral-encrusted chest that is supposed to contain the gold; then, without revealing the contents of the chest, flash back to explain how these people came to be looking for it, and tracing their efforts to the story's conclusion. In short, while a story can begin at the beginning, it is often more effective to open with some high point in the action and then flash back to reconstruct your narrative.

Another variation of the action/narrative lead is the "You" lead. This one puts you, the reader, in the driver's seat, and drags you right into the center of the action. Suppose you were writing an article on, say, the importance of checking over your car before a trip. You might begin this way: "You filled your car with gas and checked the oil and tires, and you have gotten up early to head the 174 miles to your meeting. A few minutes after you turn onto the highway it starts to rain. You turn on the windshield wipers and discover that one of them, the one in front of you, is stuck in position. You start to pull over . . ."

Not to drag out this example, the point is to put the reader in a position to identify with the argument you're making, to see how it would have an impact on his life.

Pete Hamill used the same technique in a different kind of article in *Esquire*, this one a piece about the edgy, sometimes hazardous scene along one stretch of the border between the United States and Mexico.

> You move through the hot, polluted Tijuana morning, past shops and gas stations and cantinas, past the tourist traps of the Avenida Revolución, past the egg-shaped cultural center and the new shopping malls and the government housing with bright patches of laundry hanging on the balconies; then it's through streets of painted adobe peeling in the sun, ball fields where kids play without

gloves, and you see ahead and above you ten-thousand-odd shacks perched uneasily on the Tijuana hills, and you glimpse the green road signs for the beaches as the immense luminous light of the Pacific brightens the sky. You turn, and alongside the road there's a chain link fence. It's ten feet high.

On the other side of the fence is the United States.

In this case, the "you" is a stand-in for the author, but his technique lets you share his feelings, lets you see what he saw and hear what he heard and smell what he smelled. (Notice also that 102-word first sentence, which also helps pull you along on his journey.) Hamill is doing what a writer must do — re-creating the experience he is writing about so you can share that experience with him. And by putting "you" in his shoes, you become part of his story even as you are reading it.

Yet another variation on the anecdote/action/narrative opener might be called the case history lead. Let's imagine you want to write a piece on the impact of a natural disaster, like a major hurricane. You might interview a number of people who were involved and then start off with three or four stories about what happened to each of them when the storm hit. Throughout the piece, you keep coming back to them and what they were doing, and perhaps have some comments from them at the end.

The same technique can be used with any article that seeks to describe the impact of some major event on the state or the country — the recession, Lyme disease, young children and drugs. You might want to write about the increasing amount of violence on television and begin with three or four moments of graphic and bloody action, then stop and explain what you're up to. ("These events did not take place on the mean streets of New York or Detroit or Miami, but right in your living room. They were all on recent episodes. . . .")

I have placed the anecdotal lead, the action lead and the narrative lead in the same category because they are very similar. In the anecdotal lead, we begin with a self-contained story that captures the essence of the article. An action lead starts at a highly dramatic moment in the narrative, and then will usually flash back to tell us what this is going to be about and how we got to this point. A narrative lead, however, usually begins an article that will be one continuous story. There will be no flashbacks in a narrative; the story will simply go on and build toward the climax. A narrative lead may begin more slowly than an action lead, but it will build in intensity as the story develops.

The Quote Lead

Perhaps the next most common type of lead begins with somebody talking. We love to eavesdrop on other people, and quotation marks always promise something lively and informal and interesting—particularly when the quote chosen has all of these characteristics, as well.

> "People just aren't smart anymore. We're not smart because we don't read as much. The low figures on literacy are a national disgrace. There's no way we can compete with the Germans and the Japanese. If you don't have smart people, you just cannot do it."

I used this quote as a lead in an article on the novelist John Jakes, who had just returned from a White House conference on Library and Information Services. Jakes had some harsh things to say about education and public support for libraries, and I felt that a quote was a good way to catch the reader's attention.

> "You know," said Joanne Woodward, "you've never once asked me what it's like to live with Paul Newman." True, I said, and not because I had forgotten. She thought that over for a moment and then said pensively, "I went through a period where I felt that if one more person asked me what it was like to live with Paul Newman, I was going to leave him. Or just open up and let everybody know what he's *really* like ... Why doesn't somebody ever ask him what it's like to live with *me*?"

Joe Bell's lead for this *McCall's* article works for a number of reasons. It brings both protagonists on stage in the first paragraph; it tells us that Ms. Woodward is not entirely happy with a career spent largely in her husband's shadow; it promises a lively and candid piece that will be a bit more provocative than the usual movie star puff piece.

Sometimes a quote is frankly designed to shock, and thus to set the tone for the piece that is to follow.

"Come on in, sluts," the chairman of the board of the Miss Texas Scholarship Pageant booms from inside a mauve hotel convention room in Fort Worth. Laughing gleefully, B. Don Magness watches seventy-two young women who want to be Miss America parade by in shoulders-back posture, wearing an assortment of black lace bustiers, black Lycra minidresses and tight black leather skirts.

As Jeannie Ralston explains in her interview later in the book, she felt it was important to start off with a bang. She also believed this was an effective way to begin building a picture of Magness, a man she felt strongly about.

A variation on the quote lead, which sometimes borrows the technique of the "You" lead, is the question. It can be a quote in the form of a question ("What's the worst thing you've ever heard about me?" demands James B. Holderman in the lead of an article by Alison Cook in *GQ*), but more commonly it's simply the author posing a question about the problem at hand by asking you how you feel about it. "Would you like to try a new, efficient kind of rail travel, moving three inches above the track at three hundred miles an hour?" Or, "What happens if you get sick on a flight? Well, in all probability you won't, but ..." Both of these led into articles by Glenn Eichler in his "Smart Money" column in *Esquire*, and both did the job quickly and neatly.

Think of the purpose of your lead. Do you have a quote, or can you pose a question, that neatly sums up the point of your article, and does it in a provocative way? Maybe a question is your answer.

A Scene-Setting Lead

Another variation on the "you are there" lead, the scene-setter describes the area in which the action will take place in such a way as to put you right there. These seem most favored by travel writers.

With the morning mist swirling in the valley of the Cefou like a smoky sea, the fortified town of Cordes is ethereal, other-worldly, an enchanted citadel floating above the clouds.

Charles Redman began a piece this way in the final issue of the late lamented *European Travel and Life*.

An article called "Greece on the Precipice," by Ron Hall, in the July 1992 issue of *Conde Nast Traveler*, starts off:

> Here I am in the Astrakas mountain refuge, six thousand feet up in the high Pindus Range of northwestern Greece, savoring that comforting aroma of drying socks and steaming soup, once remembered from childhood camps of long ago . . . We are on a col above a high tableland traditionally roamed by nomadic Sarakatsani shepherds. Just beyond, to the east, is the mass of Gamila (8,195 feet), a mountain that may concede something to the Alps in terms of altitude but nothing in terms of drama. Its peaks rise, gently at first, from the high plain but then, with terrifying abruptness, spill off the edge of the tableland in a near-vertical drop of more than a mile . . .

Those of us with a fear of heights are already feeling a bit queasy, but we have certainly had the scene set for us, and we are being pulled inexorably into his story.

The Statement Lead

This lead, as I define it, has many variations. The statement can be startling. It can be an expression of opinion, preferably controversial, that makes you read on to see how the author backs it up. It might philosophical, designed to show that the author has thought a lot about this subject and is prepared to tell you what he knows and also what it means. The statement lead can even be of what writer Max Gunther calls the "prose-poetry" type; a kind of poetic extension of the philosophical. Or it can be humorous; again, a straightforward piece of writing, but one designed to convey the happy news that something funny is going to happen.

A good example of the lead designed to shock was written by Sallie Tisdale, then working as a registered nurse and writing of her experiences in *Harper's*.

> We do abortions here; that is all we do. There are weary grim moments when I think I cannot bear another basin of bloody remains, utter another kind phrase of reassurance. So I leave the procedure room in the back and reach for a new chart. Soon I am talking to an eighteen-year-old

woman pregnant for the fourth time. I push up her sleeve to check her blood pressure and find row upon row of needle marks . . .

In a different vein, Lynn Hirschberg, writing about Sandra Bernhard for *Vanity Fair*, began with this vivid image:

> Sandra Bernhard likes to take her clothes off. She's naked in her new HBO special, "Sandra After Dark." A few months from now, she'll be nude — and, in one shot, painted gold — in a *Playboy* pictorial. And right now, before a quarter-empty auditorium at Balley's Casino Resort in Las Vegas, Bernhard has slipped out of her see-through sequined gown and, except for a purple thong bikini bottom, she is, yes, naked. "Take it off," someone yells. She smiles her odd, downturned smile. The thought has definitely occurred to her.

Susan Percy wanted to tell her *Atlanta* readers about what she called the real women of the city, and she decided to grab attention by playing off a familiar image:

> Dammit, Scarlett, take your seventeen-inch waist and get out of here. And tell Melanie she can go with you. You'd think the city of Atlanta never had a female population outside the pages of *Gone With the Wind*. Frankly, my dear, I want to talk about real flesh-and-blood Atlanta women, wives and mothers and daughters who had to adjust to ever-changing sets of rules about matters grave and small, play with a deck that was stacked against them, and make do.

The opinion lead can also be startling; at the very least, it should not be expressing a commonly held belief. Jamie Diamond began her piece on male vanity in *Lear's* this way:

> I hate gorgeous men. I hate it that they'd rather work out on a machine that simulates the experience of climbing the stairs to the observation deck of the Empire State Building than take me out to dinner. I fail to find conversations about high-fiber diets fascinating . . . Something has gotten into a man . . . who measures his pulse on a treadmill when he could be making his heart race in a situation that doesn't normally require shoes . . .

Terry Kay stated her opinion very firmly in a piece on education she wrote for *Atlanta* magazine:

There are wonderful teachers in America and there are teachers—far too many—who simply should not be in the presence of students. They should be organizing terrorist groups in Lebanon, inflicting fear and pain on captors with sharp-pointed red pencils, or they should be lecturing roadside rocks, which have the material composition to withstand ceaseless boredom.

And Rust Hills, writing one of his lighthearted but totally serious instructional pieces in *Esquire,* this one on how to give a dinner party, began with this blunt statement: "Everybody does everything wrong nowadays." We know that Rust is going to tell us how to do it correctly (he once wrote a book called "How To Do Things Right,") and we can be sure that while he may mince something, it won't be words.

The philosophical lead is tricky and requires a high degree of skill, and this is a type you might want to work up to. To give you something to shoot at, here is a lead from perhaps the greatest essayist of the twentieth century, E.B. White. White was writing about New York for the old *Holiday* magazine, way back in 1948, but it has been reprinted so many times that it still seems fresh:

On any person who desires such queer prizes, New York will bestow the gift of loneliness and the gift of privacy. It is this largess that accounts for the presence within the city's walls of a considerable section of the population: for the residents of Manhattan are to a large extent strangers who have pulled up stakes somewhere and come to town, seeking sanctuary or fulfillment or some greater or lesser grail. The capacity to make such dubious gifts is a mysterious quality of New York. It can destroy an individual, or it can fulfill him, depending a good deal on luck. No one should come to New York to live unless he is willing to be lucky.

One reason I think the philosophical lead is so difficult is that it requires maturity and experience, and beyond this a quality of mind that gives the writer the ability to see and understand the full meaning of his subject. White was, of course, one of our finest writers, but beyond that he had spent a good part of his life in New York. He not only loved the city but understood it, and he was steeped in its history. This essay, titled "Here Is New York," is filled with historical allusions, with a sense that White is not only telling us how it is but how it was, as well. It has emotion and feeling and wisdom, and it makes one even sadder that the city he celebrated almost fifty years ago has changed so disappointingly. The full text can be found in *Essays of E.B. White.*

Having said this, let me add that I am not suggesting the philosophical lead to the beginning writer. Don't try one unless you know your subject so well, and feel about it so deeply, that you think you can pull it off. If you do try one, put it aside for a few days and then go back and read it fresh. If it holds, give it a shot.

Another good philosophical lead was written for *Sports Illustrated* by Frank Deford. Deford was one of that magazine's best reporters and writers for a good many years, before he went on to write books, edit a national sports newspaper and branch out of the sports area. I like the following lead because it goes beyond the world of sports to make a broader point. It deals with the late-in-life attempted comeback of a former New York Yankee pitcher named Jim Bouton. After ten years out of baseball, during which he had been a sports announcer, a TV personality and the author of a best-selling book, Bouton wanted to go back to the minor leagues and find out if he could still pitch.

With this lead, Deford tells us that he is not simply telling about Bouton's comeback; his piece will be dealing with the nature of fame and success and human vanity, and with the dreams older people cling to and so seldom achieve. He started this way:

> The man born to money expects riches for a lifetime, just as the man born with good looks assumes they will always get him by. But if the gold or good looks disappear, most such men learn to accept it. Even the vainest of men succumb at last to the reality that their physical gifts are gone. But perhaps no man is so haunted as the one who was once stunned by instant success, for he lives thereafter with the illusion that tomorrow is bound to bring one more belt of good fortune.

As I have credited Max Gunther with inventing the "prose-poetry" lead, let me use as an example one he wrote for us back in the mid-sixties for the old *Saturday Evening Post*. There was at the time an upsurge of interest in the universe, what was really "out there" amidst the stars. Research projects were beginning, and we sensed that it was time to examine it all. To do that, we picked Max, who has always prided himself with being able to write any story, no matter how complex or arcane. Max talked about how he felt after getting the assignment in his excellent book *Writing the Modern Magazine Article*.

> How could I compress this subject into five thousand words? I worried about it for more than a year before finding the courage to start writing. I tried and discarded over twenty leads. All of them sounded too "small," incompatible with the massive scope and sweep of the subject matter. Finally I decided that the only way to get the article off the ground was to use prose-poetry, a patch of purple that told of my own emotions:
> "In a near-infinity of burning stars and black space so enormous that it absolutely cannot be imagined, on a speck of rock so small that to mention it seems almost ridiculous, tiny creatures called men are trying to find out where they are."

We agreed wholeheartedly with his choice of lead, and that's just the way it ran.

Before I leave the straightforward approach, let me share a few of my favorite humor leads. Here is Dave Barry, writing a piece called "Moving Madness" for *Cosmopolitan*:

> I personally have never given birth to a child, but I have seen it dramatized a number of times on television, and I would say that in terms of pain childbirth does not hold a candle to moving. For one thing childbirth has a definite end to it. The baby comes out, looking like a Vaseline-smeared ferret, and the parents get to beam at it joyfully, and that is that.

Here's another, this one in the May 1987 *Field & Stream*. It's not thigh-slapping hilarious, but it was written with a gently humorous tone that makes it a joy to read.

There are a few basic truths that a person doesn't so much learn as simply know, beyond doubt, to be so. It's warmer when the sun shines. Half the men in Mississippi (and probably a few of the women) are named Roy Bob. Nobody from Southern California owns a pair of socks. That type of thing.

He went on to develop the theme that panfishing isn't usually considered serious fishing, and then to show that it definitely can be.

Humor is good for setting the tone, and as long as that's the tone you want to set, and you have the skill to pull it off, it works marvelously. But being funny is serious stuff, and I'd approach it with caution.

While it would be possible to come up with an almost infinite number of variations on this list, I think it covers the most widely used and commonly accepted ways to get your article going. Put very simply, they are:

1. Start by telling a story
2. Start by letting somebody else talk
3. Start by thrusting us into the action
4. Start by simply telling us what you're going to be telling us about

Any one of these approaches will work, as well as many others that may occur to you as you put your article together. Just remember the thought I started with: A lead has one simple purpose—to catch the reader's attention and lure him or her into reading what you have written.

Any lead that does that is a good one.

CHAPTER SIX

How to End Your Piece in Style

Now that you have some ideas on starting your piece, let me skip ahead a bit to talk about how to end it. The ending of a magazine article is very different from the ending of a newspaper story. On a paper, you're never quite sure how much space you'll have, so you put the most important material in front and continue in descending order of importance, knowing the copyeditor will probably lop off the last few paragraphs, anyway.

But a magazine article ending is very different. It is the last thought you leave the reader with, and will have a great influence on the way he or she feels about the entire piece. A good ending can make up for a lot of sins.

One of the most effective techniques you can use in crafting a fully satisfying article is to write an ending that refers to elements you've written in your lead. By echoing a theme or idea expressed in the beginning, you give the reader a feeling of completion, a sense that a circle has been closed, and that everything has been said that needs to be said. I began a piece on leads some years ago with the first two paragraphs of the previous chapter. When I needed an ending, I went back to the duchess again with a comment that somebody had better have a hand on her knee, and he had better mean business. That completed the circle and made, I think, an effective close.

The endings of articles have not been written about very much. Bill Zinsser did include a chapter on the subject in *On Writing Well*, but it's one of the shortest chapters in the book. The fact is that few people have said much about the best ways to wind up an article. Max Gunther once asked a number of editors what kinds of endings they liked, and he got a lot of blank stares. "I know a good ending when I read one" was the almost universal response, but there were few useful suggestions.

One thought did predominate: A good ending is satisfying. The reader feels the subject has been covered, the essential points have been made and nothing more remains to be said.

John McPhee, who many think is the best magazine writer of our time, places such importance on the ending that he claims to "always know the last line of a story before I've written the first one." Barbara Raymond, a freelancer who tells of her writing experiences in a later chapter, once told me that her current assignment was going well because "I've got the lead and the ending and all I have to do is fill in the rest."

Jerome Stern, who directs the writing program at Florida State University, was not talking about magazine articles in his book *Making Shapely Fiction*, but his point about endings works for nonfiction as well. "The closer and closer you get to the ending," he writes, "the more weight each word has, so that by the time you get to the last several words each one carries an enormous meaning. A single gesture or image at the end can outweigh all that has gone before."

During my years as an editor, whenever I picked up an article from a writer who was new to me, I would usually read the lead and then skip to the end; if the writer had started well and finished strongly, I would know I was in good hands and would settle down to read with some real sense of anticipation.

Having said all this, what *is* a good ending? What are the different methods you can use to bring your piece to a satisfying conclusion? "I always try to end sooner than the reader expects me to," Zinsser says. "The perfect ending should take the reader slightly by surprise."

There are a great many ways to bring your piece to a strong finish, and I've made up an arbitrary list of ten of them. There may be a certain amount of overlapping here, and doubtless you'll find—and write—endings that don't fit any of these categories, but here are some of the most effective.

THE CIRCLE

As I said, nothing is more effective in giving the reader a sense that the subject has been covered than a return to a theme introduced in the lead. As Peter Jacobi, a long-time teacher, columnist and writing consultant, wrote in a January 1982 column in *The Ragan Report*, "The reader should be left satisfied, feel that he's read something finished, something with a point clearly made, something with a unity that has moved him from start to finish almost in a circular manner."

Some years ago, Shana Alexander wrote what may be the best piece ever done on Judy Garland. Garland had begun one of her many comebacks with a concert tour, and Alexander began as the curtain went up on a typical performance: ". . . a plump little thirty-eight-year-old woman hiding behind furls of dusty curtain knows it is again time to go to work, and to deafening billows of applause that drown out the orchestra's final crashing chords, Miss Judy Garland trots cheerfully to center stage."

After describing the concert in vivid detail, and reconstructing Garland's turbulent but wildly successful career, the writer brings her back again to the last moments before another performance: "Without warning, Judy Garland suddenly turns her back on the watchers in the wings, sets her shoulders, takes what seems like a ten-gallon deep breath, and then—astonishingly, as one looks out from the darkness directly into the footlights' glare—she appears to glide away onto the bright-lit stage like a child's pull toy, powered by the rising wave of the applause itself."

We have met this remarkable woman, and we are back where we started; the circle has been completed.

In a profile of Cybil Shepherd in *Memphis* magazine a few years back, Ed Weathers began with Shepherd on the deck of her Memphis apartment overlooking the Mississippi, "wearing a 'Memphis Country Club Member—guest 1982' visor, aviator sunglasses and a black bikini . . ." Several thousand words later Weathers is back on the deck, but this time it is late in the day. "The sky turns a deeper purple, and Shepherd turns contemplative. 'You know,' she says, 'I regret every sunset I miss here.' As she gazes across the Mississippi, the Memphis sun disappears, headed toward L.A." Weathers has closed the circle, returning to where he began, and the reader feels a sense of completion.

THE SUMMARY

If the word summary brings to mind phrases like "as I have been saying" or "as we have seen," that's not what I'm talking about.

A good summary ending can take many forms, none of which begin "in conclusion." Reading through a typical issue of *Reader's Digest*, I found several examples of summary endings in the form of quotes. At the end of a piece on people who have been swindled in phony land deals, Trevor Armbrister quotes an official of the federal Department of Housing and Urban Development: "If it sounds too good to be true, it probably is." This advice has been given a good many times, but it still makes a very apt ending.

Another *Digest* article, this one on the importance of helmets for cyclists, concluded:

> "So many things are totally out of control in a motorcycle or bicycle accident," says Dr. Donald Leslie, a head-injury specialist. "A helmet is one thing you can control."

A splendid example of the summary ending that does not sound like a summary was used by AP reporter Saul Pett in his Pulitzer-Prize-winning article on the federal bureaucracy and how it got to be so big.

> The parts multiply like the denizens of a rabbit warren on New Year's Eve. Everybody, it seems, wants something or opposes something and, in the melee, bureaucracy grows larger and more shapeless and threatens to become in itself, a government of too many people, by too many people, for too many people.

THE QUOTE

The straight quote ending does not necessarily summarize the point of the piece, but it should reiterate its theme and tone. It's a good idea to look for an appropriate quote when you're typing up your notes, some comment that seems to sum things up in a snappy and appropriate way.

One I've always liked comes from a piece Richard Gehman wrote for us at *True* magazine years ago. It was about the Dalton family, for many generations (even back to the time of Queen Victoria) the preeminent rat catchers of London. After what amounted to a short course in the history of the rat and how to catch him, Gehman concluded with a quote from Bill Dalton, elder statesman of the clan:

He has grown so fond of rats over the years that some-times, as he is sitting a lonely vigil in a dark room in the depths of this ancient city, he begins to speculate uneasily over the future. "What I wonder," he says, "is this — sup-pose I'm a rat in the next world? What am I going to do to keep away from the bloody Daltons?"

A *Vanity Fair* piece in November 1992, by Nancy Collins, began with a quote ("I don't give a shit what people think." Elizabeth Taylor, as usual, is speaking her mind.) and also ended with one. After a piece telling of her life today and her hard work raising money for AIDS research, Collins ends with another quote from Taylor.

> The world's most famous movie star is now the world's most famous AIDS activist. And once again she is center stage. "In Amsterdam, people from ACT UP [a gay activist group] were demonstrating outside the building where we held my press conferences. As I walked past them one day they yelled, 'Act up, Liz. Act up.' And I thought, Well you've got the right girl. Worry not. I will."

Another ending I'm fond of has elements of the quote ending and the one I am about to describe, the anecdotal ending. It was written by Dalma Heyn for *Mademoiselle* and was, as she put it, "about men who take off when the going gets tough, and about women who try to keep those men instead of just letting go." It ended this way:

> And if you've ever had the luxury of saying to someone, "Thanks for pulling me through this," after a tough time in your life, you'll surely crave the depth of that kind of commitment again. Which means you'll need a person of character by your side who can greet troubles like, well, like a man. So stick to your guns and do not listen to people who drone on about the man shortage, who consider attri-butes like ambulatory and heterosexual sufficient reason to hold onto a guy. Listen instead to my seventy-eight-year-old friend Evelyn. Several years ago I introduced her to a rather vague young man I knew. They spoke for several minutes; then I watched her eyes glaze over. The minute

he left I said protectively, "Well, he's a man who hasn't yet come into his own."

She looked me straight in the eye. "My dear," she announced, "that man has no own to come into."

THE ANECDOTE

Just as you looked through your notes for a good quote to wind up your story, you might also look for a good anecdote, perhaps the second best if you plan to lead with your best one. It need not be a full anecdote, just some bit of action, some little story that seems to sum up the essence of the article.

Novelist William Kennedy wound up an August 1992 GQ article about a long-ago interview with Louis Armstrong this way:

> There is one other memory, of something that happened at the beginning of our meeting, when I interrupted his warmup. Louis got dressed after I knocked, I went in and sat down, and he picked up his horn, feeling unfinished, and he said, "Wait till I hit the high note," and then he played a little while I listened—the end of "Nevada." He blew some low notes, then a few higher ones, and finally he hit the high one and held it for about a week and turned it like a corkscrew and flattened it out two or three ways and sharpened it up and blew it out the window.
>
> Then he put down the horn and smiled.
>
> "Solid," he said.
>
> Oh, yeaaahhhh.

At the close of Robert Sam Anson's November 1991 *Esquire* article on the filming of Oliver Stone's movie about the assassination of President Kennedy, Anson remembers a moment near the end of the long seventy-nine-day shoot.

> The light was fading and preparations for the final retake were finished. The action this time went flawlessly. As Costner walked off, burdened by what Mr. X has told him about the assassination and Vietnam, two pig-tailed black girls took their cue and, impossibly happy, began dancing over the knoll. And then, Oliver Stone, who'd been observing from beneath a tent that resembled nothing so much as a

GI's hutch, did something that was both crazy and wonderful: He leaped up, and, as the cameras rolled, joined in.

As he played, all-at-once young again, it seemed a different era, a time when John Kennedy was alive and the country itself seemed young. In Oliver Stone's smile was a memory of what America had been, before "the bad guys," as he called them, had stolen its hopes. By making a movie, he'd searched for those villains, and found in his work the beginnings of an answer. Perhaps to the mystery of a crime. Perhaps to the puzzle of himself.

And Joseph R. Judge, combining elements of the surprise and the ironic ending, told this little bit of history at the end of a fine piece on early exploration of the New World that appeared in *National Geographic* a few years ago. After reporting that the first European settlements were Spanish, predating the English colonization by almost a century, he wound up this way:

> Thus it was when a Spanish caravel came into the Chesapeake in 1611, under the pretext of searching for a lost ship, and captured a young English pilot named John Clark. Three from the caravel were stranded ashore and were jailed. One died of starvation; another, found to be English, was later hanged for treason. The third, Don Diego de Molina, survived four years imprisonment in Virginia, railing in letters smuggled home against English designs in a land to which Spain had such an ancient and honorable claim, and calling Jamestown "a new Algiers in America."
>
> Clark had been taken to Spain and interrogated, and in due course of time each man was returned to his native land. Clark returned to the sea and found work to his liking as first mate on a ship bound for America.
>
> Her name was *Mayflower*.

THE END OF ACTION

This is sometimes appropriate for a narrative, but not always. It, like the summary, gives a feeling that the last act has taken place and the events about which the article was written are over. In Joan Didion's classic collection of articles, *Slouching Toward Bethlehem*, she includes a memoir of coming of age in New York called "Goodbye to All That." After remembering what it was like for a young girl to come to the big city from California and try and make her fortune there, she ends:

> The last time I was in New York was in a cold January and everyone was ill and tired. Many of the people I used to know there had moved to Dallas or gone on Antabuse or had bought a farm in New Hampshire. We stayed ten days, and then we took an afternoon flight back to Los Angeles, and on the way home from the airport that night I could see the moon on the Pacific and smell jasmine all around and we both knew that there was no longer any point in keeping the apartment we still kept in New York. There were years when I called Los Angeles "the Coast," but they seemed a long time ago.

John McPhee does everything so well that it's natural that I should turn to him for an end of action ending. This is from a *New Yorker* series he wrote back in 1969 on a tennis match at the U.S. Open between Arthur Ashe and Clark Graebner. McPhee was not, of course, simply describing another tennis match. He was using the match as a device, a framework with which to write a twin profile of these two young athletes, both at the top of their game, and of the very nature of competition itself. "Arthur Ashe, his feet apart, his knees slightly bent, lifts a tennis ball into the air. The toss is high and forward . . ."

And just as he has begun with the start of the action, he ends as the action ends:

> "Match point," Ashe tells himself. "Now I'll definitely play it safe." But Graebner hits the big serve into the net, then hits his second serve to Ashe's backhand. The ball and the match are spinning into perfect range. Ashe's racquet is back. The temptation is just too great, and caution fades. He hits it for all. Game, set, match to Lieutenant Ashe. When the stroke is finished, he is standing on his toes, his arms flung open, wide, and high.

THE IRONIC

In a marvelous essay called "Journalese, or Why English Is the Second Language of the Fourth Estate," John Lee crams in many of the worst examples of newspaper writing in one nifty closing paragraph, even including the cliché of the summary ending.

In sum, journalese is a truly vital language, the last bulwark against libel, candor and fresh utterance. Its prestigious, ground-breaking, state-of-the-art lingo makes it arguably the most useful of tongues, and its untimely demise would have a chilling effect, especially on us award-winning journalists.

Irony should be used sparingly, but when the subject matter is appropriate, it can really drive home the point.

A combination of the anecdotal, the ironic and the quote comes at the end of Rex Reed's splendid profile of Ava Gardner, taken from his book *Do You Sleep in the Nude?*

It had been a long afternoon of talking and drinking, and they are all going out to dinner:

> Ava is in the middle of Park Avenue, the scarf falling around her neck and her hair blowing wildly around the Ava eyes. Lady Brett in the traffic, with a downtown bus as the bull. Three cars stop on a green light and every taxi-driver on Park Avenue begins to honk. The autograph hunters leap through the polished doors of the Regency and begin to scream . . . They (Ava and her entourage) are already turning the corner into Fifty-Seventh Street, fading into the kind of night, the color of tomato juice in the headlights, that only exists in New York when it rains.
>
> "Who was it?" asks a woman walking a poodle.
>
> "Jackie Kennedy" answers a man from his bus window.

THE SURPRISE

Surprise endings are hard to find, and most articles, particularly long ones, don't lend themselves to this sort of treatment. Truman Capote pulled it off effectively in a piece called "Mr. Jones," which appeared in his collection *Music for Chameleons*. Although Capote was best known as a novelist, he was a skilled reporter and a matchless storyteller. Jones was a neighbor of Capote's in a small Brooklyn rooming house during Capote's early years in New York. The man was both crippled and blind, with few friends and no known occupation, and no one thought him remarkable until the day he disappeared.

Then, ten years later, Capote was riding on a Moscow subway when he looked up and saw his former neighbor.

> I was about to cross the aisle and speak to him when the train pulled into a station, and Mr. Jones, on a pair of fine sturdy legs, stood up and strode out of the car. Swiftly, the train door closed behind him.

What had seemed a simple sketch of a casual acquaintance suddenly turned into a spy story — and a memorable one.

THE POETIC

In this case, the writer is allowed. to indulge in some flowery writing, perhaps even a bit of philosophy. It can be self-indulgent (be wary of this), but it can also leave an echo in the mind that the reader will not soon forget. One of the best I know is from E.B. White's classic essay on New York, which I quoted in chapter five. The New York he wrote about is gone, as is the great Mr. White, but his final image has stayed with me.

> A block or two west of the new City of Man in Turtle Bay there is an old willow tree that presides over an interior garden. It is a battered tree, long-suffering and much climbed, held together by strands of wire but beloved of those who know it. In a way it symbolizes the city; life under difficulties, growth against odds, sap-rise in the midst of concrete, and the steady reaching for the sun. Whenever I look at it nowadays, and feel the cold shadow of the planes, I think: "If it were to go, all would go — this city, this mischievous and marvelous monument which not to look upon would be like death.

White avoids the pitfall of sentimentality through his skills as a reporter. He never writes in generalities. The tree is "battered . . . long suffering and much climbed, held together by strands of wire." He uses it as a symbol of the city itself, and he calls up an image that was much in our minds in 1948 — the threat of nuclear war — to drive home the importance of every living thing.

The article is long — about eight thousand words — and it needed some closing image to symbolize his essential feelings. There is poetry in his language, but it is not a flight of fancy.

Every word is firmly rooted, like the little tree, in the reality of life in the city.

THE ECHO

This carries the circle technique to its ultimate extent by repeating a word or phrase frequently throughout the piece, so that it becomes almost a theme in itself. Max Gunther recalls an article he once wrote on the history and legends of gold. He dropped the word in frequently, in the form of one-word paragraphs, after many of his anecdotes, and closed with:

> It's the bloodstained metal. The metal that can make you rich. Or dead.
> Gold.

THE STRAIGHT STATEMENT

While this sort of ending does summarize the point of the article, it is certainly not the "as we have seen" approach. Remember that your conclusion is the final thought you want to leave with the reader, the one that reemphasizes the point and answers the question: "Why did I read this piece?"

I like to close with a thought that drives home the essence of what I have written, but definitely does not repeat it. As Zinsser says, "Every element in a piece should be doing something that hasn't been done before."

An example of the straight statement ending that I'm fond of was written by former Senator (and perennial presidential candidate) Eugene McCarthy, in an article for *Geo* magazine. His subject was political campaigning, and he concluded:

> Defeat in politics, even relative failure, is not easy to accept. Dismissing the troops, as both Napoleon and Robert E. Lee learned, is not easy. Soldiers do not want to take their horses and mules and go back to the spring plowing. It is better to win.

IN CONCLUSION . . .

This list obviously does not include every possibility, but it should give you some good ideas. The essential point to remember is that the ending is probably the second most important element in your article, after the lead, and you should be pointing toward it all the way through. A weak ending leaves a soft, squishy feeling about the article; a strong one will cover up a lot of weak spots. When you've finished writing, and waited a day or two and read your piece over again, see if you haven't gone on longer than you really need to. The best ending may be a few paragraphs back — maybe even a few pages!

I've quoted the estimable Mr. Zinsser frequently, so I think I'll just let him have the last word: "When you've finished telling what you want to tell, stop."

CHAPTER SEVEN

Putting It All Together

Bob Stein, who was editor of *McCall's* during the happiest of my seventeen years as managing editor, had one comment he invariably made when puzzled by an article we were considering: "Why is she telling me this?"

Bob was once again being frustrated by the fact that many writers, even seasoned professionals, fail to make clear just what the article is going to be about and why it was worth his—and the reader's—time to read it. This brief but vitally important section should come immediately after the lead, or perhaps even be part of the lead itself, but it has to be there. It has been called many things—establishment paragraph, thesis statement, nutgraph—but its essential purpose is to tell the reader where the article is going and why it will be worthwhile to follow along.

In my *Sandlapper* article on an innovative and remarkably successful school in Charleston, South Carolina, known as the Ashley River Creative Arts Elementary School, I inserted this sentence about the end of the fourth paragraph:

> At a time when SAT's and other test scores are dropping all over the country, when schools are accused of failing to teach our children even the basic skills and *Time* magazine charges that an "appalling number of America's schools are atrocious," Ashley River stands as a model of what can be done with imagination, dedication and a lot of very hard work.

What I was saying, of course, was that Ashley River was not only remarkable in itself, but schools throughout the country could learn from its example. In short, a message that everyone from parents to educators to school board administrators should pay heed to.

In a splendid article for *Life* magazine called "The Detective," James Mills followed New York City detective George Barrett around for weeks and reported in great detail on how he did his job. Mills inserted this sentence at the end of his lead:

> To some people George Barrett is precisely what's wrong with law enforcement. To others he is all that can save it.

In both instances, the thesis was stated very briefly. The "Why I am telling you this" section can run a paragraph or maybe even a little longer, but it should be fairly short. You know your theme by the time you're writing the piece, and it shouldn't take too long to share this with the reader. Some writers even suggest writing it out and posting it where they see it constantly as they write. (One writer told me, somewhat whimsically, that Shakespeare might have kept in mind the simple thesis: *Hamlet* is about a man who can't make up his mind.)

In an article in *Vanity Fair* a couple of years ago, Ron Rosenbaum explored the controversy surrounding Dr. Jack Kevorkian. The article started by describing Dr. Kevorkian's first use of his so-called "suicide machine," and then began to tell what he was up to.

> In one respect the trial is the revenge of the "goddanged ethicists" on a doctor who disdained their strictures. A parade of the medical profession's deepest thinkers on matters of Life and Death, Healing and Killing, took the stand here in the Pontiac, Michigan, courthouse to attack what Dr. Kevorkian had done. The defense countered by likening the doctor to the great martyrs of intellectual and medical history persecuted for advocating ideas ahead of their time. The Doctor himself compares his ordeal to the famous Scopes trial of the twenties (in which a schoolteacher was convicted for teaching evolution). Dr. K's chief defense attorney, Geoffrey Fieger, goes further: "This is more than the Scopes trial. This is the trial of Socrates."

And then Rosenbaum gave us his "why I am telling you this" statement—the question his article wants to answer, the point he wants to make.

Is this the trial of Socrates—or Dr. Mengele? Is Dr. Jack Kevorkian a brilliant if heretical philosopher or a shameless medical murderer?

Gary Smith was a National Magazine Award finalist in 1992 with a touching article about a police detective named Lt. Rick Davey who finally identified a little girl who died in a tragic circus fire in Hartford, Connecticut—forty-seven years before. Davey is going through the evidence when he hears a colleague approaching and shuts the file drawer.

What would he say if they asked him what he was doing? That an unclaimed little girl buried beneath a gravestone marked only by her morgue number, Little Miss 1565, had obsessed him? That he was on the verge of cracking open the investigation of a circus fire that killed 168 people . . . in 1944?

Smith's *Life* story then goes on to tell us how Davey solved the mystery of Little Miss 1565's identity, and laid to rest a haunting mystery.

Once you've told the reader what the story is going to be about, and why he or she should stick with you, it's time to produce on the story you promised. And now you have to answer that nasty little question your subconscious has been asking: "How do I take all of this mass of material I've accumulated, this pile of notes and clippings and books and speeches and old newspaper articles, not to mention the interviews and facts I've learned through just plain digging, and turn it into a coherent article that runs no longer than the assigned length?"

In the chapter on interviewing, I mentioned typing up your notes, and this should be done whether they're notes on an interview or on any other reporting you've done. But with all of your material at hand, how do you begin the tortuous process of transforming it into a finished article?

In her delightful book, *Poison Penmanship*, Jessica Mitford poses the same question and answers it this way:

One technique I have found useful in the early stages of an inquiry is to write letters to friends about what I am doing. In that way I perforce start editing the material for fear my correspondent's eyes will glaze over with boredom if I put in everything I have learned. Also, one's style is bound to be more relaxed than it will be at the dread moment when one writes "Page 1" on a manuscript for an editor.

Tom Wolfe (*The Right Stuff*) began as a newspaper reporter, and decided to try writing the longer magazine piece during a newspaper strike in New York. He spent a month researching his first article, one on customized cars, and then when he settled down to write, he had no idea how to begin. After several days of agonizing struggle, he telephoned his editor at *Esquire*, Byron Dobell, and told him he couldn't do it. Dobell said they had already laid out Wolfe's story and engraved the pictures, that they had to have the story, and if Wolfe couldn't write it at least he could be of some help. He asked Wolfe to write him a letter describing what he'd seen and learned, and Dobell would turn these notes over to, as Wolfe puts it, "a real writer" who could complete the story.

Wolfe rolled a sheet of paper in his machine, typed out "Dear Byron," and started writing in the informal way of one person telling another about some remarkable thing. Dobell simply cut the "Dear Byron" off the top and published it just as Wolfe had written it.

Where Wolfe found his style by writing a letter to a friend, other writers say they figure out their structure by just studying their notes and other research material and then putting it all aside and just thinking about it for a day or so. As Bill Zinsser explains it: "The job of organizing a long piece is one of the hardest tasks a writer has. My technique could be called 'just thinking'—just thinking about the shape, thinking what I'm trying to do, where I'm going next."

John McPhee has a much more complex way of organizing his material. First, I should point out that virtually all of McPhee's work appears first in *The New Yorker*, often runs in several parts totaling fifty thousand words or more, and subsequently appears in book form. McPhee spends months researching an article, and amasses a mountain of material. In his introduction to *The John McPhee Reader*, William L. Howarth explains the author's methods.

McPhee takes notes in a series of notebooks, and the first thing he does is transcribe the notebooks, in order, adding whatever details he remembers as he goes along. This may give him a hundred or more typed sheets, which he then copies for later use. He then reads and rereads these pages, looking for areas in which he might need to do more research. He is also, during this period, forming an idea of how it might all come together.

He then writes the lead and, as I said before, plans the ending. Then he goes back to his typed notes and begins to code them, so that all of the material on a given subject can be identified and located easily. Once the material is coded, he writes the name of each category on an index card and shuffles them around until he determines the order in which the different parts of the article will be presented. When he is satisfied, he tacks the cards up on a bulletin board.

With a rough structure now in mind, he takes the duplicate set of notes, codes it according to the subject categories on his index cards and cuts it up into scraps of a few sentences to a page or two, each scrap devoted to one of the coded topics. The scraps are then sorted into file folders, each folder corresponding to one of the index cards. He is now ready. He stabs a dart under the first index card, takes out the corresponding file folder and begins to write. When he has finished this section he moves the dart, opens the next folder and continues.

Having organized so carefully, he finds that the work flows easily, and when he goes back over his first draft it is mostly to trim out unnecessary words or passages and polish the style. With the article having been planned out so carefully before the writing started, he rarely makes any organizational changes and the first draft is fairly close to the final one.

This approach is probably more structured and time-consuming than you would feel is necessary for a short article, but I have gone into it in such detail because I think it represents the ideal way to get ready to write. At the very least, I think you need to type up your notes, code them by subject and rough out an outline showing the order in which you plan to present the material. By planning carefully, the actual writing will go much more easily.

This is a good time to decide what you aren't going to need. You may have acquired press releases or speeches or clippings that have been duplicated by interviews or reporting, or just aren't essential. Don't throw them away, but do put them in a separate pile. You can always refer to them later to see if you've left out anything. If you work on a word processor, you can simply put material you think you won't need at the end of the file. Then, when your draft is finished, you can go through it to make sure this discarded material is really of no use to your piece.

One small tip: You won't write it all in one session, so you need to stop at a point where you know what's coming next. The outline will help enormously. Writer's block raises its ugly head because the writer doesn't know what to say next. By planning ahead, you'll always be ready to sit down and start up again.

BUT HOW DO I STRUCTURE IT?

The approach I have outlined works fine on a narrative, in which events can be described in the order in which they happened. But suppose you are writing about, say, some state or local problem, and there is no single story line? It might be problems with toxic waste disposal, inadequate day-care facilities, racial tensions in the high school, some health care problem. Let me rough out a structure that might work.

I would start by showing how the problem first became apparent. Perhaps there is an anecdote that dramatizes this. Perhaps a quote from some local expert. Or perhaps a straight exposition lead, a statement lead, will do the job. Just remember what I said about the lead—it has to command attention.

Then you need to explain "Why I'm telling you this." Maybe the lead will cover this, and if so, you can now move on into the body of the article. This section will develop your theme through interviews, anecdotes and basic facts that support the point. You will also want to talk to the inevitable dissenters; those who feel there isn't a problem, or that the problem is not being dealt with properly.

You know what you think about the subject at hand, but unless you are an expert on this yourself, your opinions don't belong in the article. Let the experts and the anecdotes and the facts support your feelings about the extent of the problem and the solutions that might be found. And try ending on a similar note to the one with which you began; perhaps another anecdote, another quote, or whatever seems to complete the circle and leave the reader with that satisfying feeling that the subject has been thoroughly covered.

Every article, of course, is not put together in the same way. Just as form follow content in the construction of a house, with the final design being determined by the location, the different features you want, the size, etc., so is the form of an article dictated by what you want to put into it.

There is no complete list of possible structures, and I'm not going to try to create one. Just remember, you're not writing a newspaper story, where the most important facts come first and so on, in descending order, until it reaches the point where some copyeditor cuts it off to fit the available space. You need to lure the reader in, explain why it is important, build your case and end on one of your most telling pieces of evidence. Now let's examine some possible structures.

Chronological

The narrative is, of course, structured chronologically, but you might consider leading not with the beginning of the story, but at one of the climactic moments. Once that dramatic moment has the reader hooked, you can flash back to the beginning. But let's imagine a totally different kind of story: the "How-To." You're writing an article on building a toolshed, or laying out a backyard vegetable garden, or baking a cake. This obviously requires a step-by-step approach, which is not only the most useful but by far the easiest to organize.

Problem and Solution

First, as in the case of the school discipline problem, you might want to structure this as a series of questions and answers:

1. How has the problem made itself apparent?
2. How serious is it?
3. What solutions have been offered?
4. What are the advantages and drawbacks of each?
5. What do the experts say? And so on.

I mean this very specifically. You ask the question, perhaps even putting a *Q* at the beginning, and then an *A* in front of the answer.

Perhaps the goal of your article is to explain the impact of a new tax law. You might pose a series of questions that ask just what items will be taxed, who will be liable for the new tax, why the new law is necessary, etc. By focusing on what readers want to know about a problem, you can easily devise questions that will deal with their major concerns.

Compartmental

We've talked about dividing your material up into subject areas, and this can also be used to devise a structure for the finished article. When I was on the *Saturday Evening Post*, back in the late 1960s, we wanted to do an article showing the impact of the Vietnam War on the country. We finally decided to ask our writer (Joe McGinnis, who went on to write *Fatal Vision* and other bestsellers) to find three men who illustrated the effect of the war. One was to be a man who had fought in the war and was struggling to adjust to civilian life. The second was to be a wounded veteran, someone who had been disabled in combat and who would talk about how he felt. And third, we asked McGinnis to follow the body of a man who had been killed in action, telling what happened in Vietnam and showing the impact of his death on his family and the community in which he had lived. The article was extremely effective and should not be blamed for the fact that this was in the last issue of the old *Post* ever published.

The compartmental approach might take the form of a broken narrative, such as the article about the woman with multiple sclerosis who had driven herself to walk and then to run again, flashing back and forth between the story of her recovery and her agonizing effort in the marathon.

It might be used in illustrating a problem such as the shortage of adequate health care. Here, a number of case histories might dramatize the problem. A man who has lost his job, become ill, and has nothing to fall back on. A woman who has been divorced and has insufficient money to provide care for a sick child. A family in which one member develops an illness or suffers an injury requiring long-term care, and the insurance runs out. Each case will dramatize a different aspect of the problem and perhaps point the way to planning a new health care system that would cover these tragic emergencies.

I usually find it more effective to keep these case histories separate. Everybody loves to hear a story, and what you have with this approach is a series of stories, each making the point, in this case, that our health care system is not what it should be.

But the material may suggest otherwise; you may want to break up the compartments into different aspects of the same problem. Let's imagine that you're reporting on the impact of an earthquake or flood or hurricane. The opening section might tell what each of four or five different people was doing just before disaster struck. Then you need that establishment paragraph, which reminds readers of the event and tells them what they will learn from your retelling of it. Then you go back to each of these people, in turn, and tell a little more of their story. The reader thus becomes involved with each of them, and by constantly cutting from one to the next — a technique often used in the movies — the reader will stay with you to find out how each person survives, or doesn't.

Again, as I said before, the material will determine the structure. John McPhee's article on the Ashe-Graebner match used the match itself as the structure, cutting from the action into the biographies of his two protagonists. As in architecture, form follows content.

Listings

A variation on the compartmental approach might be used in a travel article on, say, what to do and see on a visit to Washington, DC, or New York. You might start by listing the attractions, tours, day trips and so on, and then going on to explain each one.

And, as I talked about earlier, you might think of organizing your material in the form of a list. Ten ways to save money on your taxes, twenty last-minute gift ideas, the ten least expensive places to visit in Europe, and so on.

TRANSITIONS

You have written your lead and your ending, you have devised the logical structure and your piece seems to be finished. But does it all hang together? Does every thought and idea lead logically into the next one? *Saturday Evening Post* editor Bill Emerson used to insist that every article read like a "seamless garment." He was talking about transitions.

Transitions are those words and phrases that keep the story moving smoothly from one subject to the next. They ensure that each paragraph flows into the next one, and they prevent the reader from stopping in confusion to wonder where he is. A reader who has to stop and think, or read back to get the connection, is a reader on the verge of turning to the next article. Or, even worse, an editor about to move on to the next submission.

Transitions have been called the nails that hold the structure together; while this is true, I think of them more as the grease that allows one part to slide easily into the next. They are the little clues that signal a change of direction, or the simple words and phrases that echo from one paragraph to the next and keep us on the track. One might conclude a paragraph in a profile of a successful businessman by listing his various achievements and ending, ". . . but his greatest source of pride was the store."

The next paragraph could then begin, "The store, an impressive white marble structure standing eight stories tall . . ." We have been carried easily from one thought (the man himself) to his crowning glory (the store).

Screenwriters joke about the cliché, "meanwhile, back at the ranch." The word "meanwhile" is a transition carrying the reader from what is happening here to what is happening somewhere else. Other words that accomplish the same purpose are *finally, but first, on the other hand, nevertheless, next, now, of course, therefore,* etc.

You might be writing about a new piece of legislation, listing various aspects of it. Then you write, "In addition, the law will have an impact on . . . ," the words *In addition* help move the reader along. Also, think of *also*. And *then*, and *besides* and *finally* and so on into the night. These are words that bridge thoughts and ideas, that contribute to Bill Emerson's seamless garment.

Look at the section you have just read on compartmental structures and note my use of *but* and *again* to move you along to the next thought. Note also the way I frequently use word or sentence bridges to carry you from one chapter to the next. These, too, are transitions.

In my article called "South of the Border," I have a section in which I talk about the ubiquitous signs along Route I-95 that promote the tourist attraction. One paragraph quotes a few of the signs, the next begins, "The signs are all written by Schafer . . ." The next tells who actually builds the signs, and the next begins, "The signs, which are South of the Border's only means of advertising . . ." I used the word *sign* to link several different pieces of information. Then I talked about how many tourists the signs pull in (fifty thousand a day) and how much these tourists buy in his shops and then went into "After checking out a few of the shops . . . I asked to see some rooms." And I am off into another piece of information, the accommodations.

In the rush to complete your first draft, you may jump from one topic to another without worrying too much about transitions. *Smithsonian* editor Tim Foote even suggests writing paragraphs on separate sheets of paper and then shuffling them around to find the right order. Then, when they all seem in place, you'll have the fun of writing transitions.

If your piece has been logically constructed, reading it over will show you where different thoughts need to be linked more strongly. Do it now. Remember, nobody gets a piece right the first time. In his book *Collecting Himself,* James Thurber wrote, "I have never written more than a dozen pieces that I thought could not have been improved. Most writers who are any good have this belief about their work." And much of this rewriting consists of weaving in the transitions, keeping the reader from getting lost and losing interest.

Two final suggestions: First, read a lot of magazines and see how other writers make their transitions. Or don't. The mechanics should not be obvious to an ordinary reader, but you are a student of writing and you will see them. Second, after you have put it aside for a day or so and then read it through again, ask a friend to read it. Ask the friend to make a mark every time he or she gets confused, or doesn't quite follow you. That's where a little invisible weaving is needed. It will pay off.

STUDY OTHER WRITERS

This is only a beginning, to give you some ideas on how to start organizing your material. Before you even begin to structure an article of your own, go through a number of magazines— preferably ones you'd like to write for—and study them to see how each author solved the problem. Go through the articles carefully, labelling the lead and the thesis statement and anecdotes and interviews and so on, so you can see just how it was put together. Make note of the different types of structures used, and see which one you might be most comfortable with.

Studying other writers is invaluable. When I used to write short detective fiction, I often sat down with a book by Raymond Chandler or Ross Macdonald to get a feel for the way they dealt with the problems I knew I'd face. I'm not talking about imitation or, God forbid, plagiarism, but about using the successful methods worked out by others to point the way to your own solutions.

And don't forget just plain old thinking. Read over your notes and research material carefully enough so that you know what pieces you have available to build your article, and then put them aside and just think about them. You'd be surprised at how often the proper structure will just "pop into your head."

Okay, you've learned how to write leads and endings, you know how an article is put together, you know all the basics. This is good news, but the bad news is that a lot of other writers know this, too. What you need to do is give your writing that something extra, that spark that marks you as more than the ordinary writer, that quality that makes editors remember you and call *you* with assignments.

CHAPTER EIGHT

How to Make Your Articles Sparkle

S ome years ago Charles Barnard, now the travel editor of *Modern Maturity* but then managing editor of a highly respected men's magazine called *True*, was asked to put together an anthology of the best articles the magazine had published over the previous quarter century. In the course of going through thousands of pieces on everything from headhunting to martini mixing, he began thinking about what might be called the best piece the magazine had ever run.

It wasn't as hard as he had expected. The story that stood out in his mind, that he had never forgotten, was not a skillful piece of investigative reporting or the dramatic story of some epic adventure. It was, instead, a quiet, thoughtful, moving report from a writer named W.C. "Bill" Heinz.

Bill's story, "The Morning They Shot the Spies," describes an incident he had witnessed while serving as a correspondent during the latter days of World War II, when three German soldiers had been executed after being found in American uniforms behind allied lines. This incident had made no news when it happened, nor did it make any when that issue of *True* was printed, yet it was the kind of story readers — and editors — remember long after the more sensational pieces have been forgotten.

One passage will give you a sense of Bill's style:

> I looked at the ground, frost-white, the grass tufts frozen, the soil hard and uneven. I wondered if it is better to die on a warm, bright day among friends, or on a day when even the weather is your enemy. I turned around and looked down into the valley. The mist still hung in the valley, but it was starting to take on a brassy tint from the sun

beginning to work through it. I could make out three white farm buildings on the valley floor—a little yellowed now from the weak sunlight—and I could envision this, in the spring, a pleasant valley.

This view I see now, I said to myself, will be the last thing their eyes ever see . . .

One of the elements that make Bill's writing so effective is his telling use of detail. The ground is "frost-white, the grass tufts frozen." The day is "warm and bright." The mist is hanging in the valley, and he sees "three white farm buildings . . . a little yellowed now from the weak sunlight . . ." Details are vital to the evoking of a sense of scene, of time and place, to the magic of re-creating the events you are describing.

His story was also memorable because of the honesty and integrity with which he told it. He simply described what happened and how it affected him and how others felt about it and that was all. He didn't hype it with words like "incredible" and "earthshaking"—words that have been so overused that they have lost whatever impact they once had. He simply let the story tell itself, as directly and cleanly as he knew how.

There are, of course, many articles that cannot be written this way. The author frequently does not have a chance to witness all the events he is writing about, and a straightforward piece on saving money on taxes or where to eat cheaply in Paris hardly needs this kind of treatment.

But Bill's story does offer one lesson: The simple, uncomplicated approach to a dramatic situation will have more impact than the kind of souped-up prose that too many writers feel is necessary. Your best/first move might be to forget everything you ever learned about "the craft of writing" and get back to the basic approach, the direct, immediate, uncluttered way of telling a story you used when you were a child.

To put it even more simply: *Don't write like a writer—just write.*

THE ESSENTIAL INGREDIENTS

Before you start writing your article, and to a considerable extent before you even write your query, there is one thing you must have: *a thorough knowledge of your subject and a clear idea of how you want to approach it.* This may seem so obvious that it shouldn't be necessary to bring it up, yet many writers don't seem to consider it as important as it is. Time and again, in my days as an editor, a writer would smile across my desk and say something like: "How about a story on Madonna . . . or the birth control pill . . . or the American Family?"

The only answer was, and is: "Okay, how about it?"

"Well," he or she would go on doggedly, "what kind of angle would you like?"

These are the words of a writer who wants somebody else to do the thinking. This writer may believe the editor will think he or she is being flexible, but nobody is ever fooled.

The moral here is something I continually tell my students: *Don't confuse a subject with a story.* Madonna and the birth control pill are subjects; there are any number of specific ideas that could be developed from either of these subjects and a great many have been. Your job is to know your magazine and to focus your idea specifically for their readers.

In addition to aiming your idea at the right target audience, you need to find an approach that will seem fresh, that won't sound like the same tired old story. If this quality of freshness and originality isn't present in the query letter, you may never have a chance to put it in the piece itself.

This leads into the second major ingredient of quality nonfiction: thinking the material out, assessing its value and arriving at a coherent point of view. It takes no great talent to gather material—just hard work and a knowledge of where to look—but that's only the beginning. You have to think about your material so long and thoroughly that it takes on a definite shape and unity in your mind. And this point of view has to be set in your mind before you can begin the harder task of putting all of your material together in the most effective way.

If you are writing about some event—a recent human interest story or something dramatic that happened in the past—you are constructing a story in almost the same way you would put together a good short story. Just as does a work of fiction, an article has a beginning (that arouses the interest and gets the action going), a middle (that develops the characters and the situation and keeps the action moving) and an end (that resolves the problems and ties up the loose ends). In any story, whether fiction or nonfiction, characterization and a sense of narrative flow are essential.

One article I remember from *McCall's* illustrates this well. It was called "A Pair of Miracles," and in it author Rochelle Distelheim told the story of a family in which two daughters had suffered heart failure and had needed heart transplants at the same time. She began at the moment of crisis, flashed back to explain what had gone before, and then picked up the story as it unfolded, climaxing with the struggle to find the heart donors and the successful operations. The article ended with the family today. Their story had all of the elements of fiction, but had the advantage of being heartbreakingly true.

One of the most famous profiles ever written for *The New Yorker* was by a writer many contemporary writers look up to as a model, Joseph Mitchell. It was about a man known as "Professor Sea Gull"—Joe Gould—described by Mitchell as a "blithe and emaciated little man who has been a notable in the cafeterias, diners, barrooms, and dumps of Greenwich Village for a quarter of a century. He sometimes brags rather wryly that he is the last of the bohemians." We would probably think of him now as a bum. Here is the way Mitchell introduces him:

> Gould is toothless, and his lower jaw swivels from side to side when he talks. He is bald on top, but the hair at the back of his head is long and frizzly, and he has a bushy, cinnamon-colored beard. He wears a pair of spectacles that are loose and lopsided and that slip down to the end of his nose a moment after he puts them on. He doesn't always wear them on the street and without them he has the wild, unfocused stare of an old scholar who has strained his eyes on small print. Even in the Village many people turn and look at him. He is stooped and he moves rapidly, grumbling to himself, with his head thrust forward and held to one side. Under his left arm he usually carries a bulging, greasy, brown pasteboard portfolio, and he swings his right arm aggressively. As he hurries along, he seems to be warding off an imaginary enemy.

In those few words, written almost without adjectives, Mitchell has created an unforgettable word picture of this eccentric little man. And do note the details that make Gould come so vividly to life. He is "toothless . . . bald on top, but the hair at the back of his head is long and frizzly." His glasses keep slipping off his nose. He walks with a stoop, "his head thrust forward and held to one side." As he walks, "he swings his right arm aggressively." These details paint a picture, allowing you to see Gould as Mitchell saw him.

Another excellent example of a writer with a sharp eye for the telling detail is Barbara Grizzuti Harrison. You can see it in anything she writes, but a piece she did for *McCall's* on Phyllis Schlafly is a particular favorite of mine. At one point in the article Barbara describes a trip she made with Mrs. Schlafly, and in a few seemingly unimportant details she sketches a real sense of the woman she is writing about.

> We have been driving a long time; Mrs. Schlafly shows no signs of wearying. She says she wants to stretch her legs. She pulls over to the side of the road, gets out, stands up, takes one deep breath and gets back in again.
>
> Is there a frivolous bone in her body? She likes Nelson Eddy musicals. She seldom watches TV, but she "knows all kinds of terrible things go on — my friends tell me it's just simply awful." She hasn't been to the movies in such a long time she "just doesn't know" who her favorite actor is. She saw *Private Benjamin* with her daughter Anne because it was about women and the draft; early in the film there was a specific reference to orgasm, and Phyllis "prayed Anne wouldn't understand it."

Many writers might have considered these details too trivial to mention, yet they give us a sense of this woman's self-discipline and obliviousness to what most of us think is the real world that we might never have gotten if the writer had not been so sensitive and so observant. By the accumulation of detail she has accomplished what every profile writer must accomplish — a genuine re-creation of a person on a printed page.

The tricky part is in deciding which details are important and which simply clutter up your story. I emphasize the importance of details to my writing students, and they often counter by filling their articles with things I don't need to know. The fact that a man smokes a pipe is a useful detail. (It would be even more useful if a woman smoked one.) The color and make of the pipe tell us nothing. The fact that he has bitten through the stem tells us that this a man under stress. The color of the rug in his den may not tell us much, but if there is a large coffee stain near a writing desk, or a worn spot in the center, this helps make the room — and the scene — come alive.

It's sometimes hard to know which details are most evocative. My rule of thumb is that a writer should note every detail and put in rather than leave out. An editor can always take out what doesn't work but can't put in things that exist only in your notes. The fact that Schlafly seems tireless and needs only to stretch and take one deep breath to revive herself seems unimportant, yet it helps tell us what she's like. Her indifference to popular culture also tells something about a woman who has strong feelings about what people should believe yet has only a passing knowledge of the world we live in.

While I have been talking about profiles, many of the points I have made apply as well to any type of nonfiction article. If you are writing about a new medical discovery or treatment, for instance, think of its final development and acceptance as a narrative. Talk to the men and women who were responsible for it, and try to re-create their moments of discouragement and triumph. Talk to other doctors who are in a position to recognize its importance, and keep your material lively through the use of quotes and anecdotes.

Bring the material home to the reader; show how this will affect that reader personally. This can sometimes be done by getting personally involved in the subject you're writing about. Some years back a young writer approached *McCall's* with a proposal to do a piece about the Moonies, young children who were joining the religious movement of Sun Myung Moon and often abandoning their families in their newfound devotion to the cult.

Many new recruits were approached near New York's Public Library on 42nd Street, so I suggested to our writer that he hang around there awhile and see if he would be invited to go away on an indoctrination weekend. He was, and his description of how the Moonies came on to lonely young people, and how intensely they worked to persuade their weekend guests to join the movement, gave an immediacy and suspense to his article that he could never have achieved had he not gone through this experience.

Some writers, like George Plimpton, have made a career of writing from the inside — of being the very thing they are writing about. George has been a professional quarterback, a baseball pitcher, a symphony conductor, a chef. Some of these began as articles, grew into books, and were even dramatized in movies and on television. You may not want to carry it as far as he has, but it's a useful way to inject something extra into your writing.

George used this approach, which was originated, I believe, by a sportswriter named Paul Gallico, as a way of finding a fresh approach to a familiar subject. You may not want to put on a pair of spikes and a pinstriped suit, but, by the same token, you can't fill your baseball article with on-the-field exploits and stock interviews, the sort of material that appears in the sports pages every day. Get the locker-room stories that weren't in the papers, the unguarded comments of your subject and his teammates, the facts that explain *why* things happen, not just *what* happened. This usually requires more than one or two trips to the press box and the locker room; it takes awhile to win confidence and get the kind of revealing interviews that you want.

Sometimes you won't get the interview at all, but patience and doggedness and thoughtful reporting can still save the day. Gay Talese was once assigned a profile of Frank Sinatra, and when he got to Las Vegas, Sinatra had changed his mind and wouldn't see him. Talese was told he could stay and watch the singer perform and make a recording, so he hung around for weeks, soaking up the kind of detail that made for a far stronger and more intimate portrait than could have come from a standard interview.

WRITING A TITLE

Many writers think the title they put on an article is unimportant ("Hell, the editors will change it, anyway"), but a title is more than a label for a story; it is a theme. It not only makes clear what you're trying to say about that subject, but it helps you focus your material as well. Nine times out of ten, when an article came in with a title like "Clint Eastwood Story," the piece itself would reflect the same unfocused approach.

Think about the basic point your article is making. Think

about what struck you most about the person or subject you're writing about. What you might say if somebody asked you why you decided to write that piece. Perhaps a study of Eastwood's films suggests a growing maturity, a stronger feeling of personal integrity, a man with more substance, more authority. You might call it "Clint Eastwood: Growing Older and Growing Better." Not a wonderful title, but it does show what your piece is going to be about.

Sometimes alliteration is effective. I remember the title I wrote for a Bill Heinz piece about the old Brooklyn Dodger player, Pete Reiser. I called it "The Rocky Road of Pistol Pete." The *R*'s and the *P*'s give the title a kind of rhythm I find effective.

Perhaps there is a quote that seems to sum up the piece, either a quote by the subject or simply a line from the article. "Music Don't Know No Age" was the title of William Kennedy's profile of Louis Armstrong in *GQ*. It was something Armstrong said during their interview. When the *Ladies Home Journal* published an article about a female naval officer who had spoken out against sexual harassment in the military, their title echoed what her colleagues felt: "You Did the Right Thing."

My point is not that you have to struggle to come up with a title the magazine will use. Some editors like to write their own titles and will change yours no matter how good it is. But a sharply written and carefully thought-out title will show the editor that you have a focus, that you know what your piece says. It's just another way to make a good first impression.

ORIGINALITY COUNTS

Another ingredient that lifts an article out of the ordinary is originality. Some people will tell you that the best way to satisfy an editor is to study the magazine and write your piece in the same style. That, in my opinion, is a sure formula for mediocrity. Of course, a writer should be familiar with a magazine's style before trying to write for it, but a blind imitation of somebody else's style is the worst possible way to go about your job. Among other things, the editors may be getting tired of a certain style about the time you come along and copy it. But more important, you have to write in your own voice. Originality never comes from imitating somebody else.

You can, and should, study other writers to learn how they

solved their problems, but just remember that while imitation may be the sincerest form of flattery, it usually doesn't sell.

Originality is a hard quality to define. If you could pinpoint the exact nature of originality, it probably wouldn't be original any more. Let's just say that the original writer goes at his story in the way that seems most logical and effective to him, no matter what other writers may have done. The standard way to construct a story might be: Opening anecdote, statement of theme or subject, anecdote, background material broken up with quotes and anecdotes, concluding anecdote that sums up the theme.

This is all right. It has been used thousands of times, and will undoubtedly be used again. But it is not going to set you apart as a really fresh voice—a Tom Wolfe or a Joan Didion—somebody who is not just adequate but for whom editors really want to find assignments.

I still remember one of the first pieces I read of Joan Didion's. It was back when she was just starting to write for the old *Saturday Evening Post*, and she had written a piece about a woman who murdered her husband by burning him up in their Volkswagen. It began this way:

> This is a story about love and death in the golden land, and begins with the country. The San Bernardino Valley lies only an hour east of Los Angeles by the San Bernardino Freeway but is in certain ways an alien place: not the coastal California of the subtropical twilights and the soft westerlies off the Pacific but a harsher California, haunted by the Mojave just beyond the mountains, devastated by the hot dry Santa Ana wind that comes down through the passes at one hundred miles an hour and whines through the eucalyptus windbreaks and works on the nerves. October is the bad month for the wind, the month when breathing is difficult and the hills blaze up spontaneously. There has been no rain since April. Every voice seems a scream. It is the season of suicide and divorce and prickly dread, wherever the wind blows.

There was no doubt that this was an original voice, and there was no doubt that we would use her again. In fact, we signed her for a regular column and continued to use her as long as the magazine was alive.

Another fresh voice popped up in the *Atlantic* a couple of years ago. The author was William Langewiesche and his subject was the Sahara. I have never been much drawn to deserts, but his lead pulled me into a journey that didn't let me go until some ten thousand words later.

> The Sahara is a desert so vast that no airplane can diminish it. Certainly this one couldn't. I sat behind the pilots in the cockpit of an Air Algeria turboprop lumbering at eighteen thousand feet across southern Algeria. The airplane was a Dutch-built Fokker 27, a stodgy forty-passenger twin, doing 220 miles an hour; it had come from the capital city, Algiers, on a roundabout three-day run to the oases. Now we were bound for Adrar, an oasis remarkable even here for heat and lack of rain. It was midday, midsummer. Outside, the Sahara stretched in naked folds to the horizon, brilliant and utterly still. It was blanketed by a haze of dust, suspended not by winds but by heat. The only sign of people was a trace of smoke rising in the distance. Below us a canyon cut through the downslope of the Hoggar Mountains. To the south lay the Tanezrouft, a plain so barren that drivers in the open desert mistake stones for diesel trucks, and so lonely that, it is said, migrating birds land beside people just for the company.

Another writer whose voice I have never been able to resist is Bil Gilbert, who tells his story later in this book. Bil's work appeared for many years in *Sports Illustrated* and is found mostly these days in *Smithsonian*. He loves all living things, although I suspect he is partial to those with four feet or wings. And he writes about what he loves with a style and individuality that cannot really be imitated.

The point of quoting him is to show how far you can go in letting your own personality show through when you write. Your voice is, as I have said elsewhere, who you are. Bil knows who he is and what he's about, and his voice gives him a tone of authority as well as making him a delightful companion to read.

In a 1979 piece called "The Missouri Kid," Bil recounts the adventures of a moose who had, at the time he wrote, been roaming from the Canadian border as far south as the outskirts of St. Louis. Not only had a moose never wandered this far, but he had been doing it for two years at the time and showed no signs of going home.

Bil introduced him as ". . . an extraordinary animal, a Marco Polo of moosedom, a Magellan of its kind . . . His travels have been so remarkable and his adventures so picaresque that it simply will not do to speak of him here simply as a moose. He must be distinguished, as he has distinguished himself, from all others. Call him the Missouri kid.

"Like those of English rock groups, flying-saucer persons, Democratic presidential candidates and many other celebrious creatures who descend on us unexpectedly, the origins of the Missouri kid are obscure . . ." and he goes on to describe his adventures in his usual delightful way.

What follows is the end of an article on the black-footed ferret, a creature that may be extinct. Bil has looked for them, and he knows people who have seen them, but the Fish and Wildlife Service finally gave up the search. Bil ends his piece this way:

> Perhaps we are now as a nation too poor to continue a public search-and-rescue operation for ferrets. If so, the general quality of life won't be endangered. In fact, if the last ferret should shuffle off this mortal coil (or already has), there will be no practical reverberations. Yet there are real limits as to how much of this sort of cost-accounting we can afford. The cost, as well as the considerable glory of being human, is that now and then we must go out into prairie-dog towns and look for ferrets. No ferret will ever come looking for us.

This is pure Gilbert, revealing a kind of resignation about the nature of man, along with a deep love of the nature of nature. The interesting thing about Bil's writing is that he writes the way he talks; what he writes is who he is. I think too many would-be writers think there is some other voice to writing. Let your own voice come through, and the writing will take care of itself.

Let me indulge myself in one more quote from Bil, this one from a piece he wrote for the "Speaking Out" column in the *Saturday Evening Post*. It was called: "I Hate Horses."

> During the course of a misspent life I have, without regret, lavished time, money and affection on raccoons, foxes,

ferrets, llamas, cheetahs, bears, hawks, crows, snakes, turtles, dogs, cats and certain even more improbable beasts. I
have also, either voluntarily or involuntarily, been bur-
dened with horses on and off since childhood, invariably to
my deep regret. I find horses less personable than crows,
more delicate than hummingbirds, less efficient than bicy-
cles and more expensive than floozies.

And while I'm dipping nostalgically into the old *Post*, where
I labored with joy and satisfaction for seven years, here is a lead
from Lewis Lapham, now editor of *Harper's*.

> Peter Ryhiner introduced himself on the afternoon of a
> blizzard. A large and florid Swiss gentleman, he wore a fur
> hat and carried a canvas satchel. His red beard needed trim-
> ming; his eyes were melancholy. He said he had lost his
> rhinoceros.

There are many ways he might have started that story, which
really was about a man who had spent many years hunting
through the jungles of Southeast Asia for a white rhinoceros, and
who had many remarkable tales to tell about his obsession, but
I found this one irresistible.

One more voice, which I discovered recently in *The New York
Times Magazine*, is that of Charles P. Pierce. The subject he is
writing about is hockey, a sport I do not follow, and specifically,
a player named Eric Lindros, a name I had never heard. But there
was something about the way he wrote that pulled me in.

> They brought him in through a back door. There are
> about twenty official ways to enter Boston Garden, the tat-
> tered old dowager arena tucked into a backwater bend near
> to where the Charles River fouls the sea. These entrances
> include the front doors, the back doors, the press doors
> and, of course, the elephant doors, through which have en-
> tered not only certain pachydermal employees of the Rin-
> gling Brothers, but also Winston Churchill. On this particu-
> lar morning, there was a crowd at the bottom of the
> elephant ramp—teenage girls, mostly, all squeals and gig-
> gles . . .

Whatever the subject, I'm not going to give up on a writer
like this. I wasn't disappointed.

I'm not suggesting that you try and imitate any of these styles. I'm simply saying that you should forget the conventional way of writing a story and not be afraid to try something different. The worst thing that can happen is that the editor will ask you what in the world you were thinking of, and suggest something else. But the editor will also respect you for having tried something different, even if he felt it didn't work. Anybody can imitate; it takes talent and imagination to try something new.

Nobody remembers the *second* person to fly alone across the Atlantic.

CHAPTER NINE

Writing the Human Interest Narrative

U p to now, I've been talking about articles in general, giving information that will apply to the writing of almost any kind of piece. The editors I interview in the book's last section talk about selling to the specific magazines they edit. What I'd like to do now is discuss a very common article type, that is relatively easy to write and in regular demand: the human interest narrative.

Reader's Digest, which publishes at least one an issue, calls them "Drama in Real Life." At *McCall's*, we used to call them human interest narratives. *Guideposts* doesn't have a special label for them, but they publish several in every issue, as do *Ladies Home Journal*, *Redbook*, *Good Housekeeping* and, in fact, most of the women's magazines.

Television has recently discovered its own version of the true-life drama with stories about women whose children were abused, kidnapped, lost, the victims of strange diseases. Women come down with diseases of their own, find they were adopted and undertake a frantic search for their real parents. It's a rare Sunday night that doesn't feature a "disease of the week" or "family crisis of the week" movie.

Whatever they're called, they are accounts of dramatic experiences in the lives of real people. And, like fiction, they are told in narrative form. These stories have always been popular, and even when editors tire of them reader demand always brings them back.

I don't think there's any real secret here. We all love to get caught up in a good story. And beyond that, such stories often perform a service. Not only can readers identify with others who have confronted serious problems and overcome them, but they can often gain hope and courage from seeing how someone else triumphed over adversity.

Reader's Digest sponsors two or more writer's conferences a year, and when their editors speak to the assembled writers, they always plead for submissions for "Drama in Real Life." Their inventory of such stories, they say, is always low, and they love to tell how they have worked with inexperienced writers through several rewrites to help bring them off successfully. In chapter twelve, Phil Osborne, one of the *Digest*'s top editors, has more to say about writing this kind of article for his magazine.

The *Digest*'s stories lean more heavily on the drama than the human interest, although this must be a strong element as well. A look at a few issues found some common elements. In one, the drama involved three hikers who had been trapped twelve thousand feet up on a rock ledge in the Colorado Rockies. In another, a young couple is swept out over the ocean in a runaway hot-air balloon.

A mother sees her car rolling away from her, headed toward a swollen river with her three youngest children locked inside. A young boy is lost in a deep mine; a couple is attacked by a grizzly bear in Montana's Glacier National Park; another man is trapped on a rock face; and a nine-year-old boy is, yes, trapped alone in another runaway balloon.

Guideposts, which is described in more detail in Mary Ann O'Roark's interview, features stories that are more spiritual and inspirational. A seven-year-old girl is washed into a drainpipe and survives for thirteen hours in a storm sewer. "God said someone's gonna come get me," she told her mother after she was rescued, and "for me to stay there." Another story describes a man's search for his lost dog, and how prayer led him to his missing pet.

(*Guideposts* is so eager for good narratives that they advertise for writers. Under the headline "ARE YOU A STORYTELLER? Then tell us a story!" they invite readers to submit "a true first-person story with a strong narrative quality." The editors pick the best fifteen entries and invite the writers to an expenses-paid workshop in which they can get more training in writing their stories for *Guideposts*.)

Inspirational narratives can be found in a wide variety of magazines. Don't look for them in *Popular Mechanics* or *Field &*

Stream, although I suspect a few may have crept in there over the years. Everybody loves a good story.

THE LOCAL STORY

As I spent a good many years searching out such tales and wrestling with writers who often had little experience with writing them, or anything else, I'd like to tell you a few stories about ones we published in *McCall's.* Many of these came from writers who were trying a national magazine for the first time. They hear about some local near-tragedy — a little girl falls in a well, a baby survives a long period underwater, a boy is lost in the woods.

These tend not to be stories that make national headlines, although sometimes they do. But in most cases they are things that happen to ordinary people, in out-of-the-way places, and get reported on, if at all, in local newspapers. These are the stories you should be watching for, and when you learn of one, waste no time in getting in touch with those involved and asking them to tell it to you. Then fire off a query. Your chances of a sale, based on years of personal experience, are excellent.

About ten years ago, *McCall's* received a query from a California writer, Paul Bagne, about a young woman who, when she was fourteen years old, had been told she had leukemia. I still remember how it began:

> Cindy Walters listened intently to the carefully measured words of Dr. William Lande. "At first it didn't hit me that anything was seriously wrong," she says. "But his voice was shaking and that began to scare me. You know you're in trouble when the doctor is almost in tears."

Dr. Lande went on to tell her that her prognosis was not good unless she was willing to try a radical new combination of drugs that would make her very sick but might help her. She and her parents decided to take the risk, and eventually her disease went into remission. Several years later, Cindy fell in love and married. She wanted a child, but was told that pregnancy — if she were able to get pregnant at all — sometimes caused the disease to return. Cindy did take the risk, and both she and the baby came through.

We didn't know Bagne and had never seen any of his writing,

but we still told him to go ahead. The story worked out successfully and was very popular with our readers. Research always told us that such stories were among the most popular, even in issues containing articles of far more importance or interviews with prominent celebrities.

Shortly after we heard from Bagne we talked with two young reporters from Chicago, Rick Soll and Gene Mustain, about a story they had uncovered for their newspaper. It involved two women. One had severe birth defects and at three months of age had been labeled as retarded and placed in a state institution. A few years later an idealistic young nurse came upon this little girl. The nurse took an interest, fought the indifference and even hostility of the institution, and finally succeeded in having the child retested and found to be normal.

The little girl was eventually placed in a foster home, grew up and graduated from high school, married and had a child of her own. Soll and Mustain wanted to tell us how the nurse and the woman she had rescued had been reunited many years later, and what that meeting had meant to them.

A writer from North Carolina named Glenn Joyner came to us with the story of a remarkable woman named Kathleen White. Mrs. White had developed multiple sclerosis and subsequently lost the use of her legs and most of the use of her arms. She had been hospitalized when, through a fluke, she saw a doctor's report on her condition. The doctor had concluded that White was in the terminal stages of her disease and had not long to live. Furious that she had not been told and determined to prove her doctors' wrong, she went on a grueling program of exercise and training that not only put her back on her feet, but also enabled her to run in — and finish — a 26.2-mile marathon.

Barbara Raymond, whose interview you will read later in this book, once wrote us about a family named Spiegel, whose youngest child, Annie, had been born with severe facial damage. The Spiegels had raised Annie as normally as possible, but her appearance was shocking to strangers, and as their child grew older they came to realize that it would become harder and harder to keep her from feeling like a freak. They finally found a surgeon who could help her and, after several operations, Annie was restored to nearly normal appearance.

And just so you don't think that all of these stories involve medical disasters, let me tell you about the writer from a small town in upstate New York, Lorene Hanley Duquin, who wrote to tell us about what happened the previous Christmas in the nearby town of Ripley. A severe snowstorm had hit the area, stranding hundreds of travelers on the highways. The people of Ripley not only rescued these families but also found them places to sleep, fed them, got Christmas presents for them and even found a Santa Claus for the children. It was, for everyone, a Christmas they would never forget.

Note that all of these stories are about triumph over adversity — about someone who faces disaster and wins out over it. Cindy Walters had her baby. Kathleen White conquered multiple sclerosis. In *Guideposts* there is a religious theme; in others, the theme may be more a tribute to the human spirit, a message that if we have to face such adversity, we can survive as well. Nobody writes about people who give up, or balloons that fly out to sea and are never heard from again.

I'd also like to point out something else; these writers all have several things in common. First, they did not live in New York City. Second, we had never met them or even heard of them before. We bought each story, and in each case it was their first sale to *McCall's*.

As I have said, some of these writers were inexperienced in writing for magazines, and their first tries were pretty shaggy. But because they had good stories to tell, we wanted very much to help them succeed. We gave them detailed rewrite instructions, talked to them a number of times about their problems and helped them through several rewrites.

Let me emphasize another point about the stories I've been talking about: *We did not know about them.* New York editors read the New York papers, and sometimes a few other big city papers; they read most of the national magazines and watch television, and when they spot a story they think would work for them, they assign it. Competition for such stories is fierce, and they know from experience that if they don't move quickly, somebody else will. And you may find yourself competing with television or a film studio.

This is where you come in. If you live outside New York, you really have an advantage. You'll hear about events and people the editors up in their New York skyscraper offices will never hear about. Jeannie Ralston, a writer who was once based in New York but now lives in Austin, Texas, tells me that when she goes to New York the editors inundate her with questions about what's going on out there beyond the Hudson River, what stories she has heard and what new perspectives she can bring to them.

STORY MATERIAL

What kind of stories should you be looking for? Here are a few suggestions.

An extraordinary experience. Such stories often involve some sort of disaster (hurricane, fire, flood, earthquake) that places a person in jeopardy. The overall story has been covered in the papers and on television; what you're looking for is the human interest story. The story that tells how one person pulled through. A woman survives the crash of a light plane. She is badly injured and the pilot is dead. She doesn't know where she is, but she knows she cannot survive long without medical help. After waiting several days to see if anyone will come, she starts crawling down the mountain . . .

It was a hell of a story, and it ran in *McCall's.*

A common problem. This kind of narrative describes how a man or woman or family dealt with the sort of experience many of us have faced or might face, and thus helps us to understand how such problems can be handled and perhaps offers guidelines to what we might do in similar circumstances. An older couple whose grandchild has been separated from them because of their son's divorce and his former wife's remarriage decided to fight for the right to see the child. They finally went to court—and won. The story of how they were awarded visitation rights had great meaning for others in their situation, as well as being a heartwarming story for everyone. Think of some universal problem and try to find one person or family whose story will make it vivid and alive for the reader.

A national issue. A few years back, *McCall's* ran an article about a woman in Alsea, Oregon, who had suffered a miscarriage and found reason to believe that it might have been caused by a chemical herbicide that had been sprayed in her area. Working virtually alone for the next three years, she managed to gather enough evidence to convince the authorities to suspend spraying until further studies could be made.

Back in the late 1970s, stories began to appear in the papers and on television about the dumping of toxic chemicals into an abandoned canal near Niagara Falls, New York, an area that became known as Love Canal. Environmental pollution was becoming a major national issue, and we felt the best way to bring the seriousness of the problem home to our readers was to tell the story of one woman's family and what they had suffered. By writing of her children's birth defects, her husband's blinding headaches and her own serious illness, we tried to make readers aware of possible threats to their own homes. (Incidentally, this is another example of a story that wasn't proposed to us by a local writer, who would have had far better contacts and knowledge of the situation than we did. We learned of this story through the national news and assigned an outside reporter.)

WHERE DO YOU FIND SUCH STORIES?

I asked each of the writers I have been talking about where they found their stories, and I think their answers offer some pointers you can use, too. Paul Bagne found out about the young woman who had recovered from leukemia by working as a volunteer for a local branch of the American Cancer Society. "It's good for a writer to stay involved with the world around him," he told me. "That's where the stories are."

Rick Soll and Gene Mustain, the two reporters who told us about the "retarded" child and the nurse who had rescued her, found their story when they were going through some back issues of the paper they worked for. One of them came upon a report of a girl who had sued her parents for abandonment, and they were curious to learn more about what had happened. They eventually wrote it up for their paper, and then contacted us.

Barbara Raymond heard about Annie Spiegel on a local TV show. Glenn Joyner discovered Kathleen White and her fight against MS in a newspaper column in a North Carolina paper. "I always check the columns when I'm in a strange town," he told me, "because you often find human interest stories there." Lorene Duquin, who told our Christmas story, read about Ripley's "miracle" in her local paper. She called the town clerk in Ripley who gave her the contacts to track down the people she needed.

"Finding ideas for true-life dramas is easy," she wrote me

afterwards. "The newspapers are full of them. Attorneys are another good source — especially if they have a hot court case that is based on some social issue. Once you become established in your community as a freelancer, people come to you with stories.

"In fact, I just got one the other day. I've met people on vacation who I've done true-life dramas about. And I try to keep in touch with friends and acquaintances who might lead me to a story because of where they work. For example, I have one friend who works in a hospital emergency room, another who is the assistant New York state attorney general in the Buffalo office, and another who in involved in local politics. I've gotten story ideas from all of them."

With a little imagination and a lot of legwork, you can sometimes discover a story that hasn't been in the papers at all. When we learned, for instance, that new medical techniques were being used to save the lives of premature babies that once would have died, we asked a writer to go to a hospital that used such techniques and see if she could find a couple whose baby had been saved in this way. She interviewed doctors, talked to a number of couples and finally found one whose story illustrated the point perfectly. She spent several days with them, re-created their experience and wove the medical facts into a gripping narrative.

The same approach has been used to illuminate such problems as finding a baby to adopt, or to illustrate the new choices available to infertile women. We used it to dramatize the new treatments that are saving so many more cancer patients. If there is some dramatic breakthrough in medical knowledge, think about how it might be made even more compelling by using the story of one person or one family to provide the narrative framework.

HOW DO YOU WRITE THEM?

The narrative form is comparatively easy for the beginning writer because the structure is largely dictated by the facts of the story itself. I used to tell writers to simply begin at the beginning and then tell what happened next — to get out of the way and let the events themselves carry the story along.

The only real decision you have to make is the lead. As I have said, the most effective way to get into the story may not be the first incident in the chain of events you're describing. Just remember the lead's purpose — to lure the reader (and this includes the editor, who will decide whether the reader gets a chance at it or not) into your story, and to capture that person's interest so firmly that he or she cannot put it down until you tell them how it comes out.

For Maxine Rock, whose story of one woman's fight to save her son from paralysis and death was published in the *McCall's* June 1985 issue, the lead went this way:

> Most of all, Alana Shepherd remembers the blood. It came gushing out of her son's throat when a tube, placed there by doctors because the young man was so paralyzed that he couldn't breathe on his own, slipped out. She recalls a horrible hissing sound, and suddenly the hospital walls were spattered with red. It cascaded over her hair, her face, her chest. Blood puddled in her lap. It shot higher and higher, erupting like an angry volcano. It was the only time, whispers Alana, her hand trembling at the memory, when she really thought her son might die.

From there, Rock went back to the boy's near-fatal accident, how his mother learned of it, and what happened next.

Soll and Mustain began in the present, years after the drama they were going to describe, with the reunion between Karen and the woman who rescued her.

> Karen Boldt, a tiny, attractive woman of thirty-two, hesitates a moment, then leaves her crutches in the car. Struggling into the icy wind of a winter day in Detroit, she limps toward a motel coffee shop. Inside, she scans the room until she recognizes an older woman sitting several booths away. Approaching her from behind, she cups her hands over the woman's eyes and kisses her cheek. The woman turns, and they embrace. It is an emotional moment for them both.

Having gotten the reader's attention, they were free to go ahead with their story in chronological order.

Glenn Joyner used a somewhat different technique. Using the marathon itself as his narrative framework, he interwove the events of the race with the story of White's fight to get to the starting line. It began this way:

> The Starting Line: It is a brisk Saturday morning in Char-

lotte, North Carolina, and 1,002 runners are nervously jog-
ging and stretching as they wait for the start of the sixth
annual *Charlotte Observer* Marathon. At exactly 10:01
there is the crack of the starter's pistol, and the pack surges
forward. At the very rear, her heart already pounding, is a
thirty-five-year-old housewife wearing lavender shorts and
shirt and a railroad engineer's cap. Waving to her four excited children along the sidewalk, she appears very ordinary
and totally relaxed. She is neither . . .

Joyner continued the action for a few more paragraphs and
cut to the background.

Kathleen White has been battling with incapacitating ill-
nesses for almost two decades. At the age of seventeen she
contracted Crohn's disease, an incurable disorder that
causes severe abdominal cramps, nausea and chronic diar-
rhea. But, with remarkable stoicism for a teenager, she
accepted her misfortune and vowed not to let it ruin her
life . . .

Cutting back and forth between the story of White's fight back
from paralysis and her agonizing effort to finish the marathon,
the first she had ever run, Joyner shaped a compelling narrative.
This technique won't work every time—you obviously need
some dramatic event to provide the framework—but it's a good
one to keep in mind.

Suppose you were writing a piece about a performer, for instance, or an athlete, or perhaps a man getting an award for
bravery. The performance, or the game, or the award ceremony,
could be used as the framework, following it for a while and
then cutting back to the person's biography, switching back and
forth to allow the performance or the game to carry the narrative
line.

As you write, keep in mind that even the most exciting story
will not hold an audience unless the characters are human and
believable, people the reader will identify with and care about.
To make someone come alive on the page you need details—
details about appearance, manner, the way he speaks or she
moves. You need those little human touches that may do nothing

to move your narrative forward, but that will make its characters real and alive.

Maxine Rock captured details by talking at length with Alana Shepherd and her son, James, about Alana's struggle to make him walk again after the paralysis. Much of what they told her could not be used in the final story, but only through hours of interviewing did she learn the little details that made the scene she was describing unforgettable.

This is Alana's memory of seeing her son for the first time after his accident: "We were in a tiny hospital, staring down at the body of our son. He was too tall for the bed, and his heels were hanging over the end. He looked like a rag doll." Instead of simply saying that he was limp and unconscious, the image of the rag doll said it for her, and in a way that allows readers to see it for themselves.

> It was a long, hard trip. James burned with fever one moment, then turned icy cold the next. When he was awake, his dark eyes were wide with pain and fear; asleep, he looked ashen and skeletal. James was nearly dead when the plane touched down in Atlanta, but he opened his eyes briefly, and his lips soundlessly formed one word: "Home."

As mentioned in the chapter on interviews, specific details like this don't just leap at you from the person you are interviewing; they have to be dragged out with lots of questions: "What did he look like?" "What did he say then?" "How did you feel?" "What is your most vivid memory of that moment?" Don't forget the old four W's and the H that all reporters are taught to remember: where, when, why, what and how. By accumulating these details, you can paint a memorable portrait of a person or an event.

Under Barbara Raymond's patient questioning, Irene Spiegel remembered the moment when her daughter first became aware of her facial deformity.

> Annie loved to sing and dance in front of the mirror. One night she stopped, leaned forward and looked at her image. With her fingers, she tried to tug her features into place. "Why does my eye look like this?" she asked me.

After hours of interviewing Jeanette Cusick, the nurse, about the little girl she had rescued, Soll and Mustain were able to re-create a touching scene that took place in Jeanette's home on the first night Karen came out of the institution.

> Karen touched everything—the furniture, the carpeting, the draperies. She was mesmerized by the ordinary comforts of Jeanette's home . . . for the first time, Karen used a fork and drank from something other than a tin cup . . . Later, after soaking in her first bubble bath, Karen snuggled into bed, then gazed intently at the painting hanging in Jeanette's bedroom. Titled "Love is Blind," it depicted a little girl hugging a doll. Sawdust tumbled from the doll's broken foot. Jeanette, conscious of how sensitive Karen was about her clubfoot, told her, "When people see your beautiful face, no one will notice your foot."
>
> The next morning Karen opened the first real Christmas presents she had ever received. Among them were a rocking chair and a doll. She examined the doll's perfect legs like a doctor examining a newborn baby. Then she named the doll "Jeanette."

Talk to your subjects as much as you can, even after you think you have all you will need. I've had writers tell me that sometimes the most revealing comments have come after the interview seemed to be over, when the recorder or the pad and pencil had been put away and everyone was beginning to relax. Over-research, overreport, learn much more than you can ever use. Only then will you fully understand the people and events you are writing about, and be able to select the details you need.

The late Dick Gehman, one of the most prolific and successful magazine writers who ever lived, put it this way: "I must emphasize the importance of extensive, exhaustive research. If the writer knows so much about the subject he cannot possibly cram it into five thousand words, so much the better. He will be bound to put in the most important details."

THE FINAL WORDS

Where do you stop? And how? In her story of Alana Shepherd's struggle to help her son, Maxine Rock decided to end on the climax, the moment everyone had been waiting for, even though much happened to James and his mother after that.

Doctors insisted on wheeling James to the hospital doors, but James got up, folded the wheelchair and handed it to his father. "I won't need it," he said. He leaned on just a cane and pushed open the hospital doors. Then, triumphantly, he walked out.

Soll and Mustain ended by coming full circle, back to the reunion between Jeanette, the nurse and Karen (now thirty-two, with a child of her own).

> "The whole experience at Dixon," (Karen) says, "was a tragedy. But I try to find good even out of bad experiences. The pregnancy hurt, but I have Michael. I look forward to watching him grow up and accomplish things I couldn't."
> Jeanette tells Karen that's what she always wanted, to watch the girl she rescued grow and become what she is now. "Karen, I loved you from the time I met you, and I love you now."
> "*That*," Karen replies, "is what saved my life."

And Lorene Duquin ended her story of Christmas with the stranded tourists in Ripley, New York, with this lovely image:

> Christmas had come and gone. But the nearly one thousand visitors did not forget. Cards, letters and donations poured into Ripley, many from people who had not even been there that night.
> Then, last spring, a man from upstate New York, whose daughter and son-in-law had spent Christmas in Ripley with their children, sent each of the women who had worked in the kitchen three beautiful rose bushes. Now, every June, when the tall shade trees form an arch over Ripley's Main Street, the townspeople will see the blooming Peace roses, and they will remember, too.

It is sometimes said that good stories tell themselves; they don't, but if you have done your job well, they will read that way. You must research the situation thoroughly, talk to everyone involved, find a focus that will hold it all together. Then you must figure out the essential ingredients of your narrative and describe them as simply and honestly and cleanly as you can.

Human interest narratives do take a lot of work, both to find and to write, but nobody ever said writing was easy. These stories are relatively less complex to put together than a profile or a straight article. And as they are always in great demand, they are an excellent way to break into a national magazine.

CHAPTER TEN

Articles Anyone Can Write

A few years ago, a writer I know, Sally Olds, asked me to speak to a meeting of ASJA, the American Society of Journalists and Authors, about some aspect of writing for women's magazines. I told her I wanted to discuss articles that anyone can write.

"What in the world are they?" she wanted to know. Well, I said, for one thing, personal pieces. Pieces that grow out of your own experience. Articles about feelings and relationships and fears and worries and ambitions. Articles about people close to you — children, husbands, wives, parents, grandparents. Furthermore, I said, such articles don't run only in women's magazines; publications like *Reader's Digest*, *Guideposts*, *Parade*, *Parents* and dozens of others all use them.

She paused a moment and then told me a story of her own. She had written a very personal article about a year and a half before, and had never sent it out because she didn't know how she felt about having it published. It dealt with the death of her mother, and the unexpected feelings this brought out in her. But perhaps she had been wrong to just sit on it, she said, and asked if I would like to see it. I said I would; we bought it and ran it a few months later.

A few years before, I had interviewed a young woman for a job, and while we didn't hire her, I was impressed with some of the pieces she'd written. Then, some months later, she called to tell me that she and her husband had recently had a baby, and that they had begun keeping a joint diary on the day they decided to have a child. Their experience was, Lord knows, as old as time, but she described it so charmingly that I encouraged her to send in some samples. It not only developed into an article for *McCall's*, but an agent encouraged her to expand it into a book outline, and they sold the rights for an impressive advance.

And, to restate a point I've made before, these were *stories that we didn't know about.*

RECOGNIZING A GOOD STORY

The bulk of the articles in a magazine—I once estimated about eighty-five percent of the articles in *McCall's*—come from ideas thought up by editors and assigned to staff or freelance writers. Editors don't do this because they're in love with their own ideas; they do it because there just aren't enough good ideas being submitted by writers.

I often think it's because many writers don't recognize an idea when they see it. Often the things we take for granted about our lives, things so personal that we think they couldn't possibly interest anyone else, express the kind of universal feelings and emotions that strike a chord with thousands of others.

ARTICLES FROM DEEP INSIDE

One of the best magazine writers I know is Joan Barthel. An interview with her appears later in this book, so I won't tell about her now, but she wrote two outstanding examples of the personal story for *Life* magazine. The first was a piece she never wanted or intended to write. A good friend was seriously ill, and Joan was thinking only of comforting her. Then, as the illness continued and Joan was told her friend was dying, she felt a strong need to keep a record of what was happening.

The record turned into a simple yet profoundly moving description of what it was like to watch someone you love die. But more than that, she made this tragically common experience into something with a universal theme. "I was afraid then," she wrote at the end, "and I still am, but for myself. I guess I projected myself onto that narrow white bed, and even to consider being so helpless, being aware without being able to communicate, leaves me almost hysterical with dread . . . I am afraid now because the inner resources I thought I had, so strong, I thought, now seem so frail and feeble . . ."

The final article, entitled "I Promise You, It Will Be All Right," turned the story of her friend's death into a deeply felt tribute that has meaning for us all.

Joan says she was very proud of that story, as she was of another very personal piece on growing up Catholic. But, of course, it was about more than that, as her lead indicates:

> You wore a medal on a chain around your neck, usually a Miraculous Medal of the Blessed Virgin Mary, with that inscription on the reverse side. If you were a Catholic and you had an accident, somebody would call a priest. If you were a priest, you would come. Roles were clear and definitions sharp, and in general it was easy in those days — those days being the 1940s and a good part of the 1950s, the days of steadily growing up and unsteadily groping out — to be either a plain Catholic or a Catholic priest.

What she was writing about was the certainties of youth and the doubts of maturity, and the changes that were affecting the church and straining the faith of priest and parishioner alike. A very personal piece, yet a piece that spoke to everyone, Catholic or not.

These are articles that come from deep inside, articles that only one person can write. And because they draw on genuine emotions, they move us in a way ordinary articles cannot. One of the best examples I can remember was written in the form of a letter from a woman whose adopted daughter was going to meet her birth mother for the first time. Because we felt that "Letter to the Other Mother" was a beautiful and universal expression of love, and because it had something important to say about what being a mother really means, we were delighted to publish it.

Another I remember was a first submission from a young woman in South Carolina who had never gotten along well with her mother. Then, when she had her own child, she gained a new understanding that led to her becoming closer to her mother than she had ever been. We later received letters from many other women who had similar experiences.

Barbara Raymond was a housewife with two very young children when she began her writing career. She had no training or experience, had never even taken a writing course, but she was bored so she sat down one day when the children were asleep and started writing little pieces about things that meant something to her. She wrote a reminiscence of her father. She wrote about her frustrations at having to give up her teaching job and stay home with two infants. She wrote about an illness she had suffered as a child. She wrote about how she felt when her first child went to school.

Personal things—things "that couldn't possibly interest anyone else"—yet they did and got her started on a successful freelance writing career. The writer Joyce Maynard sold article after article about her young family until her children finally grew old enough to read and were embarrassed by the attention and asked her to stop. I talked recently with a freelancer from Virginia named Anne Cassidy, who used to write about relationships. Since getting married and having children, she now writes almost exclusively for magazines like *Parents*, *Parenting* and *Working Mother*.

MARKETS FOR THE PERSONAL STORY

I went to our local supermarket when I started this chapter, just to see if the kinds of articles I've been talking about were still as common. Believe me, they are. *Good Housekeeping* still runs a feature called "My Problem." (It used to be called "My Problem, and How I Solved It" but presumably they came upon some problems they couldn't solve.) The issue I picked up contained a story called "My Husband Came On to Other Women," and had been written by a young wife who was near divorce because she felt her husband was more interested in other women than he was in her. Therapy revealed that he learned this behavior as a way of getting his mother's attention. The writer didn't sound entirely satisfied with this, but at least she seemed to understand.

Redbook featured an article by a young woman who had married a rabbi and felt strong pressure from the congregation to conform to their idea of what a rabbi's wife should be. She sounded even less happy than the woman whose husband flirted with other women, but I am sure it did her good to get it off her chest.

Ladies Home Journal had an article called "How I Fought the System—and Won," written by a woman who proved she had been discriminated against on her job, sued her company and won $400,000 in damages. She was not only someone that other women can identify with, but her story might inspire others to fight back against an unjust management.

Cosmopolitan had a story called "Second Thoughts . . . or, I Cancelled the Wedding." I don't need to tell you what this was about, but it was interesting to note that a *New York Times* report showed that 100,000 American couples call off weddings every year, so this approaches being a universal problem.

Cosmo also has a one-page feature called "On My Mind," which deals with personal opinions. There are similar columns in other magazines, usually carrying a title like "Back Talk" or "My Turn," and expressing strongly held and often against-the-grain opinions. These are also very personal pieces, and ideal places for new writers to break in.

In *Guideposts*, I found a great many such personal essays, more inspirational in tone but still very universal in the feelings they expressed. One woman told how she had grown so depressed that she lost the will to live after a divorce and the development of cancer, and how she found the strength to fight back. A mother told how she taught her son—and herself—to accept the fact that he was dying.

In another, a man pondering the ethical thing to do in a business situation remembered the lessons his father had taught him, and knew the decision he had to make. Another was written by a woman who had taken her young son and his new wife and child, and then her parents, into her home, and of the pressures this put on everyone. Her article told how she had worked out her problem. And in another issue, a mother told how she had learned to survive the death of a beloved son and use her experience to help others.

Special Report, a magazine for young working mothers published by Whittle Communications in Knoxville, Tennessee, presented a multitude of personal stories. One told of the problems and joys of growing up as an only child. In another, a man told of his fears of a vasectomy, and of how he had become sure he had made the right decision. Yet another told the personal saga of a family trip to Disneyland in a rented RV, and one more was a moving essay by a young woman about the father she never knew.

And finally, in *Family Circle*, I found "My Son Was a Bully," which dealt with a small boy who was later diagnosed as having what is now known as ADHD, or attention deficit hyperactivity disorder. Again, it was one woman's story of her problem and how it was solved.

When you read through magazines, keep an eye out for such stories; you'll find more of them than you might have expected. They don't make coverlines, and they're often fairly short, but magazine readers love them and editors know it.

Whenever we would run articles on women trapped in lonely marriages, or men who can't or won't express their feelings, we would get thousands of letters from readers thanking us for understanding and letting them know they were not alone. I can't tell you how many letters I read that began, "I felt that you were speaking directly to me. . . ."

Women's service magazines, and many other magazines as well, have survived and prospered because they are very close to the lives of their readers. They deal with the very real problems and worries and feelings and issues their readers face every day.

And these are not problems that anyone else is dealing with. Not their newspapers, except for columns like "Dear Abby," and not their television sets, either. The Phil Donahues and Oprah Winfreys and Sally Jesse Raphaels used to talk about common problems and concerns, but now they struggle to out-sensationalize each other with issues like lesbian adoptions and women who marry homosexuals and the like.

WRITING THE PERSONAL ARTICLE

The style of these articles tends to be fairly simple and straightforward. The author is usually telling about something that means a great deal to him or her, and understatement is more effective than overstatement. Simply tell what happened and how you feel about it, using a straight narrative form if the material lends itself to that. The diary of the young couple having their first baby was just that—a diary. It needed a few paragraphs to explain what it was going to be, and then the passing days and weeks became the structure.

The letter to the birth mother of the writer's adopted child was literally in the form of a letter. The article by the woman whose mother had died was essentially an explanation to her daughter of why she felt relief when her mother was finally freed from her pain and suffering. Joan Barthel's journal of her friend's death was broken down by days, telling what was happening and how it was affecting everyone involved.

Because these pieces are so personal, and so different, it's hard to draw up a set of guidelines for writing them. The best advice I can give is: *Think of how you would tell this to a sympathetic friend.* Tell it as simply and directly as you can, and let the facts and your feelings about them carry it.

But keep in mind that it has to adhere to the writing rules I have been discussing. The lead has to attract your reader's interest; don't be too leisurely or indirect at the beginning. You have to let the reader know early on what you're going to be talking about, and why it will be worth their time to listen. And, generally speaking, such pieces should be fairly short. I'd aim for between fifteen hundred and two thousand words.

Somebody once said that everybody's life contains one novel, and I think this is even truer of such personal articles. Many young writers feel that such things are too special for them to interest a large audience. But few of us are alone in our feelings and experiences, and things that affect us deeply will affect others as well. And they're right there in your own head, part of your own life. These are stories that only you know, and there are plenty of readers who would like to hear them.

CHAPTER ELEVEN

Fifty-Three Ways to Be a More Effective Freelancer

Let me start by saying that most of the suggestions in this chapter appear somewhere else in the book. But I have found it useful to compile them in this way. As the material begins to fade in your mind, it will be useful to read them over and remind yourself of the essential things you must remember to be a successful freelance writer. When I go over this list with my students toward the end of a course, they always ask for a copy. Here is yours.

Note: They are not arranged in order of importance; if I didn't think they were all important, I would not have included them.

1. Never submit a query to a magazine unless you've read at least two recent issues of that magazine.

2. Unless the magazine has a very small staff do not send your query to the editor or even the managing editor. Top editors are busy with the Big Picture; send your ideas to lower-ranked editors, who are hoping to find new ideas and new writers and become top editors themselves.

3. Never write a query that is longer than two pages, and keep it to one page if you can. Remember that if you want to intrigue them, don't tell them the whole story.

4. Never write anything you wouldn't feel comfortable saying.

5. Never submit an article until you've read it aloud. Listening to the words will force those awkward phrases and repetitions and redundancies to leap out at you.

6. Don't use any unnecessary words or phrases or sentences or

paragraphs. Many professional writers go over their finished pieces five or six times, looking for everything that isn't needed, that clutters up their prose, that the reader doesn't need to know.

7. Detail is vital to capturing the feeling of a person or an event. But make sure your details are revealing of character or place, not just verbal litter.

8. Don't use big words, unless they're the only way to make your point.

9. Try to avoid using jargon, but if some strange word is necessary to the understanding of your article, be sure to explain it the first time you use it.

10. Don't use three or four words when one will do. "Was witness to" is a lot lumpier than just plain "saw," and "at this point in time" is a boring way to say "now."

11. Make sure that everything you write is perfectly clear. If what you write can be misunderstood, it will be.

12. Watch word placement in a sentence. "Only I love you" is not the same as "I love you only" or even "I love only you."

13. Unless you're entering a William Faulkner sound-alike contest, don't use long sentences, as they're hard to follow and may cause your reader to give up. Try for an average of fifteen words per sentence, but don't waste a lot of time counting the words. If your sentence runs more than two or three typed lines, it's probably too long.

14. Vary the length of your sentences; if you do have one that runs twenty or more words, follow with a shorter one. When sentences are all about the same length, the writing has a jerky, staccato feeling.

15. To describe action, use short, punchy sentences. Longer sentences can be used for descriptive passages.

16. Make sure that every thought has a transition leading the reader into the next thought. If you lose your reader more than once, you may never get him back. Never forget: The easiest thing for a reader to do is stop reading.

17. Make sure there are no questions left unanswered. A friend who isn't familiar with your subject matter may be of invaluable help.

18. Use active verbs; they will make your writing move. Sometimes the passive voice is effective, but make sure it won't be even stronger in the active.

19. When you're paring out inessential words, take a hard look at those adjectives and adverbs. Can a strong noun or verb do the job by itself?

20. When you're writing dialogue, always identify the speaker after the first complete phrase or, at worst, the first full sentence. And one attribution is plenty.

21. If you're not going to write "he said," think hard about what you're going to substitute for it. "He asked" is fine, as is "he answered" or even "he explained," but never say "he opined." "He smiled" is foolish; "he said with a smile" is much better. And don't say "he believed" unless you're very sure he does believe it. We all say a lot of things we don't believe.

22. You don't have to use all of a quote you are given in an interview; sometimes it's more effective to paraphrase part or even all of what somebody says, so that you get to the point more quickly.

23. No article has ever been published in which every word spoken is printed exactly as it was said. You can cut. You can rewrite if necessary to make the speaker's meaning more clear. You can rearrange the order in which the words were spoken. But you can never, *never* distort the meaning.

24. Remember the three *I*'s and one *E*, because they should be present in everything you write. They stand for Information, Intelligence, Insight and Entertainment. No matter how important the information you have to convey, it should be done in an entertaining manner.

25. While you're thinking of letters, remember the C words, too. They should also Characterize your Composition: Correct, Clear, Concise, Complete, Constructive, Credible, Conversational and Captivating.

26. If the person you're interviewing is going too fast for you, ask a question or two that you don't want the answer to. Then catch up on jotting down what they said while they're saying something you know you won't use.

27. Even before writing the query, remember who you're talking to. How sophisticated is the audience of the magazine you're pitching an idea to? How much do they know? At every stage of the process, from query to finished manuscript, remember three little words: Audience. Audience. Audience.

28. If you're having trouble getting your piece started, think about how you'd tell your story to a friend. What were the things you learned that impressed you most? Perhaps the one fact or event that is uppermost in your mind suggests a good lead. If it's the first thing you'd tell a friend, maybe it should be the first thing you'd tell a reader.

29. There is no "right" lead on an article. The right one is any lead that grabs the reader's attention and leads him or her into your piece.

30. If you're having trouble finding the right lead, don't sweat it. Just start writing those sections of your article that you feel sure of, and eventually a lead should emerge. If worst comes to worst, just start at the beginning.

31. Never mis-lead. Don't use humorous leads for serious pieces, or vice-versa. And don't use a lead that is just an attention-grabber, and not truly an important part of your article.

32. Don't expect your reader to absorb too much at once. Pace your material, remembering that adage: Tell them what you're going to tell them, tell them, and tell them what you've just told them. This has to be done subtly, but it can be very effective in making your point.

33. Be sure and tell your reader why this story is worth his or her attention. The "why I'm telling you this" paragraph is vital to engaging and holding the reader's interest.

34. My bibliography at the end of this book begins with *The Elements of Style*, by Strunk and White. Use it regularly to re-

view the elements of good punctuation, grammar, form, composition — and style.

35. Unless you are a recognized expert, your opinion is not relevant. To support your points, quote real experts.

36. Unless you're an important figure in your story, or unless your piece is clearly labeled "personal opinion," avoid the first person. Too many uses of "I" sound like too much ego. (I make exceptions for instructional books.)

37. Overresearch. If you have too much material, you'll use only what's most important.

38. Don't put in everything you have learned. If an editor wants twenty-five hundred words, don't send thirty-five hundred.

39. Know how you feel about a story before you try to write it. And make sure the facts justify that feeling.

40. You learn to write by writing, but first you learn by reading. Study writers whose work you would like to emulate. See how they solved the problems you face. Don't imitate. And certainly don't plagiarize. But do learn from the experience of others.

41. Writing is like talking. The purpose is to communicate ideas and information as simply and clearly as possible. If you try to "write like a writer," it will sound phony.

42. When you are proposing an idea, don't confuse a subject with a story. AIDS is a subject. "How AIDS Tore My Hometown Apart" is a story.

43. The title you put on your query, or your article, is not just a label. It is a *theme*. It not only tells the editor what you're trying to say, but shows that you have focused your material. It helps you keep your focus, too.

44. Show, don't tell. "Show" the reader why a woman is beautiful, or a forest fire is terrifying. Let the reader reach his own conclusions. Don't tell him what to think.

45. The structure of your article will be determined by its content. That is, by the points you wish to make and the material you have to make them with.

46. When planning the organization of your story, there is no substitute for *thinking*.

47. Always get your pieces in on time. If you miss a deadline, it may make the editor look bad, and he won't hire you again.

48. Don't take rejection personally. Learn from it.

49. Make sure you and your editor have a clear understanding of just what your story will be like. If there is any confusion, type a synopsis of the piece you plan to write, and make sure you're on the same track.

50. Metaphors and similes can enrich your writing. But watch out for phrases like "cool as a cucumber" or "fierce as a lion." Clichés are death to good writing.

51. If a cliché is the only thing that seems to work, however, make sure the reader knows *you know* it's a cliché. Admit that it's a cliché, but argue that it's the most effective way to make your point.

52. Colloquialisms and slang in dialog can be helpful in defining a personality, but they don't belong anywhere else.

53. To avoid writer's block, always stop writing at a point when you know what's coming next.

CHAPTER TWELVE

The Writer's Life

In the course of writing this book, I turned for advice and help to a number of writers I have known and worked with over the years. They ranged from contemporaries to young people I met in the last years of my editing career, varying in age from late twenties to early sixties. I originally turned to them for samples of their work to use as examples of good writing, and for their suggestions on such matters as writing queries, doing research, organizing their material, interviewing.

But as I talked to these men and women, I began to get the feeling that their stories of breaking in and building careers in freelancing would be of value to beginning writers. I also felt they offered helpful insights into the way writers think and work, and that their examples could be both instructional and inspirational.

Accordingly, I went back and prepared a series of questions, which I asked each one, ranging from how they got started to how they do their jobs. I asked them when they first realized they wanted to write, when and how they sold their first piece, how long it took to get established. I asked about their work habits, how and where they got their ideas, how they prepared for interviews.

I asked for tips on writing successful queries, choosing leads and endings. I asked how they organized and structured their articles, how many times they rewrote before they were satisfied. I asked them to tell me some of their personal experiences, and solicited their advice to young writers trying to break in today. And finally, I asked if they liked to write and if they ever expected to stop.

There is some repetition, and some examples showing that

everyone does things a little differently, but there is also a remarkable degree of similarity in the advice they give, and in the
stories they tell. And, in the end, I think they add up to a revealing picture of what it is like to be a freelance writer today.

RICHARD MERYMAN *has been a magazine journalist for almost forty-
five years. I met him back in the days when we were first starting
out in New York, and we used to play touch football with a bunch
of other editors and writers in Central Park. I kept in touch with
him over the years, watching his career thrive and grow, and while
I was at* McCall's, *he wrote a few pieces for us.*

*Recently I talked to him at some length about his life and work.
Note that this piece — and, in fact, all of the writer interviews — are
in the voice of the writer. This is my small tribute to a technique Dick
perfected over his years at* Life *magazine and other publications, in
which the sometimes messy give-and-take of an interview is
smoothed out, made to seem as if the subject of the interview is
talking directly to you. He used this technique with articles on Sir
Laurence Olivier, the Swedish filmmaker Ingmar Bergman, Elizabeth
Taylor, the painter Andrew Wyeth, Louis Armstrong, Julie Andrews,
Joan Rivers and many others. The articles carried Richard Meryman's
byline, but were in the voice of the person being interviewed. This
is what I have done.*

I had this idea as a kid that I wanted to be a writer. I was
terrible, but I had a brother who was a scientific whiz, and
I've always thought I wanted to be a writer because this was an
area I could have for myself. I loved words and I read a hell of
a lot. I loved the music in words, the sound of them.

I took writing courses in college, fiction courses, and I always
got *C*'s and *D*'s. My writing was terrible, but I always had this
thing about words and language. I got a job on *Life* right out of
college, and it turned out that what I was was a journalist, not a
writer. I worked my way up as a reporter, getting the material
for stories others would write, and gradually I learned how to
use the material in putting stories together. And I learned just
how important the material is — the reporting. That's the beef in
what you say.

I started at *Life* in 1949 and worked for twenty-three years,
until it folded as a weekly picture magazine in 1972. Over the

last four years I worked in the text department as a writer, but I never really considered myself a "writer." I was a reporter who had learned how to write. I still feel that way.

What I really think I learned during those years was how to use the material. Fiction writers have a power of invention that I don't have. I once tried to write a film script but I just couldn't invent the scenes.

After *Life* folded I went out to freelance, and for a while it was very rough going. My first assignment was from *Playboy*. I was very fortunate because I had a byline that was known in the magazine world, and also because I had a *schtick* — the interview. The first-person monologue. That gave me a niche I could work from, and it's kept me going. It's always been something I could return to.

I have been trying to get away from this form, and I recently had a piece in *Smithsonian* on an opera singer, and I have one coming out on a social worker. They're straight reporting.

My pattern as a writer is to always have one big thing going, and to sort of do magazine work around the edges. I've done about six books, and maybe a hundred or so magazine pieces. It's hard for me to do two things at once, but you can't make a living just by writing books, unless you're a big, big star and command huge advances. And you sure can't make a decent living just doing magazine work. You really have to be able to do both.

It's also important that you not be snooty about what you'll take on. The writer Ben Hecht once described himself as a "hired pencil," and in a lot of ways that's what you are. I think the ability you must acquire along the line is to find the story in anything you're assigned to write. The editor thinks the idea is good, but he's not quite sure what the story is, and it's your job to go out and find it. That's what they hire you for.

[Author's note: Dick's point about being willing to take on anything reminds me of a story that illustrates this well. Some years ago, a writer I have quoted before, Bill Heinz, told me he couldn't take on an assignment because he had something he felt obliged to do. Bill had been a war correspondent in World War II and had received some favors from an Army doctor named Richard Hornberger. Now Hornberger had written a book about his experiences during the Korean War, and he needed some-body to put it in shape for him.

Bill said that Hornberger had some great stories to tell but he wasn't really a writer, and he had asked his friend Bill Heinz to see if he could turn it into something publishable. Bill had been putting the doctor off for over a year, as I remember, and was feeling more and more guilty and had finally decided to do the rewrite.

I can't remember how long it took Bill, but eventually he was back and available for assignments. The book was eventually published, under the pseudonym of "Dr. Richard Hooker," and it was called *M.A.S.H.*]

You must know basically what the story is before you start, but you have to be open to change. You look for material that will support the story you have in mind, but if the situation tells you that the story is different, you have to go with that. But just to start without knowing what you're after, to go in blind and fish, is terrible.

I had worked at *Life* for fifteen years before I got a byline. I think I was lucky because I didn't do it until I was ready. My name didn't appear on a piece until I'd learned to write. The funny thing is, if you wanted to be seen as more than a reporter, the best way was to write a piece for some other magazine. I did a picture story for *Life* on a B-47 mission. They were the SAC bombers that at the time stayed in the air day and night, armed in case of nuclear war. I had a lot more material than I needed so I wrote a piece for *Harper's*, and that suddenly, in the *Life* editors' eyes, made me a "writer."

That's one way to get into the freelance business. Start out as a reporter and then move on from your daily newspaper job, using the material you've gathered to sell pieces to magazines.

Being a freelancer can be frightening, and it takes a lot of discipline. I try to write almost every day. I think that everybody has a time of day that's their best time, and mine is the afternoon. My ideal day is to eat an early lunch, take a nap, and then go to work. Five hours a day is about my limit. I begin to run out of gas at about six.

The first job is, of course, is organizing the material. You must at that point know where the drama lies, the high points to be hit hard. In the piece on Julie Andrews, I knew that as a girl she had felt responsible for her erratic family, that she was the one who held it together, a fact that had major repercussions in her later life.

And as I work, I am constantly looking for an opener and an ender. Talking to or watching a person, I suddenly hear in my head, "That's the opener!" or "That's the closer!" Or, "That's the climax!" Maybe "That's the turnaround!"—a pivot that lets me take the narrative off in a new direction. If you're conscious of needing to find these milestones, they'll save you a lot of time when you start to write.

For that subject-to-subject internal structure, the specific ideas and the order of their arrangement, I let the material itself tell me their progression. And I believe in doing this physically. I don't think you can carry everything in your head, and I sure don't believe in putting it in a computer. I can't imagine how you could work off a database, everything out of sight. I think a lot of weak writing you see today may be partly an overdependence on a computer, even though I use one. For one thing, as word after word disappears into that box, you tend to write too loosely, too long.

So I tape all sit-down, face-to-face interviews and scissor up both the transcripts and any written notes. As I do this, each piece of paper tells me its category, tells me the subject to write on a manila file folder. For instance doing a piece on Diana Ross, categories written on those folders were Break With Motown . . . Audience/Performing . . . Marriages . . . Supremes . . . Motherhood, etc.

When the folders are full, I take a yellow pad and sort of look bleakly at their headings and take a pencil and figure out how one leads into the next. I already have a good sense of what's in each folder; I've been thinking about it all the time I've been filling them.

And I'm very aware of transitions—I'll make notes showing how one piece of information will be the bridge into another piece of information. *Smithsonian* editor Tim Foote once said, "Writing is transitions," and I don't think that overemphasizes their importance one bit.

When I have my categories written down, I'll arrange them in order and start writing. Sometimes the order of subjects doesn't work, and so I'll change it. Nothing is rigid. But I know where to begin and where I'm going, and I think that's terribly important.

I pay a lot of attention to openers and enders. The opener has to pay off in the piece; that is, the opener can't just be there to get attention and not be important to the piece. And I really like to have an ender that goes back to the opener. I did a piece on an opera singer for *Smithsonian*, and in the beginning she's warming up in her dressing room and thinking about what's going to happen that night. Then, after the body of the piece tells her story, at the end she's back on stage, taking her bow. Similarly, on a social worker piece, I started as she went out on a home visit and then at the end I tell what happened to the family she saw in the beginning. I don't think you can write a piece without knowing the opening and the ending.

A lot of my story ideas come from things people tell me, or things I hear about that interest me. I also look for certain key elements in a story. Let me give you an example. I met a builder who was constructing an absolutely chemical-free environment for a woman who is totally sensitive to the chemistry in everything. She is allergic to just about any material—wood, pillows, plaster—just everything. And she's had to live with this all her life. To me that's a story. To begin with, it has wider applications than just this one person. We all live with materials that put off chemical vapors. And there are hundreds of people who have this problem to some degree. But there is something else that makes this a story—*it's something most people don't know about*. And that's terribly important.

Another thing I like a story to have is a catchphrase to sell it. Something that will give an editor something that intrigues him. And the catchphrase here is: "These people are humanity's canaries." You know, like the canaries the coal miners used to keep. If the canary died, they'd know the air was getting bad.

And it's got something else that's always at the core of a good story, and that is that *somebody is being put under pressure*. I do pieces about people, and my absolute rock bottom criterion is: Are these people under pressure? Because pressure reveals the cracks in the facade—reveals a person's true being. It's fascinating to watch how people perform under pressure. This woman with the allergies has had to live a life under tremendous pressure. How does she cope with it? How has she survived? Most of my pieces are about survival, in one way or another. Originally at *Life* most of my pieces were about the creative process — profiles of Olivier and Bergman and Chaplin and Wyeth.

It's very important for a writer to have a field of interest, something that is recognized as being your area. All these men and women I wrote about have understood something and carried it to the extreme. In prep school I wrestled, and I had one hold that was rather unusual. It was called the cradle hold, and I could put it on somebody in a flash, in almost any position, and it was my thing. Bergman's thing is that he was crazy, or on the edge on insanity, let's put it that way, and he made his work into his buffer against insanity. By doing movies about it, he helped control it.

Wyeth's thing is that for him past and present exist simultaneously. An object or a person evokes his childhood — especially the emotions — so he is painting his childhood *through* the object. What he knows is that emotion is the absolutely crucial thing, and I believe that too. He taught me that. You have to have your own feeling about what you're writing. My feeling about Julie Andrews was affection because of her image, the pleasure she had given me. I think you *must* like the person. I've done very few pieces about someone I didn't like. I've always found a way to like them. I've never done a hatchet piece. I believe that negative journalism is a way for the inexpert journalist to find energy. The energy of negativism carries the piece. I think it is a crutch. I really feel very keenly about this.

You have to go through a lot to get entrée to somebody, and to go through all that and then crucify the person, that seems like such a shitty thing to do. He or she takes you in and trusts you and opens up to you. He tells you things he's never told anybody else in the press and then you take that stuff and use it against him. I'd hate myself if I did this. It's just so dishonorable.

I think, in fact, that this is also one of my things. I'm known as someone who can be trusted. That's one of the reasons I can get to all these celebrities.

I did a piece about an actress who was widely known as a bitch, and it was true. If you know this, aren't you duty-bound to say so? Well, I guess you can slip in some hints, but I wouldn't say it outright. What these pieces are is a person's vision of themselves. And people don't always realize how they sound and what they're really like. So the pieces must be true to how they see themselves. Your job as a writer is to show people your subject's psychic journey. But you'll never get such inner material unless you plan carefully before you go out on an interview.

It's really all in the preparation. To know what the story is before you start the interview, you must do a great deal of background research. In the ideal interview you pretty much know what the person's answers are going to be when you ask your questions. In that way, you can shape your interview. A trial lawyer works much the same way — he tries never to ask a question in court unless he knows the answer.

And the second thing that is crucially important is not the first question, or the second, but the third. I always go in with a prepared list of questions, although I have them pretty much in my head and sometimes I don't even look at the list while we're talking. I'll ask a question about the relationship with the mother, say, and she'll answer and out of that answer might come another question. Or maybe they'll throw out a surprising word that suggests another line of questioning.

And it doesn't matter who it is, how famous they are, they're all a little nervous. When I interviewed Julie, she surprised me afterward by thanking me for putting her at her ease.

While someone I'm interviewing is talking, I'll say things like oh, yeah, or I know, or that's happened to me. And then I'll tell them something intensely personal about myself. The more personal the better. So I make myself a little vulnerable, too. I do that several times, so it becomes not an interview but a conversation about a mutual experience. This is very effective.

You can tell during an interview if the energy is going out of it. You can feel it. And I will lean forward and I will try to summon up energy in myself and project it into the other person. The space between you is important. If one of us laughs, I lean back. If they cry, I shift the tone of my voice and lean forward. I might reach out my hand and very softly ask them, what are you feeling right now? I try to make it a very personal thing.

I think I might have had a career as an actor, because I think a lot of what interviewing is all about is acting. Interviewing was my talent, and it's one I never knew I had until I started doing it. Then, once I learned how to take the material and shape it into a story, it all came together.

I can't imagine ever stopping writing, even though I have to admit that I don't enjoy it particularly. Anytime a writer tells me that he loves to write, I get a little tickling feeling that maybe he's not very good. I think it's so hard to be good. It takes such intensity and such focus and such determination, and that's why it's no fun.

Every once in a while I get blocked, don't know what's coming next, and the only thing I know how to do is just start writing anything. I don't worry too much about it. I just take a beginning, the thing in the research that works best, and simply start writing. I don't sit around flogging myself, waiting for it all to come clear. I just write and gradually it does come clear and the problem's solved.

What I love most is the reporting. My basic thing is that I love to go out into the chaos of a situation and bring order to it. Here is this mess and you somehow get in there and do the reporting and make it all make sense. That's why I love this business. It's the reporting.

I think there's a pecking order in writing. The poets are at the top and then the fiction writers. Then there are the nonfiction writers who do big things, and then there are the journalists. People like me.

I read a piece once in *The New York Times Book Review* about accepting your limitations, and that was very good for me. Be proud of what you are and you'll do it better. I'm very proud of being a journalist.

MAXINE ROCK, *a journalist for over twenty-five years, has written four books and more than a thousand articles for such publications as* Reader's Digest, USA Today, McCall's *and* Smithsonian. *She has lived in Atlanta for many years and feels being out of the New York area can be an advantage. Her location, she says, "gives her close proximity to a wide range of readers, so I can get close to them, their problems and their need for personal help from magazine articles."*

I sold my first piece when I was in college. I was seventeen years old, and we had a class assignment to write about something new. John Kennedy was in town and he was running for president, so I asked for an interview with one of his staffers to talk about the campaign and how the press was treating Kennedy.

My professor liked my piece so much that he sent it to *The New York Times*, where it was accepted and published. But not paid for. I called the *Times* and told them that if it was good enough to be published it was good enough to be paid for. They sent me a check, and I was hooked. I put myself through college, at least partly, by writing for newspapers and magazines.

I don't remember my first big magazine sale, but I think it was *Woman's Day*. I've sold to many of the women's magazines, and *Woman's Day* is still one of them. My main local market is *Business Atlanta*, where I'm special assignments editor, and my national markets include *Reader's Digest, Inc.*, *Harper's Bazaar* and *New Choices*. I've had to cut down on magazine work lately so I can finish my new book.

I also write for a number of small publications. They're often overlooked by freelancers, but I'm a swift writer and I can make as much or more working for the smaller magazines. I turn assignments over quickly, and I work for a lot of different editors. Editors pass your name around, and this is as true in New York as it is in Atlanta. That's one reason why I'm careful about pleasing all my editors, if I can.

I got a good start from the training I received in college (New York University, B.S. in journalism, and the University of Michigan, M.A. in journalism and science) and I think too many would-be writers today try to break in without training. I think they're making a big mistake. Unless a writer is exceptionally gifted, he or she needs the professionalism that a good journalism program will provide.

The second big mistake new writers make is that they try to sell pieces without reading enough magazines. Magazine writers have to be magazine readers. You have to be a magazine fanatic. I can't tell you how many subscriptions I have, and I read them all. Maybe not all of every article, but I read at least the titles and the first few paragraphs of everything. It helps me to keep up with what editors want.

Some writers say they get their ideas from reading magazines and newspapers, and it's certainly important to keep up with what's being published, but I get my best ideas from talking to people. I'm enormously interested in people. Everybody has an interesting story, or knows someone who has an interesting story. I'd rather get my ideas this way because by the time I'm reading about a new trend, somebody else is already writing about it.

Another reason behind the success I've had as a writer is that I have a tightly organized personality. I usually work at least a nine-to-five day. Before I start to write my house is clean and my husband and I have had our breakfast and often I've also done my exercises for the day.

This ability to organize starts when I begin researching the piece. When I interview someone I'm mentally picking out the lead. As I talk to them I make notes to myself in the margins of my legal pads. I may mark the lead, and maybe the ending, and I number the paragraphs in the rough order they'll go. By the time I'm finished with the research, I know where everything is going to fit.

When it comes to queries, I don't try to write them until I've done a lot of the research. I usually don't even mention an idea to an editor until I've found out a great deal about it. Then, once I get the editor's okay, I finish the research and begin planning how it's all going to come together. So by the time I sit down to write, the piece is almost all written in my head. I may forget to pick up a quart of milk or get the dry-cleaning, but I can remember everything that happened and everything that was said during my research.

Leads aren't a big problem for me, because I usually know the lead and the conclusion before I start, and I try to tie them together. I want the reader to feel "Now I see how it all ties together. I'm satisfied. I don't have any unanswered questions."

I go at this as if it were a business, which of course it is. The fact is that successful writers are usually very ordinary people, like myself, who lead structured lives with spouses and children and houses to clean and meals to fix. Writers like to believe they are unconventional. Free spirits. But I know very few good, tightly organized writers who make money and also lead sloppy lives.

Organization is vital at every stage of an article. Before I go for an interview, for instance, I find out as much as I can about the person, so I know what questions to ask and am reasonably sure the person I'm interviewing knows the answers. If they say they don't know, and I'm pretty sure they do, I'll drop it for a while and then rephrase the question. I'll keep coming back again and again until I have the answer, because I've done enough homework to know it's there.

But while I need time to prepare, I know that the person being interviewed needs time to prepare, as well. I'll always set up the appointment in advance, and I'll set time limits — "from three to four tomorrow afternoon," for instance. I'll tell them a little of what I'm going to talk about, so they can think about some of their answers in advance.

I always write out my questions and leave a good bit of space — sometimes a whole page — for the answer. I may use up an entire legal pad in one interview. I don't want anything to distract me, so I don't drink coffee during an interview, and I've never smoked.

I don't usually use a tape recorder, because I find that people don't speak as freely with the tape running. But if I know they're going to be hostile or wary, I'll use a tape recorder for my own protection. I want to be able to prove that they said what I say they said.

But mostly I rely on my shorthand to take notes. I do it because it's faster, and it also keeps the person I'm interviewing from looking over my shoulder to see what I'm writing down. And I'm always writing. Sometimes I'll ask an extraneous question, something I don't care about the answer to. The reason is that I want the person to keep talking while I'm writing down what they said earlier. Oh, about the shorthand. I learned it in high school, and it has really come in handy.

Sometimes a person I'm interviewing will suddenly say, "This is off the record." I've gotten very tough about this. Unless they tell me in advance, I say it's not off the record. I tell them that when you invited me over here, or said I could come, you knew I was a reporter working on a story. Everything that's been said I've taken down and will use. I tell the person before I come that they can trust me with off-the-record material, but not if they tell me something first, and then change their minds later, to conceal information. If it's just a rephrase, or a clarification, that's okay.

Sometimes somebody will say that they want to tell me something that's off the record, so I can understand the situation better. When they do that, I respect it. I just put my pad and pencil down and lean back and listen. If they get into an area that I know I want to write about, I'll tell them, "Stop, don't tell me anymore." I don't want them to think I've used anything they've told me in confidence, in case I get the information somewhere else. I do tell people I intend to find out—from somebody else. And usually, I do.

But most of the time they're not telling me anything important at all. "This is off the record," they might say, "but my dog died last week," and this is to let me know why they were irritable or depressed when I talked with them on the phone. Most of what I'm told off the record is not something I want to use, anyway.

Sometimes, though, someone I'm writing about has a good reason to withhold material. Recently a man called me after our interview and said that his attorney had told him he shouldn't have given me the story because it would really damage him, and he begged me not to write it. So I didn't write the piece. What he was asking me to keep secret was something personal to him, and not a matter of public record. I lost money and I lost time, but he would have lost a lot more.

Sometimes human compassion precedes being a journalist.

BARBARA RAYMOND *has been a freelance writer for ten years. She is now working on her first book, but still writes regularly for* Good Housekeeping. *She has also contributed to* Redbook, McCall's, Parents, Working Mother, USA Today, Writer's Digest *and others.*

I always wanted to write but thought it would be too hard to get published, so for eight years I put my writing aside and taught school. Then we had two kids very close together and I had to quit my teaching job. I was very happy as a mother for a few years, but I got more and more frustrated about not working.

Then one day I sat down and wrote a little reminiscence about my father. Father's Day was coming up, and I sold it for $45 to a local newspaper. Then I joined a writers' group and they told me about query letters. I'd just sent the first piece out cold. I also started to read *Writer's Digest*. Then I sent out my first query.

I didn't know you weren't supposed to send queries to a lot of places at once, so I sent it to five. I got three acceptances. The one that paid best was *Sunday Woman*, which was distributed by King Features to a number of newspapers around the country, so that's who I wrote it for. I told the others I'd gotten an assignment from somebody else, and I never queried them again. I had quickly learned the dangers of sending out simultaneous queries.

The *Sunday Woman* piece had dealt with making the transition from working to not working and being a mother, and that had worked out, so I sent off another query to *Parents* magazine on a similar topic. They offered me $750, which was big money for me at that time. But up to then I'd just written about myself, and this new piece required that I interview a lot of women and several experts. I think I overresearched it. I accumulated a lot of information but I didn't know how to shape it into a coherent article, and the upshot was that I got rejected.

I sold it to the same local paper, for another $45, but I was so miffed that I had failed my first try at a big magazine that I thought up another idea and queried *Parents* again. This time they gave me an assignment for $1,000. I don't know whether they'd forgotten my earlier disaster, or just wanted to give me another chance. This time I studied the magazine very carefully, taking apart their articles to see how they were put together. I looked to see how many anecdotes they used, how many quotes, what kinds of structures they usually used. And this time I was ready. They bought my article and even used it as their cover story. It dealt with how a mother feels when her kids go to school for the first time.

Then I queried *Good Housekeeping* on a piece about a mysterious illness I'd had when I was a teenager. Months passed with no word, so I called them. And they wanted it! I wrote it and they really liked it and paid me $1,500. And from then on I decided I was a writer.

But all this time I'd been writing about my own life. My problem came when I decided to take on more difficult articles. I'd had no training at all. I mean none! I'd never even had a writing course. I'd learned from my reading about how to write, and also from my editors when they told me what I was doing wrong, and sometimes even what I was doing right. And I just kept reading a lot and writing a lot. I had to teach myself to research and to interview. Again, I did this by studying published writers and seeing how they gathered material and handled their interviews.

While I was trying to teach myself to write, there was a period in which I was getting some acceptances but also a lot of rejections. But I would just keep rewriting until the pieces were accepted, if not by the original magazine, then by somebody else. You just have to say, "This is my goal and I'm not going to give up." And I kept reading other writers, writers who were a lot better than I was, and gradually I stopped getting rejected. I don't recommend this method, but it worked.

One thing I had trouble with was finding the right structure for the piece. I would become overwhelmed by my research and wouldn't know what to do with it all. I would let the research drive me. Now I feel I have to own the research before I can start writing, to know exactly what I have and what I'm going to do with it. It's at the mercy of me, not me of it. I used to put things in just because I had them in my notes, not because I needed them. Now I know what I need and where it goes. You have to have a kind of vision of the piece. One thing that helps me to do this is to summarize what the piece is about in one sentence, and write that at the top of the outline. If you keep that goal in mind, the writing is much easier.

I think the best way to figure out the structure is to study your material carefully and then put it aside and think about it for a day or so. After a while you will begin to see the structure in your head. At this stage, I write a kind of long sketchy outline. I used to get nervous when I started to write, but now I just tell myself that I'm not really writing but just playing around and roughing out how it should go. The first thing I know I've written two or three or maybe even six or seven pages, and I've almost written the piece.

Now that I know the overall structure, I'll go through my notes to see how the different sections fit together. At this point I often find that things will pop into my head from my research, things I didn't even know I remembered. Now I'm ready to begin writing.

By this point, I usually have the lead in mind. If I don't, it's hard for me to get started. Writing a piece is like shooting an arrow at a target, and the lead points the way to where you want to go. Sometimes I work for a day or two on the lead, but once I get it, the piece comes easily.

The reason for the outline is that I have found that if you just go ahead and plunge in without one, you'll reach a point where you want to put something in and it doesn't exactly fit and you don't want to go back and start reorganizing. You have all those nice sentences and transitions and it's hard to go back and start over. So you don't, and the piece has problems. But if you're just sketching out an outline, it's easy to move bits of scenes and information to where they belong.

My work day usually begins at ten and goes to five or six, with some time off when the kids come home. If I have to work at night, I do. I try to do some work every day, even weekends.

I've always been good at writing queries. A query is an overview, and I think I'm better at seeing the bigger picture than the smaller one—I can see the forest, but have trouble with the trees. In the beginning my queries were sometimes better than my finished pieces, but they did get me assignments, even if they didn't all work out.

Even from the beginning, when nobody knew who I was, I always called an editor first to see if they were interested in the subject. I'd have the idea capsulized in a sentence or two. They'd either say no, or tell me they had something in the works, but sometimes they'd say yes. And sometimes in our conversation they'd say one or two things that gave me some hints on how they'd like it shaped and focused. I know most people tell you not to call an editor cold, but it's worked for me.

I have to do a lot of interviews on the phone because I can't always get away, and I've decided that in some ways phone interviews are better. Some people are shy and I think they open up more on the phone than they would if I were sitting in their living rooms.

Before I talk to someone, I read up on them as much as I can. If I'm going to be talking to them about some specific subject, like brain surgery, I read up on that beforehand. But even with all the preparation, I almost always find that I have to call back later. Once I've outlined the piece I always find holes.

Part of my problem is that I'm so careful about not hurting their feelings that I don't push beyond the comfort zone in our first talk. But then I'll realize that there are things I have to know, tough questions I have to ask, even if it does hurt them. I've always been the kind of person who wants others to like me, but I realize now, that in this business, they aren't always going to.

I don't have to do rewrites very often. I'm a very painstaking writer and very careful with the outline, so that by the time I've finished with a piece, I don't usually have to rewrite, except to tighten. But rewriting is writing. I just write in such a neurotic, slow way that I'm really rewriting as I write.

I think young writers should have some training, take some writing courses, learn as much as they can before they start. It would certainly have saved me a lot of time if I'd been better prepared. Then, once you start writing, you have to become compulsive about it. Don't take rejection for an answer. And keep reading, especially the magazines you're trying to sell to.

Don't ever stop learning. You're never going to feel that you have all the answers. The people who think they're really great writers and know everything don't always know what great writing really is. There's always somebody better. You can always improve your work.

BIL GILBERT *has been making a living as a writer for over thirty years, during which time he has produced ten books and over four hundred articles. His work has appeared in such varied publications as* Audubon, Esquire, Saturday Evening Post *and* American West, *but the bulk of it has been published in* Sports Illustrated *and, in recent years,* Smithsonian. *I first met him back in the mid-1960s when he came into the* Post *with a piece called "The Owl in the Playpen." He claimed that his daughter Lyn had been raised by an owl, and explained, with more logic than you might imagine, how this was done. We bought it, along with almost everything else of his we could get our hands on, and I don't think I ever worked with a more amiable or more talented writer. Bil was living then in a little Pennsylvania town called Fairfield, and lives there still. His son, Ky, and granddaughter, Amanda, live with Bil and his wife, Ann. Two daughters live in Tucson, Arizona, and Lyn, the owl's daughter, lives in Fairbanks, Alaska.*

Today Bil occupies a unique place among magazine writers—he just writes what he wants to write. He doesn't do queries; he doesn't do three martini lunches. He just tells the editors who know his work what he'd like to write about, and they generally tell him to go ahead. It's an enviable position to be in, and not a position that a writer achieves easily. Here's how he did it.

I'm not sure when I decided I wanted to be a writer, but it always seemed like an attractive thing to do and I kept trying to figure out how to do it. When Ann and I were married back in 1950 we took a bicycle and canoe trip and I sold a piece about it to a travel magazine. We got, I think, $125. I went to college at Georgetown, and all during the 1950s we stayed in Washington and took in writing, kind of like other people take in washing.

Some public relations work, some speech writing, some stringer work for newspapers around the country; I did it all. I wrote some pieces for the Sunday magazine of the *Washington Evening Star* newspaper and for a magazine called *Nature*, that later merged with *Natural History*. I got hundreds of rejection slips, but I kept trying and finally caught on with *Sports Illustrated*. I've been freelancing full time since the early 1960s.

I've always written about whatever interests me: nature, social commentary, environmental politics. The last ten years my writing has been fairly equally divided between social history and natural history. I do about four pieces a year for *Smithsonian*, switching between the two. When I get tired of dead people I write about live animals. I'm working now on a piece about armadillos, and I did one recently on snapping turtles.

I spend more time these days on books than I do magazines. I use magazines when I want to go someplace or do something that interests me. I'm right in the midst of a long thing now that may take me to Siberia for three or four months.

None of my ideas come from editors. I've got a reputation for not working well with other people's ideas, so the editors wait for me to tell them what I'm interested in. For instance, about every two or three months I go up to Washington to see my editors on *Smithsonian*. I'll have a list of things I'd like to write about, and we'll go over that and come out with some assignments. I usually have a stack of ten or twelve okayed ideas, but I keep thinking of new ones to add to the pile. Sometimes they say they don't know what in hell I'm talking about, but they know I usually end up with something publishable. And that's really how it goes.

I never did queries. Ideas are a dime a dozen. The success of an idea depends entirely on how you handle it. I can't outline an idea for beans. I always say that writing precedes perception. That is, I never know what I'm going to say until I sit down and start writing. Way back when I was at Georgetown, I entered one of those college short story contests. Part of the idea was that your entries got judged by a real agent. I sent in three pieces and the agent said there wasn't any point in pursuing this. I ought to looking around for some other kind of calling. I still remember exactly what he said. My writing was too slick to be taken seriously and to serious to be slick.

That was the only time I ever had anything to do with an agent, except for some television and movie offers that have come up. I figured then that no good agent would be interested in me because 10 percent of nothing is nothing. I just started submitting on my own and it worked out. By this time I know practically everybody in the business, so why should I start giving an agent 10 percent for material I can sell myself?

I don't mean to make it sound as if it's been easy. Writing is hard work and it takes a long time to learn. And the only way you really learn to write is by writing. I don't have much use for journalism schools. You can take one summer course on the fundamentals and then you ought to just start doing it.

When I'm getting ready to write a piece, I don't try and organize my material in advance. I just start writing. I usually do six or seven drafts. I'll admit that this is a slow and inefficient way of organizing material. It takes me about three weeks to write a *Smithsonian* piece, but most of that is spent in the first two or three drafts. Fooling around, throwing things away. To me, writing is kind of a process of self-hypnosis. You have to get so immersed in the thing that you can't think about anything else. The first week isn't worth a damn because I'm still thinking about the garden or what else I'm doing. Then I reach a point where I get so disgusted with myself and say I'm not going to spend the rest of my life working on this. At that point I begin emptying my mind, thinking about nothing. I walk around like a zombie. Nobody likes those two weeks. Somebody might tell me that a couple of my kids had died or part of my house had burned down and I'll just say oh, yeah, and not even hear them. You get so concentrated that everything else is blocked out. I think that's a lot of what writing is—focus. As you focus, things will come out. I'll think of things I'd forgotten, or hadn't planned to use, and they're just right.

I don't worry about the lead in advance. I just start from the beginning and keep going. People tell me that I should use a word processor because you can move paragraphs around, and I say that I don't want to move paragraphs around. One paragraph comes and then the next one and the next . . .

Let me give you an example of how I work. I used to coach the women's tennis team at this little college in town. And we were down at the court one day and it had been raining and the whole damn thing was covered with angleworms. The players were all asking why they were there, and I said because of the rain, and they said what difference does that make? I said I don't know but I'm going to find out.

I was up in New York a week or so later and I happened to see my editor at *Sports Illustrated*, Gil Rogin, and I said I'm going to do six thousand words on angleworms.

"Oh, Jesus Christ," he said.

His reaction became a kind of legend around the magazine. But he didn't try and talk me out of it. He was one of those editors who has confidence that you can do something that can be published, and feels there's no point in asking you to explain how you're going to do it. The angelworm piece, which was titled "They Crawl by Night," was reprinted in *Reader's Digest* and picked up in Europe and ran in anthologies and I used it in one of my books.

Of course, if a new writer comes in off the street and says, "I want to do an angleworm story," the editor will say get out of here. But they know me, and they know this is the kind of peculiar way I go about things.

There are a number of pieces I'm particularly proud of, and one is the four-part series I did on women in sports for *Sports Illustrated*. It won a National Magazine Award, and I think it had a lot to do with gaining more respect for women athletes and getting more money put into sports programs for women.

I'm also proud of a three-part series I did about ten years ago on Interior Secretary James Watt, who I thought was a real threat to the environment. I spent six months on it, and Watt still claims that my series was what drove him out of office.

I like to write long pieces. I just don't think you can say anything substantial in a thousand words, and the *Smithsonian* is one of the few magazines left where you can write at a decent length.

There's absolutely no point in being a writer unless you write about things that you think are worthwhile. It's a poor way to make money. To become rich and famous. I always tell young writers that there are three things that can strike out writers. The first is booze. The second is alimony payments. The third is celebrity-hood. I think that if you're looking for a glamorous lifestyle, you ought to pick something else. Sell real estate.

But if you have a compulsion to write, then do it. It makes absolutely no sense to write something you don't believe in, just because a magazine wants it. You've got to write about what you want, and you learn how to do this well by doing it.

People sometimes ask me what it takes to be a writer. Do you need a large vocabulary, or something? And I tell them you have to have arrogance. A writer is somebody who comes up to a stranger and grabs him by the elbow and says now listen to me. I'm going to make you laugh or I'm going to make you cry or I'm going to make you better informed. And you've got to stand still and listen and then you have to pay me for it. Now that is arrogance.

But there's no point in trying to become a writer unless you're demented in that way. People *ought* to want to know what I want to tell them about. I think too many publications are devoted to telling people what they want to know. They print the weather and the box scores and what starlet is sleeping with whom. I've always believed that one of the purposes of a publication is to tell people what they *should* know. And publications that do this are almost disappearing. *Smithsonian* in one of the last places that agree with me.

Will I ever stop writing? Well, no. I can't stand writers who sit around and whine about how much work it is to write. It *is* work, but it's never seemed like work to me. And this is because I've always written about what interests me. I think that if somebody hadn't been paying me to go down to Florida to look at armadillos I might very well have taken three weeks and gone down there and looked at armadillos anyway.

JEANNIE RALSTON *has been a freelance writer for less than six years. Her first full-time job was for* McCall's *and she later edited a magazine for teenagers before deciding to devote herself entirely to writing. She has sold to* National Geographic, Life, Ms., Glamour, Conde Nast Traveler *and* Travel & Leisure, *among others. In 1992*

*she married Robb Kendrick, a professional photographer she met on
assignment for* Life, *and now lives in Austin, Texas.*

When I was in the fifth or sixth grade I used to write really
dumb little poems. That was the first real writing I'd
done, and I was very proud of them. Then in the eighth grade I
edited the junior high school yearbook, and later the high school
paper. I wanted to study journalism so I went to the University
of South Carolina, where I worked on the newspaper, the literary
magazine, and had several internships.

I got a summer job at *McCall's* after I graduated, and it turned
into a full-time job. I had another editing job after that one, and
in both places I got a chance to write for other magazines. It
really helped to work on a magazine staff because the people I
got to know there spread out to a lot of different magazines. I
started working for *Time, Inc.,* because of a summer internship
at the *Time* bureau in London. The bureau chief was transferred
to New York, and she wanted me to work for her there. I've
always tried to stay in touch with people, and when they move
around I follow them.

I started freelancing full time in 1987, and there have only
been two times since then when I felt panicky because I didn't
have an assignment. I've been lucky because of the contacts I've
made, and because I keep sending out query letters. There are
times when I have too many assignments, but that's better than
having too few.

My major markets now are *National Geographic,* where I'm
hoping to do one big story a year, and *Life.* I've done three pieces
for *Travel & Leisure,* several for *Ms.* and *Glamour* and the other
women's magazines, and I'm a contributing editor for *Allure.*
I've done a lot of traveling with my husband, and that's given
me a number of travel ideas, some of which I've sold to *Conde
Nast Traveler.*

The most satisfying piece I've ever done was for *Life.* It was
about the head of the Miss Texas beauty pageant. This was when
I met my husband, but that's not the only reason it was so satisfying. This piece had the biggest impact of any article I've written.
It told how the head of the pageant was using his power and
influence over young women in questionable ways.

The first line of the piece was "Come on in, sluts!" At first I wasn't going to start off that way, because it seemed too strong, but I found that the piece wasn't going to be as long as I'd hoped so I didn't want to waste a lot of time getting to the point. That quote really set the mood because this guy was kind of a crude good-old-boy type. He was joking, and I made it clear that he was joking, but he was talking to a group of young women and it wasn't at all clear that *they* knew he was joking.

The article was picked up by Associated Press and *The New York Times* and TV shows like *Inside Edition* and *A Current Affair* and *Hard Copy*. The Miss America Pageant did some investigation and learned more about his methods and the end result was that he had to resign. It wasn't satisfying because I disrupted somebody's life, but because I thought I'd done some good. Sometimes you write a piece and never hear anything more about it, and this was one time when I really felt I had an impact.

The *Life* story grew out of an assignment I had for *Glamour*, and the *Glamour* piece was satisfying in a different way. They gave it lots of space, and it was the kind of story I like to do — building a story through scenes and dialogue. They allowed me the room to show how a beauty pageant trainer works, how she molds a young girl and trains her to win. I had written twenty pages and I think they cut no more than four paragraphs, so it came out just the way I wanted.

I also felt good about a piece I did for *Travel & Leisure*, describing a trip along the Texas/Mexico border. It was the kind of piece where you read it over after it comes out and you're happy with the way it's written and proud you came up with those good lines and you kind of ask yourself, "Wow, I wonder if somebody else wrote that?"

I guess it's all part of the feeling that I don't enjoy the writing itself, but I really enjoy it when it's done. I like the reporting, but I find the actual writing very painful. There is always a moment when I just think it's terrible and I feel lost. And then I just go through that and finally it starts coming around. But it's a painful process.

My work habits depend on what phase I'm in on a story. If I'm doing the reporting, I may work anytime, depending on where I am and who's available to interview. If I'm in the writing phase, I spend many evenings at it because I feel like I write better at night. I play music very loud to get myself energized. I usually play U2. It's a strange habit, but it seems to help.

Many of my ideas come from reading magazines and newspapers, but I also find that a lot of ideas grow out of other stories. When I covered an abortion protest story for *Life*, in Buffalo, I stayed with the *Operation Rescue* people for two-and-a-half weeks, up to sixteen hours a day. I had a lot of information left over, including my personal feelings about the protest, which didn't belong in a piece of straight reporting. So I called *Ms.* — I'd never worked for them before — and they gave me an assignment.

The same thing happened with a piece I was doing on Appalachia for *National Geographic*. I spent eight weeks there, and I was really struck with the women of Appalachia. They are very strong. They don't use the word "feminist" because they don't like that label, but many have become feminists because the conditions are so bad in their area and many of their husbands have lost their jobs. The women have had to step forward and really become leaders. I also went to *Ms.* with this one, and they said okay.

You have to train yourself to recognize story ideas when you see them. When I hear something interesting I start turning it over in my mind, looking at it from different angles, trying to figure out what kind of magazine it might be right for.

I also have a whole library full of clips and notes that might turn into stories someday. For instance, I have a whole file on gambling, but I haven't found the right angle yet. I keep files on lots of things. Women and guns, for instance. Living in Texas, you hear a lot about that. I might never do it because I'm afraid it's been done to death, but as soon as I throw that file out I know I'm going to need it. One whole drawer of a file cabinet is filled with folders containing story ideas and clips. I have them in categories like social issues, women's issues, environmental problems, travel and so on. I have it all broken down so that I can get at these things easily.

Also, my husband is one of the best idea people I've ever met. So he's a good influence on me.

I have two different kinds of queries that I like to write. If I know the editor well, the query is part of a letter. But if I'm trying a new magazine, I'll write the query as a small piece and use a cover letter. I pay a lot of attention to the lead and may write a page-and-a-half proposal. But before I even write that,

I'll do a lot of background digging on the subject, reading everything I can, as well as lining up my sources. If the idea is based on a newspaper story, and I have only that one source, I'll make some phone calls to make sure the original story had the facts right. [Author's note: To see one of Jeannie's queries, turn to chapter two.]

The one I'm working on now grew out of a newspaper story about American men who send for Russian girls to marry. I made some calls and found this terrific couple. The idea is to do enough work in advance so that the query doesn't sound like something that was just torn out of the paper.

When I'm reporting on a story I take a lot of notes. After my eight weeks in Appalachia, for instance, I had filled sixty-one notebooks. The story on the abortion protest in Buffalo filled twenty notebooks. I take such copious notes because I like to be able to re-create scenes and dialogue and conversations so the reader sees and feels what I did. If possible, I go through the notes the same day I take them, because my handwriting is very bad and if I wait I might not be able to figure out what I wrote.

I use those little yellow stick-ons to highlight things I want to be sure and use in the story. Then I actually type out an index, using scenes, good quotes and statistics, and mark them to show where they are in the notes. On the bigger pieces, like one for the *Geographic*, I also do an outline.

When I'm preparing for an interview I'll read everything I can about the person and then make up a list of questions. I won't actually refer to the questions during the interview, but mentally the questions are registered in my mind. The conversation always flows more easily than it would if I were just reading off a list. But at the end, I always check back over the questions to make sure I haven't forgotten something I wanted to ask.

I don't use a tape recorder on a story in which I'm going to be interviewing a lot of people, because I do write pretty fast and I feel confident about getting down all the quotes that are relevant. But if I'm doing a profile and will need a lot of quotes and detail, I'll tape it. I'll also tape it if the person being interviewed is a really important person and if you misquote them it will be a disaster, or if the subject we're talking about is very controversial. My problem with taping is that when I'm through

I know I'm going to have to transcribe it, and that drives me nuts.

When I start the actual writing, I try to do the lead first because I feel that if I can get that down, everything else will flow from it. Sometimes I have to change it later, but I normally stick with a lead once it's down. I usually look for a scene that will put the reader right there, but it has to be a scene that will be a good launching point for the main points I want to make.

I did one story for *Manhattan, Inc.*, on Nancy Kahan of Crown Publishers, a woman who's big in the publishing industry and is known for her big publishing parties. I went to one she gave for the writer Dominick Dunne, and it was such a scene. It was full of society types and celebrities, and I felt that describing it captured the whole literary scene. And that's the scene I started off with:

> As Nancy Kahan walks into Mortimer's for a party cele-brating Dominick Dunne's new book, Ronald Perelman and Claudia Cohen are obligingly doing a society grin-gnash inside a wreath of photographers. The restaurant's rarified air shudders with flashes of light, much like the sky on this stormy night. Two socialites with skin pulled tightly over yesterday's-deb bone structure are gushing over the author who writes about people like them. Mighty agent Owen Laster is explaining to huddled listeners how he got his black eye.
>
> Nancy Kahan sees it all, and for one moment goes through what she calls "a wave of ugh!" The veteran of hundreds of these affairs, who has earned a reputation as the uncrowned queen of publishing parties, feels a splinter of apprehension about dancing into this swirl of people. But the anxiety doesn't faze her—it always comes, at least for a moment. Kahan knows better than anyone else that for all the lightness and laughing, all the salmon mousse and vodka tonics, parties—business parties—are about nothing if not tension and fear. On both sides: party giver, partygoer.

Endings are so hard for me. You've said everything you want to say and then you have to finish it off without regurgitating anything. I try not to end on a quotation, because that seems too easy, too predictable. I'd rather end on my own take, my own kicker, instead of letting somebody else speak my ending for me.

(When the article on Nancy Kahan ran in July 1990, she was looking ahead to bringing out a book of her own on business entertaining, and the article ended with her thoughts on the party she would give for that one. Echoing a theme from the lead, it went this way: " 'I want it to say everything I say in my book and be full of fun and magic and delight people,' Kahan says, acknowledging that her book, her business, and her reputation will be on the line. *Good Morning America* is planning to cover it, and she's expecting plenty of other press. 'The eyes of the world are definitely going to be on this party.' Of course she'll be nervous, but she knows it will pass.")

When I'm ready to start writing I plan on doing three drafts of my story. The first is just to get it all down on paper. There are no rules. I don't make any judgments about how good or bad I'm writing. I just want to see how it actually plays out on the screen. The next version is for structure, and to go back and make sure everything flows. This is when the transitions go in. I make sure I get all the names and facts right. I put in those missing statistics, and all the TK's. (That stands for "to come" and I use them when I haven't got the right fact or statistic in front of me when I'm writing that first draft.) The second draft fills in all the missing parts.

The third draft is for style. For smoothing. To make sure it's singing, if I can get it to that point.

Even after this, I know there's about one chance in three that I'll have to do some rewriting. Some editors prepare you for a rewrite in advance. *Travel & Leisure* tells me that 90 percent of their pieces go back for a rewrite. *The New York Times Magazine* is the same way and prepares you by saying that you shouldn't be upset if they ask for more work.

Sometimes you have to do some pretty weird things to make sure the story is as good as it can be. When I was in Buffalo on the abortion protest story, there were a lot of other reporters there. The event was not only being covered by the major newspapers and news magazines, but CNN and all the networks were there. I knew I had to get something everybody else didn't have.

Since I was doing only half the story—I was with Operation Rescue and another reporter was covering the abortion clinic side—I was able to spend a lot of time with these people. One of the big things they talk about is getting arrested. I wouldn't say it was their goal, but it's kind of a badge of honor, and other people respect you if you're willing to make that kind of sacrifice for the cause.

I tried to get the police to let me go into the holding area where the people who get arrested are taken, just to see how they were treated and what kind of spirit there was. But there was no way. I even went to the head of the police department in Buffalo, and he said absolutely not. My husband said he would get arrested to get pictures for the story, but a police lieutenant told Robb not to do it because the first thing they'd do would be to take his cameras, and of course that would have defeated the whole point.

I still wanted to be arrested, though. I knelt down in front of this lieutenant on the street and they arrested me. I had been told that this was the sort of thing they arrested you for. So they took me and handcuffed me and put me on the bus, but they allowed me to keep my notebooks, so I was taking notes the whole time with my handcuffs on.

I was glad I'd gone in because I got to see the solidarity among the protesters who had been arrested, and I got to see first hand the kind of commitment they have to the cause. I felt the leaders of the anti-abortion movement were manipulative and not always honest about their goals, but those people I met in jail, the foot soldiers, are really wonderful. They really believe in their hearts that abortion is murder and that they have to do these things. After I got out everyone looked at me differently. They felt that if I was that committed to get the whole story, they would respect that, and they really opened up to me. As it happened, I was charged but the charge ended up being dismissed. And I ended up feeling that I never wanted to be inside a jail again.

An even more frightening time came when I was doing that story about Appalachia, and I decided to go down in a coal mine. Before I went I had nightmares about being trapped underground. The next morning we went down this elevator shaft five hundred feet below ground—that's about the height of a fifty-story building—and then once we were at the bottom we rode a tram car for three-and-a-half miles through those dark tunnels.

The whole time I kept looking up at the roof because those rocks looked ready to drop, and I'd heard terrible stories about people being crushed by falling rocks.

Anyway, we were down there about four hours and while we were heading back to the elevator, the guy driving the tram was showing us the area where there had been an explosion seven years before because of a build-up of methane gas, and that wasn't making me feel any better. Then suddenly we heard this strange noise like *Whoop . . . Whoop . . . Whoop*, and I started getting even more tense.

The driver said, "Oh, they're just testing the fan alarm. You don't have to worry unless it keeps going off." We went on a little further and it goes off again. "Oh," he says, "they must be testing it twice." And then a minute later it goes off again and he says, "I guess I'd better call upstairs."

He learns that the fan that is used to bring up the methane gas has broken down and he says we'd better get back to that elevator shaft. We get to the elevator and we hear a disembodied voice saying, "Get them out of there!" They were evacuating the entire mine.

So we get in the elevator and the door won't shut. My worst nightmares are coming true, and I'm about ready to have a heart attack. Finally he gets it shut and we get up above ground and I just whooped and jumped around in relief. We found out later that this was the first time in four years that the mine had to be evacuated, and it had to be the day I was down there. Needless to say, I'm never going to go down in a mine again, but it's sure a story to tell my grandchildren.

A happier story involves the time I was sent to Morocco to do a story on Malcolm Forbes' birthday for *US* magazine. There were so many media people there, and I was working for a bi-monthly magazine, so like the abortion story, I knew I had to get something for *US* that would be different from what everybody else got.

There was a big press conference that Forbes and Elizabeth Taylor were having, and I realized there was no use going to that one because it would be in the news that next day. So I hired a driver to take me to the area where Rupert Murdoch was having a party on his yacht. I was the only journalist. Robert Maxwell, the British press lord who died mysteriously last year, was there, and he was upset because nobody was coming to *his* party. So he sailed his yacht in and parked it next to Murdoch's yacht. The *Giannini Agnelli* came into the harbor and sailed right up to us and did this dramatic coming about and almost hit us. It was just Big Boys with their toys.

Anyway, I decided I'd better get back to the press conference to see what I'd missed and when we got there we saw Forbes and Taylor pulling out so — and I really said this, just so I could say I said it — I said, "Follow that car!"

So we went careening through the streets of Tangiers and I was never so happy, thinking "Wow, this is what it's all about." We lost them, but it was sure fun.

You don't always get to do that sort of thing, of course, but you can see why I enjoy the reporting. I try to balance my work between stories about big social issues and stories that are more fun. I also try and balance my assignments between large circulation magazines, where you don't have as much control, and stories for smaller magazines. I couldn't do big issue-oriented pieces all the time. They take too much out of you.

While it's valuable for me to get to New York every now and then to see editors, living outside of New York is definitely a benefit. I'm exposed to a different part of the country than the New York editors, and they're always asking things like, "So, what's happening out there?" It's important to keep up on what's happening in your area, the big stories and the small ones, and they'll start thinking of you whenever something happens where you live.

Will I every stop writing? No, I know I'll always be writing something, but I may change to books or screenplays or something else. But I can't imagine ever stopping completely. I *can* imagine stopping this heavy deadline schedule, where you just jump from one story to another, although I'll have to admit that magazine work has let me do much better financially. But I'd still like to do something where you get to spend more time thinking — but maybe I'd just spend more time procrastinating. But no matter what I do, I'd still want to be able to take off and do a magazine piece that really interested me.

DALMA HEYN *has been both an editor and a writer, but for the past seven years has concentrated entirely on writing. She has appeared* *in* Mademoiselle, Glamour, McCall's *and* Ms., *among others, and last year (1992) her first book,* The Erotic Silence of the American Wife, *was published to considerable acclaim.*

I guess I really decided to become a writer when it became clear that when I wrote, I always did well in school. I was in high school then and I wanted to be a psychiatrist, but I kept getting kudos for my writing and finally I realized it was bringing me as much pleasure as my ostensible goal. I began to get the sense that writing was not just something I was good at and *could* do, but was something I really *wanted* to do.

I got my first job when I was just out of college and working for a travel magazine in California. *Family Weekly* asked me to do a piece on Marilyn Monroe's psychiatrist, who lived near me. I had written something for the travel magazine, which *Family Weekly's* editor, Mort Persky, had seen and liked.

I kept writing travel pieces and editors began to recognize my name and I just kept getting assignments. Once you break in with a few published pieces, it's a lot easier to get other ones.

The secret to getting your ideas accepted is to know the market. A lot of writers don't bother to find out how each magazine differs, what each magazine needs, what the different departments are, what they're looking for, which pieces are done by staff writers and which are open to freelancers. Some don't take the trouble to study the magazine or even learn whom to query.

Before I can begin writing a piece, I have to write my lead. Some people can write in chunks but I can't; I cannot move on until I've finished my first paragraph. I'm obsessive; it has to be perfect. I think this must be the way I organize and orient myself, because once I have the lead, I know where to go. After that, it all comes fairly easily. The lead gives me the tone I want and sets me on the course to where I want to go.

If I can't get the lead, I'll literally tear my hair. I'll think I shouldn't have taken the assignment, that I can't do it. But once I do get the lead, I rarely change it.

I revise obsessively before I submit an article. I can't let go of it until I think it's right rhythmically. It's got to read well when I pick it up again the next day. I'll even edit it on the way to the mailbox. Because I am so compulsive about getting it to read smoothly, I don't usually have to do rewrites.

The only times I've had trouble with a piece is when an editor says, "Just play with it, I'm not sure what I want." Or when it's a subject they've tried before and it hasn't worked out, or when an editor wants an edgy, mean tone. I'd much rather work on my own ideas, as long as I'm very sure I know what the editor expects from me.

If an editor turns down one of my ideas, I really do keep trying; if I'm sure it's a good idea, I know it's my presentation that's at fault. So I shake it up and try and come at it a different way, and usually I can sell it.

One story I did for *McCall's* that could have been a complete flop was the Paul McCartney story. What I didn't realize was that McCartney had been interviewed by about 250,000 other reporters and was giving everybody the same interview. I had been totally charmed by this glib and seductive guy, and what he gave me was a story that had been published a dozen times.

But his wife saved me. Linda McCartney gave me this funny little take on who he was and what their marriage was and what their life was like, and it saved me. She was more willing to speak from the heart, telling me sad and shocking things that were a total contrast to Paul's glib, "everything's great" view of their life. I would have printed anecdotes that had been being used for two decades if it hadn't been for her.

When you're sent out on an interview, learn as much as you can about the subject from other people, and read as much as you can before you form your questions. Straight interviews aren't hard, but celebrity interviews can be tough. I always used to think I was going to make some kind of personal contact and get the celebrity to tell me things they hadn't told other people. Which is just ridiculous. It's happened to me a few times—as it did with Loretta Lynn—but usually you end up playing by their rules.

Everybody's work habits are different. I have to get up and write. I can't do other things and then write. When I start off early I seem to get the benefit of my subconscious, which has been at work all night and is still in operation in those first few waking hours. And my energy level is higher in the morning.

My husband, Richard Marek, is writing a novel, his second, and his way of working is to get up every morning and write one page before he goes to work. Just one page. At the end of the year has 365 pages. I couldn't work that way. I could write five pages or half a page, but I'm just not that regular in my production or my habits.

I don't think young writers should think there are many who can just sit down and create like Mozart or Joyce Carol Oates. I've never know anybody who doesn't have spurts of productivity followed by blocks, and who doesn't have any dry spells.

ANNE CASSIDY *sold her first article in 1983, and now writes regularly for* Working Mother, Family Circle *and* Good Housekeeping, *plus several different magazines devoted to parenting. She is married to Tom Capehart, with a two-and-a-half-year-old child and a five-year-old child, and lives in Herndon, Virginia. She says it took her about a year of work to begin selling regularly, and has now reached a point where "I have something due every three or four weeks, so I feel I have a pretty full schedule."*

I always liked to write, even as a child. I harbored dreams of being a writer when I was in college, and I even transferred from a small college in Indiana to Northwestern because I was so serious about journalism. After I graduated I taught high school English for five years, but I was always doing some writing— poems and essays, mostly—and I knew teaching wasn't *it* for me.

About that time my mother started her first publishing venture, a local magazine for Kentucky women called *Bluegrass Woman*, which got me even more into the journalism side of writing. I did a lot of writing and editing for her and also helped her define what the magazine was going to be. I learned the magazine business by the seat of my pants, so to speak, because none of us knew what we were doing.

Then in 1979 I left my teaching job in Chicago to get another teaching job in Kentucky and also help out on the magazine. I would do both jobs, and decide which I really liked best. So I kept my day job as a teacher and then about 3:30 every afternoon I'd rush over to the magazine office. And it soon became apparent to me that I was excited about the writing and editing and not so excited about the teaching. So that's when it really clicked.

I quit teaching and worked full time for another year on the magazine, but finally I decided that I needed more professional training, so I went up to New York and enrolled at Columbia

Journalism School for a year. After I finished the program, I got a job on a magazine, although I continued to write and edit for *Bluegrass Woman* by mail.

My first piece was sold to *Working Mother* in early 1983. I'd written a lot for my mother's magazine, of course, but this was the first I'd sold on my own. It was about grinding your teeth, technically known as *bruxism*. I'd worked on it as a class assignment at journalism school, so it was pretty much finished. At first *Working Mother* wasn't too ecstatic about the idea, but I stood up for it. I argued that the subject was important for working mothers because it was about tension and stress, and I finally talked them into publishing it. After that I began getting an assignment from them every few months, and eventually took on a new product column that I did every month.

I was also selling pieces to *Family Circle* and I sold one to *Health* and another to an in-flight magazine, and it finally got to the point where I was getting enough assignments so I could think of quitting my job and just freelance, which had always been my goal. It was nice being a writer and also having an editing job at the same time, but there was no question but that I enjoyed writing more than editing.

It also happened that about this time I was thinking about getting married, and because Tom had moved to Arkansas, I knew I'd have to leave the city anyway. I started writing full time in 1987, and I got a break then because I got a chance to be a co-author with a woman who was writing a book on the single life. I'd done some articles on the subject, and even though I was about to leave that life, it was good to have a book contract. It really took the heat off during those early months when there weren't enough assignments coming in.

One article I remember from those early years was one I still get letters about. It's funny how you'll get remembered for the thing you'd least like to be remembered for, but I'm still hearing about a piece I wrote for *Redbook* called "Toilet Training for Adults." It dealt with the things you can catch in a public restroom, and it was really a challenge because there isn't all that much you *can* catch in a restroom. Colds and flu, of course, but you can catch them anywhere. Definitely not venereal disease from a toilet seat, as a lot of people think. It turned out that the most contaminated part of a restroom is the hot water faucet handle, because that's the first thing people touch when their hands are dirty, and the warmth of the handle causes the bacteria to grow. Anyway, people still write me about that story six years later. I'm not sure I'll ever get away from it.

I did a lot of health pieces during these years and then in 1988 we had Suzanne, and I began doing more articles about children. Now it's evolved to a point where I'm doing mostly kid stuff. I get calls from *Working Mother*, *Family Circle* and *Good House-keeping*, and I don't really have to write queries anymore. But this means I'm always writing somebody else's ideas. Most pieces get interesting as you get into them, but I'd rather work on my own ideas, so I'm starting to write more proposals. I'm trying to cultivate new territory, too; do more things that are out of the children's ghetto.

But the fact is that having children gives me most of my ideas, so maybe I'm stuck with it for awhile. About the time Suzanne was getting to be fifteen to eighteen months old I began to worry that she was getting spoiled, so I proposed an article on spoiling. I did another piece on surviving the first six weeks after a baby comes right after our second daughter Claire was born. I was literally taking notes on my own experiences as subject matter for the article. Now I'm doing a piece on children and television, a subject I've always wanted to investigate.

Researching a story is a good way of finding out more about subjects that interest me. I've now done so many pieces on children that I know all the sources, the people to call, the right journals to turn to. I suppose I stay in it because it's easier for me. I guess you could say that kids are my beat.

I always wanted to be more of a generalist, but I find that my time for writing is so limited that if I don't zero in on one area, I'll spend a lot of time spinning my wheels. It's always a good idea to have an area you're known for, so that editors will think of you when they need a story in that area. I know I'm in a rut, but it's a money-making rut so I guess it's not so bad.

When I'm ready to plan the organization of a piece, I'll start by going over my notes. I always take notes, even when I use my tape recorder, because I basically don't trust the machine to keep working. Then, as I'm listening to the tape, I'm writing down things I've missed. I'm also looking for quotes and anecdotes I know I'll want to put in the story. And during this process, it begins to take some shape in my mind.

Sometimes I try to wing it and start writing without an outline, but I find when I do that I often get into trouble. Outlining is important to me, even if it's very rough. If I don't have some idea of the structure, I can veer off on a tangent and have real problems getting back on course.

Most of my interviews are informational interviews, not profiles, and I can do them by telephone. If you're doing a full profile you have to be able to sit down with somebody, but if all you need to do is ask about a study they've done, that can be handled just as well on the phone. I always read what the person has written before I talk to them, and if they've done a story, I read that. I feel that if I don't do my homework, I'm not being respectful of that person.

I also interview a lot of parents, who haven't really written anything or had anything written about them, so with them I try and put them at their ease by talking to them as personally as I can. I tell them about my own parenting experiences, so they will be confident enough to talk to me about difficulties they've had, something they might not have done if I hadn't admitted my own shortcomings first.

I work on a computer, so I'm always revising, which I'm coming to think is not always that good. Every time I go back into the story I see things I want to change, so I keep revising instead of simply going back to where I left off. Sometimes the first way I wrote it was better, and I'm beginning to wonder if it might not be better to just sit down and write the piece straight through.

This is something I'm going to be doing with essays, which I've started writing a lot of recently. They don't pay as much, and you have to do the whole thing because you can't really send out a query on an essay. But I love doing them, and I'm trying to set aside more time for them.

What I'm going to do is write them out in longhand first, before using the computer at all. I keep a journal and I write in it in longhand two or three times a week and when I go back and re-read the entries they don't need much revising. And I got to thinking, how come I'm always revising what I write on the computer? And I've decided it might go better if I just wrote my pieces in longhand first.

I never have any trouble getting started on a piece I'm writing. I feel if you have a deadline, you just have to get going. And I'm so grateful when somebody's taking care of the kids and I *can* work, that when I finally get a chance, I just plunge right in. I do get the munchies when I have to write—I have to eat pretzels or something—but fortunately that doesn't last during the *entire* stage of writing.

My advice to young writers is to look around at the publications in their own area. There are so many city and regional magazines today, and many of them are very good and will give you excellent clips. They're much more amenable to writers who are just starting out, and I think they're a really good way to break in. I guess I feel that way in part because that's how I got my start. It worked for me.

Also, writers should always try to be on time. I try to write my articles as fast as I can, and I know from my experience as an editor that there aren't many writers who do that.

And don't feel offended if you're asked to revise your piece. A lot of new writers are reluctant to do revisions, almost acting as if it's an insult to be asked to do something over. Just work with your editor on what he or she wants, and don't take the criticism personally.

I can't imagine that I'll ever stop writing, although I may try different things. I don't feel up to a novel yet. I'll just have to keep writing and work myself up to that. But I know I'll always be writing something.

[Author's note: Here is one of Anne Cassidy's "Children's ghetto" queries that "worked out well."]

BIG-PICTURE PARENTING
A Proposal for Family Circle Magazine
By Anne Cassidy

For most parents, what drives us through the day is pure momentum. We must get our kids fed, washed, dressed, off to daycare or school, then to soccer practice or violin lessons and back home again to study, play, eat and sleep. Most of the time, we find ourselves reacting instead of shaping, following rather than leading. We see the inevitable blips of child-rearing as obstacles rather than challenges.

This article would remind readers of the Big Picture: Of the original excitement they felt at starting a family; at the dreams they had for their kids before they spent most of their energy telling them to pick up the towels off the bathroom floor; at the qualities they'd like their kids to have.

I would do this by describing seven to ten "big picture" strategies parents can use to instill in their children traits like responsibility, respect, resilience, adaptability, empathy, truthfulness and self-reliance. I don't know for sure what these strategies will be — that's what my reporting will uncover — but I do know they will be long-term rather than quick-fix.

The article will concentrate on real parents who've made specific changes in how they're rearing their kids. But it wouldn't be a story on the mechanics of child-rearing as much as a piece on how to rekindle a vision of how you want your family to be. Comments from experts would bolster the piece by emphasizing the universal, essential element of the change each family made so that readers can try them, too. I'd also use experts to give a richness to the story by talking about what in their opinion are the most important characteristics parents need to cultivate in their children.

Here's an example Stephen Covey used in his book *The Seven Habits of Highly Effective People*. In a meeting about sharing family chores, Covey's seven-year-old son volunteered to water the lawn and keep it free from litter. Covey used what he calls "stewardship delegation." He put his son in charge of the yard, trained him for two weeks and then gave him total responsibility for keeping it "green and clean." His son could do the job any way he wanted — except painting it — and Covey himself volunteered to help. But the primary responsibility was his son's. After a bad start — the lawn languished in the Utah sun for a few days — Covey reminded his son of the agreement and volunteered to help. His son began to cry when he realized how he had broken his part of the agreement, but he finally realized that the yard, which everyone enjoyed, belonged to him. That was when he "signed the agreement in his heart," Covey says. "It became his yard, his stewardship." And for Covey, it was an opportunity to get to know his son better.

Covey is a professional people-changer, so he's obviously going to have more ideas about how to make big-picture transformations than most people. But then again, he has *nine* kids . . . so he really is "in the trenches." What I hope to uncover in my reporting are more examples of parents who've had a "Eureka!" experience with their children. They certainly don't have everything figured out, but they've had success in one area. And it's not superficial success. Their children are complying more with their wishes than they were before, but they've also learned a crucial skill that will serve them well throughout life.

For example, a high school acquaintance of mine decided to make her two daughters responsible for solving their own squabbles. She drew up a chart of privileges, such as playing outside after school and watching a favorite TV show, and told her daughters, six and eight, that every time one of them complained to her about the other's behavior each would lose a privilege. "I gave *them* responsibility for their actions," she said. The strategy was not always easy to follow—she had to hear a lot of "it's not fair" when she took away privileges, for example. But adapting this principle of personal responsibility has made her children more self-reliant.

As a mother of two girls (three-and-a half and eleven months), I know that scarcely a day goes by that I don't try to figure out some "better way" to teach and guide them. And I know that my friends and acquaintances do the same. I'd like to tap into some of these parents for the story. I would also try to find parents through counselors who regularly deal with them in workshops, counseling sessions, etc., or through an organization such as Family Service America, a network of community-based family counseling and support agencies.

(A list of expert sources followed)

[Anne's query seems a bit long, but this is not an easy concept to explain, and she felt she needed the number of examples she used to show how her piece would be developed. And, of course, it worked. The article, which ran in *Family Circle* in the February 2, 1993 issue, was called "The Happy Family, How to Make It Yours."]

DIANNE HALES *has been a freelance writer for fifteen years, contributing to such magazines as* Reader's Digest, McCall's, Ladies Home Journal, Seventeen, Redbook *and, since the birth of her daughter* *seven years ago, magazines devoted to parenting. As you will see, she loves her work.*

I was one of those kids who loved to read, and writing is the only thing I've ever been able to do well. I always thought I'd grow up and become a writer. I come from a working-class family and my mother wanted me to become a teacher, so I'd always have a job. I think she feels that way to this day, although she does feel better now that I've been married to a doctor for fifteen years.

The dream of being a freelance writer began early. I remember when I was in high school I read a first-person piece about what a great life it was to be a freelance writer, and I remember thinking "That's for me," but I also remember wondering how in the world I'd ever pull it off. So I set out to become a magazine editor and do some writing on staff, and just live out my life in New York. But writing always drew me, and I always liked it more than editing.

Then to my surprise I married a man in the military, and I knew we were going to be moving around and living in places that didn't have magazines for me to work on, so I went back to my old dream of freelancing. And behold, I had been right about writing in the first place—it just absolutely suited me! Now I can't imagine having a real job.

When I graduated from Columbia University in New York, I got a job on a magazine for young doctors and residents, so I began to learn a lot about medicine. Then when I got married and moved to San Francisco, there were a lot of medical meetings there. Because my connections were all in medicine, I was given a chance to cover these meetings for trade magazines like *Medical Tribune* and *Medical News*. And I realized one day that a lot of the material I was getting would be just as interesting to a lay audience. I had had to learn it as a layperson, so my writing always had a layperson's orientation.

I started sending off queries to small magazines that covered health topics, and things began moving right along from there. I began to sell to bigger and better magazines, and then I did a textbook, and suddenly one day I realized I had all the work I could handle. Since then I have never not been too busy. Today

I feel busier than I've ever been, but this is, of course, the problem freelancers want to have.

And it does cause problems. I mean, I have a child—I have a life—and sometimes my life interferes with my work. So I juggle. As soon as my husband takes my daughter to school, about 7:30, I go downstairs to my office and start working. I take a break for lunch, and I do sometimes talk to my friends, but basically I spend all day writing.

But even though I write as hard and fast as I can, there are still times when I have to turn down assignments. Even so, I always overbook somewhat, the same principles as the airlines. I don't write queries much anymore because I always have enough assignments.

I've also gotten to the point where I don't feel I have to take on assignments unless they interest me. I used to do everything I was asked, but now I can be more choosy. Most of my ideas come from editors, but I also get ideas from medical meetings, medical journals and news releases, and from local papers. I do a lot of true-life dramas, and I often find ideas in the stories and columns in small local papers.

There are also stories that come out of my own life. In the early years of my marriage I did a lot of relationship pieces, and now I do more parenting pieces. I figure that I'm an ordinary person and if a problem is of concern to me, it's probably a problem that others have to deal with as well.

I guess I don't think too much about how my pieces are going to be structured. I'm usually doing two or three things at once, and I just go on doing the research without thinking very much about where everything I get is going. But I run every day, and I think while I'm running. As I clear my mind, things begin to fall into place. I trust my intuition and when things like leads just come to me, I go with them.

When I'm doing one of my true-life dramas, which are intensely personal, I can often hear my leads as the person I'm interviewing is talking. When I was doing relationship pieces, I usually started with a case history, and I would often use my husband in the lead. Now that I'm doing parenting pieces, I often use my daughter. She's old enough now to be learning to read, and I'm sure the day will come when she'll read what I've written and tell me to leave her life alone. But you do get material from people who are close to you. I think every writer does.

Then, once I get my material, I focus on getting everything into the computer. Using my fingers and getting it down helps to lock the material in my head, and as I work, the organization begins to emerge. And I do make outlines. But mostly it's a matter of getting myself familiar with the material.

Then I do a lot of rewriting. Every time I get up from the computer for whatever reason and sit down again, I start back at the beginning. I don't know the number of rewrites I do, but I'd say they number in the dozens before a single draft gets to an editor. All during this process I print it out on paper several times, because I'm still of that precomputer generation that needs to see things on paper. I keep repeating this process right to the end.

How far I go depends on the editor I'm writing for. There are some editors who like to be like Ross Perot and get down and fiddle under the hood. So I give them something to fiddle with. I also like to get some feedback before the final polishing, so I don't find myself fiddling in the wrong direction.

Then there are other editors who really want the piece as polished and perfect as possible, so they can send it right off to the printer. With those editors, I have to polish harder before I submit. Even then, editors rarely say anything is right just as it is. They always want something changed, and I accept that as part of the process.

Before you go out on an interview, you have to think through just what you want from that person. I used to write out all my questions in advance, but now I often do phone interviews. Sometimes they'll call me at 6:30 in the morning because they can't get the hang of the fact that in California we're three hours earlier, and they'll say they have to talk right then. So I'll just do the interview spontaneously, and I've done so many of them this way that it usually works out pretty well. But I do have to know before I ever contact them just what I want to find out from them.

Sometimes I'm amazed at what people tell me, personal things I wouldn't think they'd want to reveal. But the fact is that as I talk, I also share things about my life with them, so we establish a kind of bond of shared experience and interest. I find that works very effectively. I am not an adversarial reporter and even when I'm doing an investigative piece, I stay laid back and cool.

When I was starting out I never said no to an assignment. You've got to start getting those clips. Take the long view, and realize that the clips are going to be what helps you get the next assignment.

There are many rewards to this business. You call your own shots. You set your own hours. And it's always different. A lot of my friends have reached the age where they're burning out, they're tired of their jobs and asking themselves if this is really what they want to do with their lives.

I don't feel that way because every week brings different challenges, different things to write about. This is the easiest way I know to make a living.

And it does have strong satisfactions. I recently did a piece on a woman who had breast cancer, and when it was published she called me and asked: "How did you know? I hadn't felt I did a good job of telling you what it was like," she said, "but you got it right."

Those are the pieces that mean the most to me—the ones where I tell one person's story, and they tell me that I got it right.

JUDITH STONE *has been working as a writer and editor for close to twenty years, and for the past seven has devoted herself almost entirely to writing. She is a contributing editor to* Glamour, Discover *and* Health, *and writes for a number of others. She has published one book,* Light Elements: Essays on Science from Gravity to Levity, *and has another coming out in August, written with collaborator Nicole Gregory. She says it is a parody of the inner child movement and is called* Healing Your Inner Dog: A Self-Whelp Book. *As you will see, humor is an important part of her style.*

When I was three I dictated a story to my mother called "The Fox and the Princess." I was attracted to rather conventional themes at that age. When I was in the sixth grade I decided that I wanted to be a laboratory technician. I didn't have the slightest idea what a laboratory technician did, and that phase passed before I found out. Except for that brief period I've absolutely wanted to be a writer.

I was editor of my high school paper and started college as a journalism major, but later switched to literature. I got my master's and decided to teach English. But after three years at a community college, I realized I was dodging my destiny. I moved to Chicago in the name of romance.

I had been thinking about getting another master's, this one in psychology, so I went to work in a psychiatric halfway house. I was new in town, and for a while 90 percent of the people I knew in Chicago hallucinated or heard strange voices.

Then I decided to go back to writing, but I had to make a living, so I began looking for a job. I got my first job in the wackiest way. I just looked through the phone book and began calling publishing houses. I finally reached a company that was starting a psychology magazine for high school students, and the woman who answered the phone was the editorial director of the company. She needed someone with teaching experience and some kind of psychology background, both of which I had. She asked me to write a test story, which was to be the lead piece in the first issue. She liked what I did and hired me to run the magazine. So my first job in publishing was as editor-in-chief, and I've been working my way down the masthead ever since.

My job was to write every story in the issue but two. I wrote six full-length pieces in nine issues a year. I made $11,000 and I was too stupid to know that what I was doing was impossible.

While I was working there, I sold a couple of pieces to *Seventeen*, and they were my first pieces for a consumer publication. I had been a newspaper stringer in high school and had gotten paid for that, but they were my first grown-up pieces. When I finally decided to leave my job at the psychology magazine, I made a deal to continue writing the lead piece of each issue for the next year, so I had some income. It was a good way to make the transition.

My now ex-husband was doing a lot of freelancing, too, and when it became clear that more and more of our work was coming from New York, we decided to have an adventure and move there. I did a few more pieces for *Seventeen* and one for the late lamented *Savvy*, and then we took the plunge.

When we got to New York I was almost out of money, so once again I decided to get a job. I did something everybody told me was pointless—I answered an ad in *The New York Times*. I got a job as senior editor of a magazine called *Sexual Medicine Today*, which sounds more interesting than it was. Basically, my job was to take the juiciest subject in the world and make sure it was completely desiccated by the time it reached the urologists and gynecologists who read the magazine.

I got the job because when I was working on the psychology magazine for teenagers, I'd also edited a four-page optional insert called the *Human Sexuality Supplement*, which I always thought sounded like a vitamin. (And because I could answer the only question that the big boss asked on my second interview: "Who wrote the song 'Crazy'?" The fact that I knew it was Willie Nelson seemed to clinch the deal.)

The man who hired me left after two weeks to go to *Science Digest*, and six months later hired me away as a senior editor. My science background was minimal. I was the specimen humanities person; they figured that if I understood a story, anyone in America could understand it.

While at *Science Digest* I began to do more freelancing, including my first piece for *Glamour* and some travel pieces for *Diversion*. I had decided to leave and freelance full time when an editor I knew at *Mademoiselle* called to tell me about an opening at *McCall's*. The editor-in-chief hadn't decided whether or not he wanted to fill the position, but I was asked to submit story ideas. At the end of the story meeting the editor, Bob Stein, said, "Would I ruin your life if I offered you a job?"

I spent three very happy years as articles editor of *McCall's* before leaving to devote full time to writing. I was so anxious at first that I had insomnia for about a year. Because I was nervous about making a go of it, I really overloaded myself with work. Then *Glamour* asked me to take over a column called "On Your Own," aimed at the very youngest *Glamour* reader, the woman fresh out of college. It basically covered everything I wish somebody had told me when I was twenty-two. Not that I'd have listened to them.

At about the same time I started the *Glamour* column, Paul Hoffman, the editor-in-chief of *Discover*, called to say that the man who did the magazine's humor column was leaving and asked if I'd like to take it over.

Doing two columns a month was terrifically hard work, especially since the *Discover* column was actually a 2,000- to 2,500-word article, which had to be heavily researched but highly amusing. And being funny in print is the hardest thing there is.

After doing the column for four-and-a-half years and winning a National Headliner Award for it, I told my editor, "I don't see what's so darn funny about science anymore." And I stopped doing the column. I feel it's important to cease doing something *before* you go stale, not after.

One of the best things about freelancing has been traveling. I've been sent to India, Burma, Thailand, Egypt, the Galapagos Islands, Ecuador, Vietnam, Russia, Greece, Hawaii and the Caribbean — extraordinary trips I probably wouldn't have been able to make if I weren't on assignment.

I don't know how many hours a day I work. How do you decide? I could say I work twenty-four hours a day if you count the anxiety time. Do you count the time when you put an idea on the back burner of your brain and let it simmer? Do you count the time when you're making notes? Do you count the time when you're rearranging your underwear drawer to avoid writing?

And do you count the time when you're asleep? I dream leads a lot. I have some notion about what the lead might be, and my ideas sort themselves out while I'm asleep.

Ideas aren't a problem; the world seems to be teeming with them. My friends are always suggesting things to me. And I follow my own interests. For instance, I've always wondered why some people get the willies when they hear fingernails scraping on a blackboard. I happen to get the chills when I see someone biting paper. So I collected a lot of anecdotes, talked to neurobiologists and did a piece for *Discover*. Writing is a way for me to find out what I want to know. It gives me access to information I want, so I have the double pleasure of gathering the material, a process which I love, and then sharing it.

Once I've gathered the material, I'll either call an editor I know well or write a query, particularly if I'm aiming at a new magazine that doesn't know my work. Time put in on a good query is well spent, because once you get the assignment, a good deal of your work is done.

And, of course, queries are your audition for an editor. If they're sloppy or carelessly written, the editor is going to think you're a sloppy, careless writer. When I was an editor I judged a writer's style and ability more by her query than by her clips.

When I finish my reporting, if it's that sort of piece, I type up my notes on the computer and then read them over in hard copy, underlining things I think are important and making marginal notes. Then I do a rough draft, removing things I don't think I'll use and shaping the order of what's left. But I don't delete passages I might need later. Instead of consigning them to the outer realms of darkness, I just move the extra material to the bottom of the file, creating a collection of outtakes I can pick through later.

Writing is, of course, rewriting. That's the process. First, I do a really rough version of the piece so I can work out the general shape of it. I'll write "transition TK" or "blah blah blah" to indicate places that need fleshing out later. But this rough draft gives me a chance to see the rhythm and order of the piece. Then I work like a sculptor, doing successively finer chiseling with each draft.

Although I do these drafts on the computer, there comes a time when I have to do a pencil edit on an actual piece of paper. Then I'm ready for the electronic grand finale.

Getting back to the preparation for the article, I prepare thoroughly before each interview, reading a respectable amount of background material. If it is an author, I read as much as I can of his or her work. If it's an actor or actress, I see the movies. If I'm interviewing an expert, I'll do enough homework so that I can ask good, intelligent questions.

I prepare my questions in advance, but I'm not nervous about winging it if the person goes off on a tangent. I'll just follow along, if it seems to be leading somewhere interesting. I like an interview that lasts a long time because that little nugget I'm looking for may be buried in a lot of other stuff. Sometimes people have to get really warmed up before they say something important.

Sometimes I hear the lead or the ending when I'm interviewing or doing my research, but I don't worry too much if I don't. Some writers I know have to know the lead before they can proceed. But I can shape other parts of the story and find the lead later. By the way, I think a good lead is as vital to a query as it is to the finished piece.

If I were advising a young writer, trying to break into the big magazines, I'd tell him or her to consider selling to the small, local publications first, to gather a set of clips. Then study the markets, and pick your target magazines carefully to suit your style and expertise. Make sure that the subject and tone of your query are right for the magazine, and make sure they haven't covered the subject recently. A good way to break into major magazines is by doing shorter, front-of-the-book features first, so an editor comes to know you.

You asked about leads. Here are some of my favorites, all from my column in *Discover*:

Susan Schiffman has been hired to come up with an aroma that could be sprayed in New York City's subways to reduce commuter aggression and increase friendliness. Because of a confidentiality agreement, the Duke University psychologist can't reveal the identity of her client or the fragrance that she thinks will soothe the savage straphanger. But I'd say her best bet is chloroform.

"Good gorilla sperm is so hard to find," sighs Francine "Penny" Patterson, Ph.D., and I guess there's not a woman in America who'd disagree with her.

Japanese astronauts worry that the Americans aboard space station *Freedom* will make ill-considered, split-second decisions. The Americans fear that the Japanese preference for protracted group deliberations could prove fatal in an emergency. The Italians are anxious about whether their privacy will be respected. And I'm terrified the French will make everyone watch Jerry Lewis movies.

And one more, from a travel article about Thailand:

This was my first pig sacrifice, so I wasn't certain about etiquette. Were we dressed right? Was the pig the only one allowed to squeal? Should we tip the shaman?

WILLIAM ZINSSER *began his professional writing career in the mid-1940s as a reporter and editor for the old* New York Herald Tribune. *He left in 1959 to become a freelance writer and has pursued that career ever since, although he has interrupted it at times to teach writing and to work for the Book-of-the-Month Club. His fourteen books include the popular* On Writing Well, *now in its fourth edi-*

tion. His latest, American Places, *appeared in 1992. What follows is based on a talk we had a few years ago, when I was beginning my own teaching career, and while he does talk about his writing he also talks about teaching writing skills to others. As that is what I am trying to do, I felt our interview was a highly appropriate addition to this book.*

W riters shouldn't worry so much about where their piece will be printed, but should just write as well as they can. They need to master their craft before they think too much about selling. I've never been interested in telling people how to sell what they write. I want to teach them how to write, on the theory that if they master their craft well enough they will damn well find an editor who wants to publish their work.

Once you have learned to write, there's no excuse for losing the reader for reasons of failure of craft—for not writing a decent lead, for not telling the reader why he or she is being asked to read your piece. The writer must be conscious of all the forms of disarray in magazine writing: losing the reader because from one sentence to the next you change tense, you change time, you change place. You must always stop to think where you left the reader in the previous sentence.

One way to find out whether you have lost the reader is by reading your piece aloud. All the incongruities, all the false trails will jump out at you when you hear them. Reading aloud is a way for me to hear ambiguity, to detect all the ways a sentence can be misread, misunderstood, read in different ways. When I read it aloud I hear clunkiness; I hear repetition; I hear when I've lost the reader. There's almost always some way to rewrite a sentence to make it more clear, more harmonious, more rhythmical, a little more pleasing. I always read my stuff aloud, and I always find things that strike me as wrong and must be changed.

To me, surprise is the most refreshing commodity in writing. The essence of humor is something that takes you by surprise. Humor writing is an extremely hard thing to do. Writers should always try to put humor into their pieces, because readers are desperate for humor. Editors can always take it out if it doesn't work—and it mostly won't work, because it's the hardest kind of writing to do—but only a writer can put it in.

Humor is an act of risk. It's also an act of intelligence. People think humor has to be more outlandish or comic or grotesque than life itself. But humor is just a way of looking at life and saying, "This is outlandish." It's not an act of tremendous exaggeration. Most humor is just a slight turning of the knob—up. Think of the pieces in James Thurber's *My Life and Hard Times*, or Woody Allen's *Without Feathers* and *Getting Even*. They are hilarious, but also very close to what we recognize as the truth.

I rewrite and rewrite and rewrite. This is just to satisfy myself. E.B. White and James Thurber rewrote eight or nine times. Rewriting is when you finally get rid of all the stuff that shouldn't be there. Thurber used to show his wife his fourth draft and she would say, "That's high school stuff, Thurber," calling him Thurber, which may be part of the problem he wrote about in all those pieces about men and women. When I've finished that eighth or ninth rewrite, I read it over again aloud, just to make sure I've taken everything out that needs to be taken out. And I usually haven't.

When people ask me how I learned to write I tell them it was by reading writers who were doing the kind of writing I wanted to do, and trying to figure out how they did it. Other writers have their Faulkners and their Walker Percy's, but my mentors were the men who wrote about baseball and other sports for *The New York Times* and the *Herald Tribune* and the *Sun*. Fortunately, they were good writers. But it doesn't really matter what subject the writer you learn from is writing about. What matters is that they are writing well about it. There's no good or bad subject; there's only good and bad writing.

The job of organizing a long piece is one of the hardest tasks a writer has. My technique could be called "just thinking"—just thinking about the shape, thinking what I'm trying to do, where I'm going next. Sometimes I'll start with the lead, get the reader hooked and flashback to fill the reader in on what has led up to that lead. But this has to be done gracefully, so the reader isn't lost. Many writers don't give enough thought to all the transitions that carry the reader from one sentence to the next, from one paragraph to the next. If all the transitions are in place the reader doesn't realize he's being pulled along. I spend a tremendous amount of time and labor on transitions. But the reader should never be conscious that you're doing this.

When it comes to endings, I try to end sooner than the reader expects me to. I never crank up and say, "and therefore, in summary . . . " This is insulting to a reader. Every element in a piece should be doing work that hasn't been done before. When you've finished saying what you want to say, stop. Often the ending will just occur to you. I often look for a quote. Or I try to close the circle that I began with the lead—to echo what I started with. I think this provides a subconscious satisfaction for the reader.

Never tell your readers what they should think about something. You may write about amazing things, but never tell them that something is going to be amazing. Just lay out the facts and let the reader say, "Wow! Imagine that!" The writer's job is to present the facts as cleanly as possible, so that the reader has the pleasure of making these discoveries himself. The reader needs to be given room to play some part in the act of writing. One difference between the amateur and the professional is that the amateur spells it out and the professional lets you find out for yourself.

Along this line, never quote something funny and say "he joked." This is insulting as hell. If it isn't obvious that he's joking, the quote shouldn't be in there at all. There always has to be a way of constructing the piece so that the material makes its own point, and the reader has the pleasure of discovering that point, and the humor, for himself.

Not only should you never say "he joked," you should think hard about using any attribution except "he said" or "he asked," or maybe "he explained." But never say "he opined" or "he averred." Another thing I often see is "he smiled." You don't hear much smiling these days.

I don't like to write; I like to have written. Then I can't wait for people to read it and say, "That's wonderful." And of course I think it is, but only because I've sweated blood to get it that way.

JOAN BARTHEL *has been making her living as a writer for thirty years. Her first pieces were sold to the Arts and Leisure section of* The New York Times, *and her first magazine piece was in that paper's magazine section. She was a staff writer on* Life *for several years, after which she began selling regularly to such publications as* TV Guide, McCall's, Cosmopolitan, Lear's, New Choices *and others.*

She is currently completing her fourth book, a biography of TV star Oprah Winfrey.

I was hired by the *Times* right out of college and was working in a kind of pool, mostly typing letters for editors. I'd gone to a convent school in St. Louis where the nuns said you can be anything you want, a doctor or lawyer or even president, but in the meantime you'd better learn to type and take shorthand. It was good advice.

But by 1963 it became obvious that the *Times* wasn't going to give me much chance to write and by that time I'd married, so I quit. Then, about two or three weeks later, I got a call from the editor of the Arts and Leisure section asking me to write a piece for them. There's this woman, the editor said, who's funny and interesting and has a cooking show on TV, and her name is Julia Child. I did it and after that I began doing a piece almost every week. And after about a year of this they wanted to hire me back as a writer. I said no thanks, I'm having too much fun freelancing.

They paid very little—only $125 per piece—but their rationale was that I was getting good exposure and some big time editor was going to see my work and ask me to write for him. And that's exactly what happened. Steve Gelman of *Life* called and said he'd seen my work in the *Times* and wanted me to come over and write for them. And it turned out to be one of the best places to work in all of American journalism.

But I didn't start with the title of writer, even though that's all I did. I was listed on the masthead as assistant editor, which was odd because I wasn't an editor. It finally got to me and I wrote a memo and said I want to be listed as a writer. My memo got passed on to Ralph Graves, who was then running *Life*, and he asked me to come and see him.

He said, first of all, you are going to be a staff writer. He explained that I hadn't been there long enough to have the title, but I was definitely going to be one. The classy thing is that he told me first that I had it, instead of going through a long discussion of why I didn't have it already. I've never forgotten that because I thought it was such a sensitive and graceful way to handle the situation.

You know, people now think of the old weekly *Life* as just a picture magazine. I wrote some of my favorite pieces for them, and some of them didn't even have pictures. One I particularly remember was about a friend I had on the *Times* who was dying. I hadn't planned on writing about her, but I used to go see her a lot because I loved her. She was the first person I'd known who was so sick, and after a while I began taking notes on what was happening. After she'd died I said to Steve, I'd like to write this. And he let me. It was simply the journal of a friend dying.

After *Life* folded as a weekly, I went with *New Times* as a staff writer. It was a great magazine, although it lasted only a few years. That's where I did my first Peter Reilly piece. We had bought a house in Canaan, Connecticut, and I read an article in the local paper about this boy who was in jail and accused of killing his mother. The article wasn't about the murder, though, but about the fact that the people in this small town were saying that something was wrong, that they thought he was innocent.

I began checking into the story and found that there were all sorts of things that didn't add up, that there was strong evidence that Reilly was not guilty. The piece I wrote led to Peter getting out of jail. Later the charges were dropped and the judge called it a "grave injustice."

So that piece was satisfying because it showed me what a magazine piece can do. You don't often write something that gets such immediate results. From a personal point of view, a couple of other articles meant a great deal to me, too. The one on my friend who died. Another on the experience of growing up Catholic in St. Louis that I did for *Life*, and another for *The New York Times Magazine* called "Five Priests in Search of a Calling." It dealt with priests who felt serious conflicts between the Church's position and their own, and were struggling to resolve them. I was proud of that piece, and I think that I've been very lucky to be able to do articles like that.

Another piece I'll never forget was a profile of the actor George C. Scott that I did for *Life*. Scott was making a movie in Arizona called, very appropriately, as it turned out, "Rage." He was a very, very unhappy man, and I wrote about an unhappy man who was also one of our best actors.

This was in 1973. Eleven years later *TV Guide* asked me if I'd like to go to France and England and do a few pieces for them. Scott was making a new version of "A Christmas Carol" in a little English town called Shrewsbury, and they wanted a piece on him. I went over and was driven up to Shrewsbury by two public relations people. I browsed around the town and read clips from the local papers and talked to the director, all the things you do before starting a story like this. I was to see Scott the next day. I had dinner with some of the people connected with the film and got back to my room about ten, to find a call for the PR person asking me to meet him in the bar. He told me that Scott had recognized me and didn't want to talk to me. He remembered that old piece I'd done on him. I'd been honest about Scott, and apparently he didn't like that.

I wrote the *TV Guide* story anyway. It was about how he hadn't changed, and argued that perhaps his unhappiness was what had made him such a great actor. I thought it turned out well, but I've never seen Scott again.

Another memorable interview was with Mel Brooks for the *Times*. He was making a movie called "The Producers." I loved the idea of doing a piece on Brooks, because I'd always thought he was one of the funniest men around. I went to see him and this is the first thing he said. I know it's right, because I used it as the lead of my piece.

> "What do you want to know, honey?" Mel Brooks asked me. "Want me to tell you the truth? Want me to give you the real dirt? Want me to tell you what's in my heart?"
>
> I said yes.
>
> "What would I tell you, really?" he snapped, with what had to be called a sneer. "That this is movie is the worst movie I've ever seen?"

He went on to throw in a number of four-letter words and was so obnoxious that even I, novice that I was, realized this interview wasn't going to work. As I headed for the door, he asked, "Do you fool around?"

The fact that I continued as a freelance writer says something about my perseverance, or my optimism.

Most of the time I don't use a tape recorder, relying on the shorthand the nuns taught me, but one time I did use one. It was a cover story for *Life* on Bob Hope. Boy, do I remember that one.

I'd gone along with Hope on a two- or three-day trip through the Midwest — this was in the early 1970s and he was very hawk-ish on the Vietnam war. He gave a one-man show in Flint, Michigan, and during it he said that the war was a beautiful thing. I knew what he meant — we were fighting Communism, and so on — and I thought I made that clear in the piece.

Sometime later I read in a gossip column that Hope said I had misquoted him. I was furious, and this is where I made my big mistake. Steve Gelman had always said that if somebody accused you of misquoting them, just have a stiff drink and go on to the next assignment. But I was on my high horse and I called the PR man and said Hope did say it, and I have it on tape. I even volunteered to bring the tape over and prove it to him.

But I couldn't. The tape had run out before he said it. He had been talking in a big, noisy auditorium, and I'd never heard that little click when the tape stopped. I can still see myself sitting on my floor and playing that tape over and over and hoping that this time I'd hear him say it. But it just wasn't there. Fortunately, there were some other volatile remarks Hope had made that we didn't use, and we pointed that out to the lawyers. So it ended in a kind of standoff, and nothing more was ever said about it. But you can see why I'd much rather rely on my own notes than a tape recorder.

My work habits are pretty ordinary. I'm not one of those romantic writers who start at sunset and write all night. Larry King, who was on the staff with me at *New Times* and later wrote "Best Little Whorehouse in Texas," used to do that. He said he would write all night and come up with a finished six-thousand-word piece in the morning. I can't do that.

What I do is really pretty boring. I get up, take a shower, walk, coffee, go to work. Of course, when you're working on a story you're really working on it all the time. Nights, weekends, it's always part of you. Writing doesn't fit neatly into a nine-to-five routine. Sometimes I'll work fifteen hours a day on a story, but usually eight or nine hours is my working day. I like to go to bed early, thinking about what I'm going to write, and then get up early and start.

When I get ready to organize my material, I just sit down and read it over and over again. I always have a great deal of material, because I overresearch. I do lots of interviews and read everything I can find and collect everything that relates to my subject.

From reading all of this many times, a piece begins to take shape in my mind. And a lead will usually emerge. I almost always know how I'm going to start before I begin writing.

I like to get a sense of motion in the lead, a sense that things are moving forward. Leads are very important; if the reader doesn't like the lead, he probably won't finish the piece. Sometimes I like to take chances, stretch the normal limits of a lead. I did a piece a few years back for *Cosmopolitan* on Joan Lunden. Everybody thinks of her as a morning TV person, but few people know that she once did a gig as a stand-up comic. So I started the piece with some one-liners from her routine. My editor, Guy Flatley, wasn't sure this would work, because it wasn't what readers would be expecting, but he finally went along with it.

I also remember a piece I did for the *Times* on Ingrid Bergman. This was a long time ago, right after she'd come back from her "disgraceful" affair with Roberto Rossellini. I was impressed with her but I was skeptical, too. And I was bothered by some of the contradictions in her. She seemed very magisterial and yet in a way she was very girlish and not what I expected. So my lead was just a list of adjectives.

> Girlish and austere. Wistful and imperious. Seductive and maternal. Talkative and frank, yet surprisingly uncommunicative. Basic and complicated. Earthy and fragile. Bergman.

You can only do that kind of lead every twenty years or so, but sometimes you can take a chance like that. I'd been going over my material and suddenly it just clicked and I thought that approach would be more interesting than a traditional opening. And I think it was.

I give a lot of thought to endings, too. I've always loved it if I can find within the piece some subtle thing, not something that hits the reader over the head but will make him say, "Oh, wow." I'm not talking about a moral message, but something that sums up the point of the piece.

I was able to do that with the piece on Joan Lunden. As we talked, it became clear to me how driven she was. She's a workaholic. And toward the end she was on the treadmill in her garage and she didn't want to stop. So I just ended the piece with her walking away on the treadmill, still talking and not wanting to get off. That seemed to say it. It wasn't obvious, but it did make the reader say, wow, that's what she's all about.

Once a piece is finished, I rewrite very little. But what I do is rewrite as I go along. I may take two days on a couple of pages. I simply cannot go from paragraph three to paragraph four unless three is right. So while I don't do an entire rewrite once a piece is finished, I agonize over every paragraph as I go along.

What advice would I give a writer starting out today? Well, it's tough. My best advice is to just write. Write a page a day. Just do it. If you can't think of anything to write about, then write that. Look out the window. Describe the weather. Talk about how rotten you feel because you don't know what to write about. But write something. My great writing teacher at St. Louis University, Dr. Cronin, used to say that inspiration is far more likely to come to you after you've been at the typewriter for two hours, and it's true.

One of the things that people always expect me to tell them is some great secret about writing. They think there's a trick to being a freelance writer. But the answer is that there isn't. Freelance writing is kind of like a bad news/good news joke. The bad news is that you just have to keep at it, no matter what kind of rejection you get or how hopeless it seems. But in a way that's the good news, too. Because if writing is what you want to do, then it's got to be good news that you're doing it.

Writing becomes a part of your life. It's not just a job, just something you do. I remember that I did a couple of pieces on homelessness back in the early 1980s, before it became trendy to write about it. I did one for *Family Circle* and one for *Redbook*. I had been told not to do homeless in New York because everybody thinks New York is full of homeless, so I found a nun in Springfield, Massachusetts, to help me. I'm a middle-aged writer, and I was dressed like a middle-aged writer. My daughter Annie was with me, and she was wearing jeans.

So anyway, the nun sent us to a shelter in Holyoke, Massachusetts, a very nice town that you don't think of as being a haven for the homeless. Sister Margaret said go up there and talk to them because they have a shelter, so Annie and I walked up the steps of this lovely Victorian house on a side street in Holyoke and rang the bell. A woman came to the door and looked at us, and I said Sister Margaret McCleary sent us and her face fell.

For that one moment she thought we were homeless, that we were seeking shelter. I've never forgotten that and neither has Annie.

Telling that story is a way of saying that writing isn't just a job, that it is somehow a life as well. Writers really do get caught up in the world they're writing about. I love doing it. I would love to write even if it didn't get published. Once when I was talking with Oprah, she said that the test of success in life—not fame, because that's different, but success—is being able to say that you would do what you do even if you didn't have to, even if you didn't need the money.

For me, writing is my job and my livelihood, but as precarious as it is, it's a privilege.

CHAPTER THIRTEEN

How to Get Started

I n the course of writing this book, I interviewed a number of top editors of magazines that accept freelance submissions. I asked them a series of questions designed to discover any tips or tricks that would be helpful in selling articles to them. I wanted to know what kinds of pieces they had trouble finding, and thus the types of ideas they would be most receptive to. I asked them what impressed them most about a query from a new writer, and what things about a proposal turned them off. I asked if they required written queries, and if they liked to see clips. Finally, I asked them what advice they would have for a writer trying to break into magazines today.

While everyone answered a little differently, depending on the needs of their particular publication, there were certain key points of advice that were common to all of them.

1. *Read the magazine*! They all complained about ideas from would-be writers who had obviously not read any recent issues of the publication and thereby identified themselves immediately as amateurs.

2. *Don't make mistakes*! Editors complained about misspelled names, careless punctuation, incorrect facts. As Rona Cherry of *Fitness* magazine says, "A query is a freelancer's resume." It is your introduction to the editor and is virtually all he or she knows about you and your ability to produce a successful article. And in addition to getting all your facts right, present them in a clean, professional manner. Neatness does count.

3. *The idea counts much more than the credentials*. A record of sales to major publications does tell an editor that you have a proven track record. But one after another, they told me that a

well-presented, on-target idea was what they were looking for, whether it came from an old hand or a new face. Every editor is hungry for new faces, new ideas. And no matter what your experience, that editor will work with you to make the piece succeed. As Phil Osborne of *Reader's Digest* told me, "We're not here to shoot down your ideas."

MIDGE RICHARDSON, *Editor-in-Chief,* Seventeen

For us, the hardest articles to find are those dealing with very current topics, sensitively written and directed to our readers. AIDS, for example. Contraception. It's difficult to find someone who will write with a balanced view. We consider ourselves a magazine that educates as well as entertains. We are sensitive to young people and don't try to sway them emotionally, because they're swayed so easily at that age.

I'm impressed by a new writer if he or she takes a fresh approach, who understands and can write about the subject from a young person's point of view. It's important that writers not talk down to our readers. Writers for *Seventeen* must avoid being too simplistic, because young people today are a lot more sophisticated than they used to be, and they know immediately when a writer is being condescending.

We absolutely require queries if the writer is new to us. We have to see if somebody can write, and the query is one of the best indicators. We also want to see clips, as they will show us a writer's strengths. If you haven't been published before, don't send us school papers; the academic approach won't tell us anything about your ability to write for us. I'd prefer a short piece from a school publication, where at least some reporting has been done.

My best advice to young writers is: Just do it! You aren't going to get anywhere sitting around and thinking about what you might like to write about. Study the magazine, develop and focus your ideas, and send out queries. We're more than willing to try first-time writers. In fact, about 30 percent of our articles are by writers who are being published for the first time. We will work with you if you have a good idea for us, and present it intelligently and well. But you won't get anywhere if you keep your ideas and your abilities to yourself.

STEPHANIE STOKES OLIVER, *Editor,* Essence

M ost of the people who query us want to write about people — somebody the writer knows, somebody they've met and been impressed by, somebody they admire. We get a lot of those, and we don't usually assign them to untried writers.

The hardest pieces to find are those on health, politics and social issues. Also, we need more fillers. More service journalism. Study the magazine to see the kind of things we're publishing. And don't query me; look at the masthead to find the editor of the section you're interested in, and write them directly.

We insist on written queries, even from writers we've worked with before. Writing a query helps a writer focus the idea, figure out what he or she wants to say.

And don't try too many ideas at once. We had one writer who would submit about fifty at a time. And a lot of them had good titles, like "How to Find Your Teenager a Job — For Sure!" We got seduced by some of the titles and several times we gave the writer a try, but none of the pieces ever worked out. I think that when writers present too many ideas at once it's a good sign that they haven't thought enough about any one of them.

I'm impressed by a writer who gets right to the point in the query, a writer who has obviously read our magazine, and has some very specific ideas that have been tailored to our audience.

I'm turned off by what are obviously form letters. By laundry lists of ideas. By queries in which the paragraphs are not indented. By queries that come in single-spaced, or with all capital letters. I'm turned off by sloppiness and obvious mistakes. But most of all I'm turned off by people who have obviously never written before, and haven't taken the trouble to find out how to present an idea professionally.

And I do want to see clips. This is not only to see how well you write, but to see if the publications you've sold to are on the same professional level as ours. A lot of the writers we hear from are not ready for prime time. They need to have tested the waters with smaller publications and worked their way up.

RONA CHERRY, *Editor-in-Chief,* Fitness

M y magazine is for women with a median age of thirty, so we reach women in their twenties and thirties. The audience is interested in staying fit and healthy, as well as looking good and feeling good.

I'm turned off by queries from writers who haven't taken the time to read our magazine. If you have trouble finding a copy, write and I'll send you one, along with a set of writer's guidelines. Don't try to write for us without knowing our magazine and our audience.

My magazine is almost entirely freelance written, and we're wide open to new writers. If somebody has a good idea and can present it well on paper, I'll give them a chance. When I was at *Longevity*, a young woman sent us a lot of ideas, but none of them was quite right. I was impressed that she kept trying, so finally I assigned her a short piece of a few hundred words. We liked the result so much that we asked her to expand it, and it finally ran as a two-page feature.

I do want to see clips, although they're something of a mixed blessing. If the clip comes from a major publication, I know it may have been heavily edited. I'm impressed by a sale to a major magazine, but I know a clip from a local publication may be a better indicator of the writer's style because it probably hasn't been edited at all.

I am certainly impressed by an interesting idea, but I'm even more impressed by a proposal that is interesting to read. And one that has no mistakes. If the query is sloppy, I know I can't trust the writer. How can you trust a writer who makes mistakes even in a query?

My best advice to any would-be writer is to keep trying. Keep believing. The easiest thing in the world to do is give up. Don't be discouraged by rejections. There's not a person in the business today who hasn't received a ton of rejection letters. Don't be discouraged and eventually you'll make it.

[Author's note: When I first talked with Ms. Cherry, she was editor of *Longevity*, which she described this way: "My magazine is for baby boomers, men and women from age thirty-five to their early fifties. They're basically people who are interested in life extension research and in learning how to live longer, healthier lives. They want to stay as young as possible for as long as possible. Do not make the mistake many freelancers make of targeting your ideas for seniors in their eighties or nineties; this is not my audience, and tells me immediately that you do not read the magazine."]

ERIC SCHRIER, *Editor,* Health

I think any good reporter can handle any subject. A good health story is just a good story that happens to be about health. I'm not so much interested in expertise as I am in curiosity about the subject. I like writers who aren't afraid to keep digging. Most of our regular writers aren't health experts, but people who want to know more about the subject they're dealing with. They respond much as an interested reader would, and ask the kinds of questions curious readers would want to ask.

The queries that really excite me are those with a good bit of personality and voice. Ones with a touch of humor. What I'm really looking for is writers who can deliver a solid and useful service piece without being boring. Medical narratives are easy to find. It's good solid service information, presented in an interesting way, that we always need.

And I definitely need queries from new writers. But before you query us, study our magazine. Then write and ask for guidelines, and we'll indicate those areas of the magazine that are most in demand.

Concentrate particularly on the lead of your query: If that doesn't grab me, you're in trouble. It should be a fresh idea, and I also want a couple of anecdotes, to show you can get them. And get to the point quickly.

And do send clips. They're really important, and I'd like to see as many as a half dozen of them. And don't worry about where your piece appeared; I'm more impressed by the quality of the writing than I am the place it was published.

What turns me off? Misspellings, errors, sloppiness. Stale ideas. Proposals that beat around the bush and make me work hard to find the point.

It's hard to make a living as a freelance writer, but there are not enough good professional writers out there, and everybody's looking for them. Study your craft, study the magazines. Establish a relationship with an editor. Send ideas. Keep trying. And don't give up.

JANET CHAN, *Executive Editor,* Redbook

I think the major concern here at *Redbook* is not being too much of a New York publication. We are a national magazine for working mothers, and we need to reflect the entire country, not just New York. We are often asked who our major competitor is, and we say our biggest competitor is time. I don't mean *Time* the magazine; I'm saying that the reader barely has enough time to read any magazine at all. She's too busy. She loves her husband, she loves her kids, she loves her job. Sometimes she doesn't love her job, and there are days when she doesn't love her husband, but the kids always come first. She ends up coming last.

But it's not a magazine for victims. The *Redbook* reader likes her life very much, and she is interested in the world. So we're talking about articles that help her understand things and even deal with things, but not "cope." It's not "poor her." She can handle it, and we just want to help.

We also want it to be a magazine that is fun to read. So we publish a lot of material that's just interesting, that's fun to escape with. Sometimes our service articles are as direct as "Healthy Fast-Cooking Meals." Sometimes they're more implicit, as in "Make-Up Lessons for Beauty Klutzes." There was a recent piece telling why you should take your money out of the bank and invest it, and how to do that. There was a news piece on breast feeding taboos. The sad fact is that breast feeding is good for both the baby and the mother, and is done widely in other cultures, but American society doesn't like it.

So *Redbook* is really into a wide range of topics. We're always trying to get away from the ethnocentricity of New York, and are very interested in people and interests and trends from all over the country. And, of course, in writers from all over the country.

I have certain pet hates in terms of queries. The ones I hate most are queries that don't give you any information, that tease you without really telling you what the idea is. Maybe these writers think you're going to steal it, or maybe they just think they're being provocative. One query I received asked, "Are you interested in the most improved contraceptive technique since the pill?" Well, maybe, but what about it? The query didn't say.

I'm also tired of writers who write me, "I proposed an article on the pill and you rejected it, and then I saw that this month's issue has something about the pill." In this case, the article we ran was on ambivalence about using birth control. What they proposed was something along the lines of: "The Pill: All About It." What these writers don't realize is that a subject is not necessarily an idea.

What we love having is an idea accompanied by a working title. This helps us see how you have focused your idea, as well as helping you sell it to us. I'm also impressed by a well-thought-out idea. It should be long enough to let us see what the idea is, whether a page or more. But the writer doesn't have to do all the research before submitting the query. Often, at *Redbook*, the editor and writer will work out the shape of the piece together. That's assuming we find the proposal sufficiently impressive in the first place.

Clips are helpful. I do need a sense of how the writer writes. But sometimes I'll get a query from a writer proposing a profile, say, and the clips are all straight service pieces. They don't really help me.

On the other hand, if the writer tells me he or she has never done a profile before, has access to a hard-to-reach celebrity, and seems to have an interesting slant on the story, it might work. We'll ask the writer to deliver two or three paragraphs giving a sense of how he or she would write in the profile style, and that might be enough to go ahead with.

But while I think it's a serious mistake to not give enough of a story, it's even worse if your proposal shows that you don't understand our magazine. I don't expect a writer to know everything the magazine has ever published, although if the story you're proposing is a big coverline in the current issue, it does show you're not paying attention. But if we have to turn an idea down because it's too close to something we've done, I consider that a successful submission. That writer clearly knows what we're looking for, and I'd encourage them to try again.

Our readers are primarily working women in their thirties with young children, and the writer should know that. We're not interested in "When Your Grown Children Move Back Home," because our readers are too young to face that problem. But we think more in terms of what their lives are like than in how old they are. We have stretched our parameters at times, if the idea is very much in the air, because we know every piece can't be about a thirty-one-year-old woman with a two-year-old child. We're looking for real voices, stories about real people. Everything doesn't have to be about how Jane Pauley does it. We do one or two celebrity pieces an issue, but we're equally interested in how real women deal with the problems all of our readers face.

I would advise new writers to avoid the celebrity profile, and stick with subjects you know about or have dealt with personally. Try us with a news-oriented piece, or with a service piece or, best of all, one with a light touch.

TIMOTHY FOOTE, *Senior Writer and Member of the Board of Editors,* Smithsonian

In the magazine business you keep getting suggestions for stories that essentially you've read over and over again. You know what the reporting is going to turn up. You know what the writer has on his mind. At *Smithsonian* we don't need another suggestion about the joys of building a wooden boat, or a science story about gorilla behavior that everybody read in *The New York Times* a few weeks back. Or those perennial suggestions about the Flying Doctor Service in Australia, the Annual Hobo Convention in Brett, Iowa. Not to mention one of many favorite fests—the Annual Vulture Fest in Hinkley, Ohio.

What we're looking for is a story we haven't read before. Or an old subject with an unexpected point of view. At the same time, and it sounds a bit like a Catch-22, we'd also like a story that will make readers exclaim (not with a groan but with approval) "Only in *Smithsonian* would you find a story like that!"

The magazine deals with art, history, some theater, general culture, the environment, conservation, architecture, astronomy, anthropology, primatology, not to mention a lot of pieces on birds and small animals examined in detail. Also occasional literary figures from Shaw and Joyce to Beatrix Potter and Tony Hillerman, with emphasis on biography and anecdote. Rarely medicine. Never health, sex, current politics, popular showbiz or *People* magazine people—though we do portraits of individuals (living and dead) whose lives and works seem amusing and/or significant.

Talking about what's wanted, you have to be specific. Because I'm especially involved in history, I tend to think of an ideal *Smithsonian* story as one that deals with a fascinating and unexpected historical event or situation that has sharp resonances with the present. This is an age of lawyer-bashing, so we did a story about a time (it's hard for Americans to imagine) when there *were* no lawyers. In fact, in ancient Athens citizens were forbidden to hire anyone else to defend them in contests of law.

Another story told how the U.S. Marines occupied Haiti from 1915 to 1934, trying to stabilize the place, and failed. We ran it in the midst of island's current difficulties. Come to think of it, regardless of subject, *Smithsonian* stories often have an historical element, a moment in which the writer briefly delves into the past to see how things got the way they are today.

History tends to repeat itself. But Americans don't know much history and can easily be surprised by the parallels there are between the present and the pains and problems and, yes, the scandals of the past. Which is why we smuggle history into the magazine on the back of storytelling and personal anecdote, with as much detailed reporting from the past as possible. Not too long ago, we discovered a celebrated group of Shiite assassins who had operated in the Middle East a thousand years ago, using exactly the same terrorist principles and techniques that Shiite terrorists and assassins use today, and there was plenty of reportorial detail.

A story on failed summit meetings of the past (run when Reagan and Gorbachev had just failed at Rykjavik) offered anecdotes about Richard the Lionheart's meeting with Saladin and Napoleon's sparring with Tsar Alexander. We're just now working on the story of Homer Plessy, a New Orleans shoemaker whose challenge of a railway Jim Crow law led to the landmark Plessy vs. Ferguson Supreme Court decision. That decision declared separate but equal facilities legal under the Constitution, and wasn't reversed until Thurgood Marshall argued Brown vs. Board of Education before the High Court in 1954.

When it comes to history, some of our stories could appear in *American Heritage* and vice versa. But they are a magazine of American history and politics, and their editors can assume (as we cannot) that subscribers have a definite interest in and knowledge of the subject. It's a fine magazine and I read it regularly with admiration, but we are much bigger (more than two million subscribers) and deal with all sorts of subjects. Even with regard to history, we range all over, from Greece and Rome and the Middle East up through the Renaissance and modern European history. Both magazines would run stories on the Oklahoma Land Rush, or World War II, or the Constitutional Convention. But obviously you wouldn't see a story on the Black Death, or Mata Hari, in *American Heritage.*

The range of our stories, and the kind of story it makes sense to suggest, should be clear to anyone who reads even a few issues of the magazine carefully. But one perennial problem about suggestions — I think every magazine has it — is that new writers will suggest a story though they clearly *haven't* read the magazine. That can be provoking. I mean, if we never do stories on contemporary politics or cutting edge medicine and a writer suggests one, it's hard to take his interest seriously. If he can't bother to read your magazine, why is he bothering you?

Of course (Catch-22 again) some writers sedulously study the magazine and then offer an uninteresting journeyman's carbon copy suggestion for the kind of story we run all the time. Like every magazine, we're drowning in suggestions, most of them run-of-the-mill. No magazine simply wants okay duplicates of its usual pieces. There are already too many of those. So why assign another to a new writer whose prose is either unknown or unimpressive? We look for a little class in the prose, some sense that the writer has an idea or two to rub together or a pressing interest in the subject that he can communicate. That last is important.

We do read and want query letters — i.e., story suggestions — even though the suggestion is one of the hardest and most ghastly literary forms a professional writer has to deal with. Personally, I would rather walk to the Yukon barefoot, report the story and write it, than to sit down and write a query trying to tell somebody why a good story is good. But query letters are selling tools, and new writers (all writers) should work very hard on them. One problem with most queries is that there's not nearly enough selling done in them. Ideas tend to come in laid out briefly, and matter-of-factly, without communicating any excitement.

These days every magazine has to compete hard for a reader's time, establishing compelling contact in the first few paragraphs. Once a reader is with you, he may stay to the end, and be willing to absorb all kinds of demanding material. But if you lose him right off he's gone for good.

This is less true of editors reading suggestions. But it is a good idea to show some flare in your first paragraphs and some of the writing skills necessary for the lead paragraphs of a magazine article. Among them is change-of-pace, since you can't explain everything with the same amount of detail. I define it as the ability to sum up the sweeping history of Western Civilization on the head of a pin so you'll have time and space to describe the precise moment in which a man slowly reaches up, picks and peels a banana. It also helps, somewhere in the suggestion, to demonstrate that you are aware of what kinds of difficulties the reporting of the story may offer and that you've figured out a way to deal with them.

I think writing any magazine article, or a suggestion, is a lot like telling a story at a dinner party. You have to get peoples' attention, then intrigue them into listening further.

Smithsonian has no objection to long suggestion letters. Some magazines, I gather, feel that a suggestion should be no more than a page, but we don't necessarily care if it's a lot longer. Not long as in "I didn't have time to write it short," but long enough to make it interesting and to do the story justice. Most editors aren't desperate for stories; they're desperate for great stories. The writer needs to stir curiosity, get you involved, get across the feeling that you'd like to listen to him/her tell the whole story.

Unlike many editors, I'm perfectly happy to talk to nearly anyone on the phone. If I'm busy I'll say so, take your number and call back. You can save us both a lot of time that way, in that you'll find out right away if an idea has any chance. But obviously don't call an editor unless you've thought through the idea pretty carefully and can explain it compellingly on the phone. Even if an idea *seems* promising, we'd still want something on paper — and writing samples. A telephone conversation won't eliminate the need for writing a query later, but at least it will tell you if there's any interest at all.

One of the best proposal letters we ever got from a writer we didn't know came from Jim Chiles, who has since become a regular contributor to the magazine. His proposal noted that we're always thinking about ancient monuments and buildings and how they're being destroyed by wind, weather, decay and industrial pollution. What he wanted to explore was just how well the great structures of the twentieth century, made from steel and with the latest thing in modern design and technology, will stand the test of time. What condition will they be in a hundred, a thousand years from now?

This was clearly an architecture and construction story with a difference. Among others, Chiles eventually examined how, and with what, the World Trade Center and the St. Louis arch were built, and, with help from engineers, then explained how decay would get at them. Would they last as long as the Pyramids or the Louvre or the Leaning Tower of Pisa? If they collapsed how would it happen?

Chiles is very good at writing query letters. So is Bruce Watson, one of the best proposal writers and best magazine writers I've ever met. You can read his initial query on the Luddites, or the Navajo Code Talkers in World War II, both of which subsequently appeared in *Smithsonian*, and know that he understood the nuances and possibilities—and the difficulties in reporting—these stories, and was really excited about them.

Here is Watson's query on the Luddites:

On May 9, 1812, residents of Nottingham awoke to find a paper posted in plain sight.

"Welcome, Ned Ludd, your cause is good,

Make Perceval your aim;

For by this Bill, 'tis understood

His death, so break a Frame—

That night a small band of men gathered at dusk in the forest north of town. They carried hammers and axes. Their faces were blackened. Their leader called the roll by numbers, not names. When the numbers reached fifty, the excitement grew. Then the leader fired a pistol in the air and the men set off in perfect military order, towards the mills.

Their leader called himself Ned Ludd, sometimes General Ludd. For months, Ludd had sent threatening letters to mill owners, especially those using the hated steam looms which when employed could cut the labor force in half. Desist in the use of these looms, as well as the Gig mills and the shearing frames, or grave consequences would result, General Ludd said. But though overseas markets for cloth had dried up due to British wars in America and France, mill owners ignored the warnings. The machines, which had once been banned by royal decree, were moving quickly into the mills, and Ludd's consequences raged across central England for five bloody years.

The Luddites have given their name to anyone who opposes technology. Yet the birth of the movement was much more complex. Contemporary Luddites are scattered throughout the globe, but their namesakes were a paramilitary organization whose small bands terrorized mills, broke machines, and after their own members were killed, sometimes murdered mill owners.

Though Parliament focused on its wars with Napoleon and with America, another war was being fought in the Midlands. While some of its soldiers proclaimed revolution, it was a war against a revolution — the Industrial Revolution. On one side were the embattled workers whose wages had dropped by a third even as grain prices doubled. Croppers, shearers, and weavers, driven to the breaking point by poverty and the creeping installation of machines, took up arms against their enemy, the machine. Staging late night raids, leaders like John Stones of Westhoughton and James Towles of Loughborough confounded the opposing army of General Maitland. Though General Maitland believed his opposing General Ludd a real person, there were really hundreds, each assuming the leader's name.

Before the war was finished, thousands of looms, stocking frames, and other machines would lie broken across the rolling hills. Mills would be torched. Several mill owners would be killed and hundreds of Luddites, including Stones and Towles, would be executed. Yet peace was only won by rising economic conditions which brought more employment to the region. And the hated machines which the Luddites had broken were negotiated into use by trade unions and owners. Luddism had brief outbreaks in the 1820s and 30s, but its name and spirit are all that remain of General Ned Ludd.

In telling the story of the Luddites, I will use accounts by British historians, including newspaper accounts. I will focus heavily on specific incidents and the group's unusual rituals which included oaths, poems, and the mystical cult through which the name of a Nottingham youth, Ludlum, who broke his knitting needles rather than work, metamorphosed into that of General Ludd.

If you're a young writer and trying to break into the magazine, it doesn't make much sense to suggest a very ambitious story that involves a lot of reporting, a lot of money, a lot of time. We sometimes take a chance. But more likely we won't assign it because it is far too complicated to take a chance on a writer whose work is unknown to us. It makes more sense for a young writer to start with a subject that not only looks like a natural fit, but is simple to report and write, saving more ambitious projects for later.

Along with query letters we tend to like to see some clips. They don't have to be of published articles, although one is naturally encouraged if a writer has appeared in other good magazines. When I was at *Time* interviewing writers, I tended to look for people who had written short stories or skillful novels but who (as often is the case) find it hard to make a living at fiction. If a candidate has writing talent, he or she can be trained to be a good journalist — i.e., magazine writer — but if they don't start with that edge of talent, they'll have a harder row to hoe. I still sometimes ask young writers to send in short stories, or even poetry that they've written. It's not a matter of looking for publishing credits, it's a matter of talent and the search for a fresh voice. A writer may not be able to show what kind of a voice he has in a newspaper, although newspaper reporting does show that he/she knows how to go out and get a story. The voice may be more clearly there in something that was never published.

I'd suggest that new writers start out with an idea they really like, that really interests them, that they really want to do. The enthusiasm will show in any query letter. Then see if you can find a name on the masthead that you have some connection with; somebody who's a friend of a friend. If not, read through enough issues to find some things an editor may have written that makes you think he/she might be a kindred spirit, or interested in your subject, and make your pitch to that person. You might begin by making reference to the piece of writing you liked.

Especially if the comment is cogent, you're likely to get the editor's attention.

Smithsonian gets a thousand query letters a month, so anything you can do to stand out from the crowd will help. And it's true that once in a blue moon we buy unsolicited pieces that come in over the transom. The source isn't important. Every editor is hungry for a piece of writing that really interests him, and will go to considerable trouble to try to find it, or poke it and push it into shape.

So read the magazine. See the kinds of stories we run. You may be surprised at how broad *Smithsonian*'s range of interest is. Then pick a topic that *you'd* like to explore personally, that has enough interest for *you* so that, if you had the spare time and money, you'd like to dig into it, report it and write it without an assignment—something that few of us have the leisure or the cash to do. Then send us a suggestion letter, enclosing some samples of your writing. Quite often I call up new writers after getting a suggestion to explore it and talk over ways in which it might work as a story for us.

Editors are depressed by messy copy. We get nervous about a suggestion with spelling mistakes or obvious errors of fact. Such things are not a measure of talent, but they're always a bad sign. Genius may or may not consist, as has been said, in the ability to take pains. But who needs a writer who can't be bothered to look up a word or, these days, use the spellcheck on his computer?

Journalism has been defined as the occupation of the vaguely talented. My advice to most would-be writers is to get a good education and then go to law school instead. Or, as Flannery O'Connor once put it in a slightly different connection (I paraphrase), "College writing courses stifle a lot of young talent—but not half enough." Don't become a writer unless you absolutely *have* to. Don't become a writer unless you can write fast—and better than all your classmates. Don't become a writer unless you can't imagine doing anything else.

PAMELA FIORI, *Executive Vice-President/Editorial Director, American Express Publishing Corporation (*Travel & Leisure, Food & Wine, *etc.)*

The best travel articles, at least the best for *Travel & Leisure*, have a definite angle or point of view. At the very minimum, an article proposal for T&L should indicate clearly why the story belongs in T&L in the first place, and what the payoff is for the reader.

Instead, what often happens is that a writer sends in a roster of places where he has been or destinations where she is about to go — as if the mere listing of locations were enough to warrant an assignment. Imagine, for example, how many times in its twenty-two-year history T&L has covered Paris, or any other major European capital for that matter. Unless the idea is compelling, the chances are that it will be turned down.

So, yes, we look for writers with bright ideas. That's a given. We further appreciate writers who have a style that suits the magazine. This assumes a certain level of sophistication and experience, both as traveler and as writer. If it's not there, the reader will notice instantly.

The query letter should be short — one or two paragraphs per idea, and no more than three ideas in one letter. The surest way to the bottom of an editor's mountain of work is to send a long-winded query letter.

The proposal should also indicate, somehow, that the writer is familiar with the magazine — and that the idea or ideas have been created specifically with T&L, and no other travel magazine, in mind. It always surprises me how often story proposals come in that could just as well be addressed "Occupant."

Just as bad are ideas that come close to what has already run in a previous edition. Much time and embarrassment can be spared by looking at the last two or three issues of the magazine being queried.

The condition of the proposal is important; that means no misspelled words, no punctuation mistakes and no grammatical errors. Neatness counts, even in 1993.

Penultimately, send along one or two examples of recently published articles (unless your credentials are already known to the magazine). That doesn't mean a collection of all the pieces ever written; it slows down an already lengthy process.

Finally, keep at it, even if you get a "no" in the beginning.

Many widely published magazine writers have received their share of rejections—including this one.

JOHN MACK CARTER, *Editor-in-Chief,* Good Housekeeping

The hardest pieces for us to find are not the stories you read in the paper or hear about on television. The hardest ones are the soft pieces, what I call the "meaning of life" stories. Stories on relationships. On feelings. Writers need to be able to write and talk about the emotional life of the reader in terms of a woman and her family, a woman who has had a problem and faced it and triumphed over it.

These are the stories we don't know about until writers tell us about them. They're not in the papers. They're the stories only the writers out in the rest of the country know about.

My advice to young writers is to write. Write all the time. Get a job on a newspaper, or some other place that involves writing. When writers ask me for advice I say, don't go to graduate school. Go on a newspaper. Write on anything. The most important thing is not the subject, but learning the craft of writing.

If I had one last word of advice I'd say: There's a future in this business, and it's worth working on.

MARY MCLAUGHLIN, *Executive Editor,* Working Mother

What we need most are article ideas that are based on new research, new information. Findings that illuminate a common problem and give us a new way to think about it.

And we do want our ideas in writing, particularly if you're new to us. But even when a writer has some publishing history with us, I'll ask them to put anything we're interested in down on paper. I have to see if they have the idea worked out, if they know how to shape it into a good article.

I'm turned off by fatuous queries, letters that begin: "Hello, how are you? You don't know me, but . . . " I won't even try a writer who begins a proposal this way, because I know they lack judgment and are not professional.

It helps if you have some personal experience with our subject matter, so you have a genuine feeling for the problems our readers share. It also helps if you know a good deal about child psychology. And, of course, it helps if you read the magazine carefully. In fact, if you don't, I think you have almost no chance at all.

MARY ANN O'ROARK, *Senior Editor,* Guideposts

Anyone writing for a religious or inspirational publication has to have some spiritual orientation that conforms to the beliefs of that magazine's audience. A writer has to hone the material to be of meaning to that particular audience, and to give them information and ideas that apply to their lives, to their culture and to their religious framework.

In the case of *Guideposts*, that is a Judeo-Christian orientation. This is not specifically stated in the magazine, but that is what studies show our audience to be, so that is the way we orient our material. We call ourselves an interfaith inspirational magazine, but demographic studies show that our audience is mainly Christian with a smaller percentage of Jewish readers. A few years ago a study showed that we had a fairly large number of Buddhist readers, which caused us all to be quite astonished, but it turned out that this was just a typo and was supposed to be Baptists.

Knowing our readership, we know that we must in some way reflect or respect that Judeo-Christian readership. This does not mean that we have to employ specific religious terminology. In fact, God or Jesus Christ do not even have to be mentioned. One recent story that did not mention God brought some complaints, and we responded by pointing out that Jesus himself, in his parables, often does not specifically mention God. God's messages, we said, are conveyed in people's lives and through their actions, so it is not necessary to continually invoke God's name.

We feel that our magazine is often read by people who are just discovering religion, and we don't want them to be put off by too strong a religious content. We did a story recently with Katie Kelley, who left her job as a highly paid reporter on a New York TV channel to go to Vietnam and work with Vietnamese children who had been fathered by American servicemen. Katie's story, which was featured on our cover, wasn't a story of personal faith; in fact, she did not have a strong religious orientation herself. This was a powerful story because her life was displaying faith in action.

There are also, of course, articles that are much more specifically religious. And other religious magazines are more overtly religious, particularly when it comes to supporting their own denomination. The more fundamentalist magazines argue strongly for their beliefs. On the other hand, there are magazines like *Christianity Today* that are more intellectual and scholarly. *Writer's Market* shows almost a hundred religious magazines, and they cover a wide gamut. As in the case of proposing ideas to any magazine, it's vitally important to study the market before trying to sell any ideas to it.

While the style of writing for a religious publication is very much the style you would use for any magazine, you need to study each magazine to see if there is anything unique about the way their pieces are written. *Guideposts*, for instance, uses the first person entirely. It's important to note, though, that people who have very dramatic and spiritual experiences are often not writers and are unable to produce the pieces themselves. For that reason, *Guideposts* pieces are often ghostwritten. If you know of someone whose story might interest us, let us know about it and think about writing their story for them.

All of our stories are told in a narrative style, using fiction techniques to tell true stories. There are scenes and dialogue, the crisis builds, there is usually a turning point. Our stories are specifically designed to be strong narratives that are fun to read. And we always want what we call a "takeaway."

By that we mean that they must contain something the reader can take away from the story and apply to his or her everyday life. The stories should contain a lesson, almost like a parable. The reader is not simply reading for entertainment, although they must be entertaining, but is also learning some kind of lesson showing them how to change their lives, how to deal with some problem, how to grow spiritually. The stories should show someone coping with a problem and growing because of the lessons they have learned in solving it. We make a real point to have this element in every piece we do.

If this sounds difficult, it might help if you think about why you want to tell this story. What point are you trying to share with your readers? If you think this through before you start, you'll have an easier time keeping your story focused, and thus getting across that lesson more effectively.

We are very open to ideas from new writers. In fact, we receive good stories all the time from writers we have never heard of before. A recent one came from a woman in Oklahoma who had written very little. She wanted to ghost write a story about a woman whose son had been killed by his father-in-law. The man had gone to prison, and she had been serving as a volunteer in the prison when she happened to meet him. It's a story of forgiveness.

This proposal caught our eye because it was presented dramatically, with a strong lead and enough specific details to show us what the story would be like.

We're always on the lookout for solid dramatic narratives like this one. We're specifically looking right now for stories with a Jewish orientation. We're also looking for humor, but it's always hard to find. If you can write with humor, and it seems to fit our audience, do send it to us.

Another good way to break in, and this applies to any magazine you might want to approach, is by writing shorter material—for regular features, front-of-the-book articles, fillers. We're doing a lot more shorter pieces, and we're always looking for such material.

When you're thinking about an idea for *Guideposts*, avoid anything that might be divisive or so controversial that it could get readers in such a rage that no point would be made. Instead, focus on subjects that will unite people rather than divide them.

We do deal with controversial subjects, but we don't take sides or make judgments. We have dealt with AIDS and homosexuality and abortion, but our story is always focused on the fact that you must love the person, no matter what. We don't want to get into the question of whether this person is right or wrong, but simply accept that they are trying to work out their problem and our job is to help them.

Our message is to love people and to help them, not to judge them. We focus on Christ's commandment to "Love one another."

If you want to sell to us, you have to write a query letter that really gets our attention. It should have a very dramatic lead, with quotes, and enough details so we can see how the story will be developed. The main fault that we see in queries from new writers is that they don't give enough specific details. They're too abstract rather than being specific.

Many people who want to write spiritual material think it can be dreamy and unfocused, that it can simply be a sort of testimony or praise report. This promises a dreamy, unfocused piece, and will not get our attention. Writers like this often act as if they have some specific insight, some special relationship with God, which they would like to share with our readers. Sometimes they seem to be talking down to those readers, and our audience can spot that at once.

What we want are writers who are struggling with doubt, with fear, with anger. Readers don't want to be preached to, but do want to hear from a writer who's in the thick of the fray right along with them, struggling with the same things they're struggling with.

If the idea sounds promising, we'll work with a writer through as many revisions as they're willing to make. Most people who want to write for us are very motivated, and they're eager for a chance to do another revision even when we can't promise an eventual sale. But we do everything *we* can to make sure that the story will work out successfully.

I would definitely start with a query. I will look at finished manuscripts, but I'd rather see a short proposal that tells me enough so that I can see if I might be interested in having the idea developed further. I don't want the writer to do all the work if we're not going to be interested. If we are interested, we might ask for more information before making an assignment.

This doesn't mean, however, that you shouldn't invest a good deal of work on that query letter, because it is your introduction to us. It tells a lot about you, and you want to make the best possible impression. You don't have to do all of the research and interviewing before writing a query, but you do have to provide enough information so we can determine if it's something we want to encourage.

For example, if you say you want to write an article on forgiveness, that tells us nothing. But if you tell us that a woman's only son was shot dead by a man she knew and trusted, his father-in-law, that will get our blood racing. How was this woman able to get past her rage and anger to forgive this man? That's what the story is.

Always send your ideas to a specific name on the masthead, not just to "The Editor." We get a great deal of material, and it will get read faster if it is directed to one specific editor. If you have clips, send them. It's better if they are in the same style as the idea you're proposing, but they don't have to be. Also, bear in mind that while we don't buy rights to pieces that have already been published, we might take a piece that had appeared in a local publication and suggest ways in which it could be adapted or revised for us.

If you're just trying to break into print, whether it's for a religious publication or not, I'd advise you to aim for subjects that people have on their minds — things that scare them, things they're perplexed about, things they can identify with quickly and deeply, things that connect them to other people.

What are they worried about? What are their neighbors worried about? What's on their minds? If they're worried about it, and their neighbors are worried about it, then others are worried about it, too. And if they can provide any new kind of insight into the problem, or some strategy for dealing with it, that will be very welcome. People are really looking for material like that.

If you don't succeed at first, be persistent. You've got to keep at it and at it and at it. I have something I call the Green Thumb Theory. People are always seeing all the plants I have in my office and saying, "Oh, you must have a green thumb." And I always think to myself, "No it's not that I have a green thumb. It's just that I have a lot of plants. It's not that I have any God-given gift, but that I keep having enough plants so that even if some fail, others will thrive."

So you can't say someone else is a gifted writer and I'm not, simply because you sent out three pieces that were rejected. What you've got to do is have a lot of pieces in the works. Some of them are going to wither and die on the vine, but others are going to prosper and bloom. As a writer, you can't have one little plant and pin your hopes on that, but you have to have a lot of things growing.

That doesn't mean bombarding editors with a lot of undeveloped ideas, because that will annoy them and won't accomplish anything. It does mean keeping a lot of queries going out, knowing that you'll have some positive responses. And then one day somebody will say to you, "Oh, you must be a natural writer."

And you'll know the real secret of your success.

RON KING, *Contributing Editor, and* **JIM SEXTON**, *Executive Editor,* Special Report

Author's note: Whittle Communications of Knoxville, Tennessee, used to be known by some as "the best unknown freelance market in America." While it's not that anymore, as the company has moved away from print journalism toward electronic media, it still publishes a magazine that is an excellent freelance market. In fact 90 percent of it is freelance written. You can't buy it on the newsstands, although you can subscribe. But where you typically find it is in the waiting rooms of obstetricians, gynecologists and pediatricians. This is where you'll also find the *Special Report* reader.

"Our reader is the family gatekeeper — a busy mom. She is one of the forty million women with kids younger than eighteen. Most of our audience is between twenty-five and forty years old, with a combined family income of $30,000 + annually . . . We demand strong writing, enterprising reporting . . . We don't underestimate our audience. These are busy women who are skeptical of experts, quick fixes and empty hype ('Ten Days to a Slimmer You.') As we've always said, top of mind is the question: 'Is there a better way?' We provide the answer."

The above description comes from a four-page guideline to writing for *Special Report*. You might also be interested in writing for the *Special Report* Home Library, a series of sixteen-page service-oriented booklets published and distributed along with each bimonthly issue. Some recent titles were: "How to Speak Your Child's Language," "The Best Family Vacations" and "The Headache Survival Guide." Here is what Ron King and Jim Sexton told me about writing for *Special Report*.]

Send us a cover letter and some clips, and let us know what your background is. We'll send you our guidelines and a sample issue. Once you've had a chance to really read the magazine, send us some ideas. We can usually tell immediately if the writer has ideas that are appropriate for us. The biggest mistake most writers make is to write us without knowing anything about our audience or what we publish.

We're impressed by detailed, in-depth reporting. The challenge in all magazine writing is providing the kind of vivid detail that paints a sharp picture for the reader. The other day we got an unsolicited piece from a woman who was married to a man twenty years younger than she was. They had been married a long time, so you might have expected some real insights. Instead, it was full of clichés about autumn/spring relationships, the importance of being honest with each other, the problems of explaining their marriage to their friends. There was nothing that was particularly surprising or unusual. Even in first-person pieces like this one, we want something fresh and original, something that has that hook.

On the other hand, we got another proposal recently from a woman who wanted to write a story about how to answer your kid's toughest questions. It's not necessarily a new idea, but her twist on it was to cover questions that kids raised in the 1990s would ask. Things like: "What is gay? Mom, did you use drugs?" She wanted to use some of her experiences as a mother of three sons as well as to pull in the latest advice from a group of national experts. This impressed us because it included both personal and professional advice, and because these are questions most young moms would like some help on.

We're always willing to consider assigning a piece to someone we don't know, but not if they tell us nothing about themselves. If they send no clips. If they provide no background information about who they are and what they've done in the past.

Writers also need to be realistic about the kinds of pieces they can expect to be assigned. If you don't have a pile of good clips, you might as well not waste your time pitching us a five thousand-word feature. We just won't take the chance, even on speculation.

And your clips have to be from comparable magazines. We often get excerpts from papers or books by professionals, and they're usually so esoteric that we can't make heads or tails of them. You have to show that you know how to speak to the ordinary reader.

We do need written queries, and they should be as short as possible. A minimum of three paragraphs, and one page is about all most editors will read. Get in, make your pitch fast and get out. You can't expect an editor to spend ten minutes reading a query from you, any more than you'd spend ten minutes watching a TV commercial.

We got a good query the other day. It came from Ann Japenga, a woman we'd never heard of, who lives in Tacoma, Washington. After explaining that she had been a reporter for the *Los Angeles Times* for eight years, was a contributing editor of *Health*, and had also written for *Self*, *Redbook* and *The New York Times*, she explained her idea this way:

> Despite years in the business, I still get excited when I stumble across a lively idea that the media hordes have somehow missed. Here's my current object of infatuation:
>
> It's the kind of literature no mother wants to find hidden away in Junior's trombone case: "The Teenage Liberation Handbook: How to Quit School and Get a Real Life and Education."
>
> This provocative underground manual, self-published by a former English teacher from Eugene, Oregon, has indeed given lots of parents and principals fits. But it has also inspired plenty of teenagers to abandon their rigid opinions about education and pursue learning for the love of it—whether or not they stay in school.
>
> Grace Llewellyn argues that all teenagers—not just the gifted ones—have the natural ability to educate themselves outside the system, often, with magnificent results. This is, of course, a venerable notion. Ansel Adams, Mark Twain, Thomas Edison, Jack London, Beatrix Potter and other famous figures were all at least partially self-taught.
>
> Following up on the popularity of the "Teenage Liberation Handbook," Llewellyn has compiled a collection of stories by self-educated teenagers, due out this spring. One example:
>
> Kyla Wetherell dropped out of her Oregon high school, where she was editor of the newspaper and the top student in her junior class. Once on her own, she studied physics and history, organized recycling projects, published essays and editorials and bicycled alone through South America. She is currently volunteering as a research assistant on a rain forest project in Ecuador.
>
> Some ideas are valuable largely because they rattle the cages that contain us. A story on Llewellyn and several teenagers who

have successfully pursued life outside high school would be mind-opening and enjoyable reading for parents.

I live within a half day's drive of Llewellyn, so would have easy access to her and several of the "unschooling" students she has worked with.

Thanks for considering a piece on Teenage Liberation. I've enclosed clips.

The author had good clips, so it was a perfect package: A good writer with a good idea. She had studied the magazine and had a real idea of what we're all about, and we've given her an assignment for a fifteen-hundred-word profile. We see too many writers who just want to be beautiful writers, but it's hard to find good reporters. The best freelancer is somebody who is willing to be a thorough and dogged researcher. People like that will definitely get assignments from us.

PHILIP OSBORNE, *Assistant Managing Editor*, Reader's Digest

If you're going to sell a piece to the *Digest*, the most important thing you have to do is establish a relationship with an editor. Pick out a specific editor on the masthead and write a letter containing your idea. Even if the idea is from an unknown writer, if it's a good idea I'm willing to look at a piece on speculation. I'll send samples of similar articles we've done, and steer the writer as much as I can. I'm not put off by lack of credentials, if the idea is presented compellingly — and professionally. The query should do a good selling job and should be written with enthusiasm, selling both the idea and the ability of the writer.

I like the initial proposal of an idea to be fairly brief, perhaps no more than one or two paragraphs. The point of the first contact is to see if the proposal warrants further development. We have to determine four things: Have we published the same idea before? Is another writer currently assigned to the same story? Has another writer gotten a go-ahead to develop a fuller proposal on the same idea? And finally, of course, are we interested in the first place?

If these criteria are met, we ask for a fully developed proposal, which might run as long as six or seven pages. If that is approved, we'll work with the writer as long as he or she has the determination to keep writing. I've gone to five drafts with some writers and wound up getting almost all of what I wanted. And getting a piece we wanted to publish.

But getting back to that first letter, it's the one that makes all the difference. I can't tell you how many letters I get that don't even have my name spelled right. I had one recently that misspelled my first name, my last name, had my title wrong, and actually misspelled *Reader's Digest*. (They left out the apostrophe in "Reader's.") If somebody can't get these basic facts right, how can they be expected to get anything else right?

I'm also impressed by a query that shows the writer is clearly determined. The query should demonstrate, as well, that the writer reads the magazine. We're much more focused than most other general interest magazines, and more targeted than most people think we are.

The most important advice I can give is to study the magazine—and I mean *really* study it. It's easy to assume you understand the *Digest*, but you can't really understand it without reading a number of issues very carefully. One way you can demonstrate your familiarity with us is to cite previous articles on the same general subject. You might say, for instance, "I know you did a recent roundup story on child abuse, but I have a different approach in mind. I want to do a first-person story about an actual case . . ."

If you study old issues of the *Digest*, you'll see that it hasn't changed dramatically over the years, and I think this is because our basic values haven't changed. There's a strong element of inspiration in our articles. We try to find solutions to problems. We try to show that the individual can make a difference, in his own life and in the lives of others. We like personal stories that teach a strong lesson.

Above all, we're storytellers, so we're always looking for strong narratives. You can make your point much more powerfully in a strong story than in a straight roundup or survey article. But even in roundup articles, we want plenty of anecdotes. We want the writer to emotionalize every story, putting the reader there at the scene.

One of our most popular features is "Drama in Real Life." "On a Wind of Terror" told a woman's story of being swept out to sea in a runaway hot-air balloon. "Grizzly Attack" recounted the horrifying experience of a young couple on a hike in Glacier

National Park. "Lost Beneath the Mountain" was the story of a young camper trapped in an abandoned mine. "My Babies Are in That Car!" was a young mother's story of the day her car, with three of her young children aboard, began coasting toward a fast-flowing river.

The element that all these dramas share—and we try to run a drama in every issue—is that we want to show what makes people hold on and survive when faced with crushing odds. Dramas have a strong message that gives meaning to the experience, that shows others that people can survive horrifying experiences and triumph over them.

We also need articles in the "Art of Living" area. A successful "Art of Living" article demands two things: a common experience that touches everyone's life, and the discipline to get it down on paper.

We need articles on self-help, on the problems and concerns of daily living, showing ways some people have dealt successfully with them. We are always receptive to articles dealing with religion or faith. But we want no sermons, no preachiness. These pieces should be inspirational, showing how religious belief can help us to gain the courage to deal with problems that might otherwise be unbearable.

One final note. We are looking for materials in two key categories—original and reprint. We are a magazine that digests material from other magazines, after all, and we will often pick up a piece from another magazine that we would not assign as original. So no matter who you are writing your article for, if it fits the *Digest* style and approach, keep us in mind for a secondary sale. We're also in the market for short fillers and items for our departments. This is all explained in the front of the magazine.

PETER MOORE, *Senior Editor,* Playboy

W hen I receive a proposal letter I don't even care what the idea is. I want to see who the writer has written for, and the quality of his or her writing. I'm looking for the intensity of the reporting effort that is evident in the writing. We've got plenty of ideas; what we're looking for are writers who can execute them. At *Playboy,* the idea is of less importance than the writer's style and initiative and reporting skills. And this can best be seen through examples of previous writing.

This doesn't mean the writer has to have published in *The New Yorker* or *Atlantic*. I don't care what publication the writer has appeared in. What I need to see is firm evidence of a strong author's voice and the will to do good reporting. There's a whole great vast gray world of mediocre writing out there, and we can't afford to have people with an uninteresting, colorless, non-explosive writing style. The stylist is who I'm after, and this is just as evident in a clip from the *Chicago Reader* as one from *The New Yorker*.

Every editor here is an omnivorous reader. That's what editors live to do, and we're always prospecting for new writers. No editor I know ever has enough good writers in his stable. And it's definitely a wonderful feeling to find and promote a writer who hasn't had national exposure and who deserves it. I'm not against new writers. But I don't expect someone to write his or her first published piece for *Playboy*.

The greatest mistake new writers make is approaching *Playboy* when what they should be doing is getting a firm grounding in the craft of writing. Writers think they can start off their careers writing for us, when in fact virtually no one does that. A baseball player has to play Class A ball and AA ball before he gets to the majors, and *Playboy* is the majors.

You have to have solid evidence, meaning three or four clips, clips that show you're capable of doing the sort of piece you're proposing. I'm more impressed by a solid eight-thousand-word piece in the *Chicago Reader* than a brightly written three-hundred-word, front-of-the-book piece in *Esquire*. I need to see what a writer can do when he stretches his legs. I assign longer pieces, so I need to see longer pieces.

Another crucial mistake writers often make is to propose a long piece of writing and then send as their clip a Q&A interview. That doesn't tell me anything. Writers need to prove that they can do a long professional investigation of an idea or a problem in society, because that's the sort of pieces we do.

One new writer we did try was a college student, whose college application had somehow found its way into those little snippets that run in the front of *Harper's*. There was so much tone and humor and brightness in this guy's writing that I turned right around and gave him an assignment. Again, it had to do with seeing a special mind at work and seeing the evidence of that shining luminously from some copy he'd written.

Another writer I'd been following in *Chicago* magazine had been doing some great writing and reporting on crime. I had a crime story I wanted to assign in Milwaukee, and it was great to have somebody familiar with the local scene to assign it to.

This is a good tip for a new writer. Say a heinous crime or some spectacular event happens in your hometown and you're an enterprising writer with some good clips but who has never sold anything on a national level. If you've been lucky enough to have a major story break right next to you, then you ought to be able to sell me. Access is a great advantage for a writer trying to break in.

There's a sportswriter in Chicago who over the years has been writing for the *Chicago Sun-Times* and the *Tribune* on the basketball beat, and who got to know Michael Jordan very well. He called me up and said he thought he could get Jordan for the *Playboy* interview. I said "Go for it," and he did, and it turned out to be one of the most popular features we'd done in years.

Access. Access is really the key thing for a new writer. If you can get me someone I might not be able to get on my own, that's definitely a way to break in with us.

One of my favorite writers is a guy named Michael Kelly, who works in the Washington bureau of *The New York Times*. He did a piece for us on John Sununu, who was then President Bush's Chief of Staff. It was a profile assigned at five thousand to seven thousand words, and Kelly must have interviewed fifty to seventy-five people to get Sununu stories. Clearly he went way beyond what any other sane reporter would do, but because he interviewed that many people, the material was better than anybody else had gotten, and it resulted in the best piece ever done on Sununu.

Especially in the early years of their careers, when they're trying to distinguish themselves from the pack, writers have to show that they're willing to do more than anyone else, to do more leg work, more interviewing, to think more carefully and originally than their peers. One way you can do that is to out-report everyone else. And that will always show up in the quality of the final piece.

For young writers trying to get published, my best advice is to do the kind of writing you want to do, not just *any* kind of writing to make a living. If you see yourself as a political reporter, for instance, then you have to start out your career saying "I am a political reporter," whether anyone else acknowledges that fact or not. And do it. Find your outlets as they come along, but make sure you are living in that world — read all of the political publications, know who's buying what kind of stuff, subscribe to *The New Republic*, immerse yourself in the same world political reporters are in so that your references are the same as their references. Understand the kinds of pieces that are being bought by the magazines that run political reporting. Develop the savvy and instincts of the field you want to be in, even before anyone else sees you as being in that field.

I also think young writers make a mistake in focusing on the idea of being published as opposed to focusing on becoming a well-rounded, well-read, well-informed individual. I think the more important thing for a young writer to do is travel the world and read, read, read. And write.

Live the life of a writer, even if you're not being published, and do whatever you need to do to make enough money to live that life. Too many people come at this with an insufficient grounding in literature and an insufficient number of hours actually spent putting pen to paper.

Devote three years to that kind of life in the beginning of your career — that will pay dividends for your whole career as a writer.

A PERSONAL BIBLIOGRAPHY

This is not a complete bibliography of books for writers, but a list of books I have found helpful in my forty-odd years as a teacher, as an editor and as a writer. Most of them are on the shelves to the left of my desk as I write this. Some of them are in print and some aren't, but any good library should have them.

These books fall into two categories. The first are how-to books, designed to help you write more professionally and sell your material more consistently. There are a great many books like this, but I have included only the ones I have read and used myself.

The second category contains books that I admire because of the skill with which they were written, and which I feel stand as examples of how a real craftsman has solved the problems we all face. As I have said elsewhere, one way we learn to write is by imitation—by studying the work of writers we admire and seeing how they dealt with the problems we are still struggling to solve.

I am not, obviously, talking about copying anyone else's content or style. A writer's voice is his or her trademark, easily recognized, and it will avail you nothing to copy some other distinctive voice. "When we say we like a writer's style," as Bill Zinsser says in the latest edition of *On Writing Well*, "what we mean is that we like his personality as he expresses it on paper."

But while you cannot copy someone's personality, by studying their writing, by seeing how they found their voice, you may discover your own.

How-To

The Elements of Style, by William Strunk, Jr., and E.B. White (Macmillan)

I have rarely known a writer who did not have this book and refer to it constantly. It contains all the information you need to write properly and well, and if you buy no other book, buy this one.

On Writing Well, An Informal Guide to Writing Nonfiction, by William Zinsser (HarperCollins)

Freelancer Don Murray has called this "The single best book on writing available today," and I can think of nothing to add to that.

Writing for Magazines, by Myrick E. Land (Prentice-Hall)
Where Zinsser is primarily concerned with teaching the craft of writing, Land is aiming specifically at the mechanics of constructing a magazine article and selling it to an editor. The best "how-to" book I know of, I have used it as a text for seven years.

Writing the Modern Magazine Article, by Max Gunther (The Writer, Inc.)
A rich compendium of tips and advice from a man who has earned his living as a freelance writer for over forty years. Out of print, but well worth the search.

The Magazine Article, How to Think It, Plan It, Write It, by Peter Jacobi (Writer's Digest Books)
Another excellent guide to magazine writing, crammed with examples illustrating absolutely everything.

Feature Writing for Newspapers and Magazines, by Edward J. Friedlander and John Lee (HarperCollege)
What makes this excellent book unique is the fact that they have included nine Pulitzer-Prize-winning newspaper and magazine feature stories, complete with the author's explanation of how the article was reported and written. A truly splendid guide.

Magazine Article Writing, by Betsy P. Graham (Harcourt, Brace, Jovanovich)
Another excellent guide to the basics of writing and selling.

How to Write Like a Pro, by Barry Tarshis (New American Library)
Valuable tips and advice from someone who really is an old pro—a professional freelance writer for thirty years.

Writing to Learn, by William Zinsser (HarperCollege)
Essentially a book for people who do not want to be professional writers, but who do want to write clearly about their

own field, whether it be business, science, mathematics, music, etc.

The Craft of Interviewing, by John Brady (Random House)
Everything you could ever possibly want to know about the fine art of asking questions and getting the answers you want.

Handbook of Magazine Article Writing, edited by Jean M. Fredette (Writer's Digest Books)
An anthology of articles from the magazine on every conceivable aspect of writing every type of article.

Words, Words, Words: A Dictionary for Writers and Others Who Care About Words, by John B. Bremner (Columbia University Press)
A unique dictionary, filled with wit and common sense, that covers the history and etymology (look it up) of words. It is not only a dictionary you'll enjoy reading, but a rich store of article ideas.

How to Write and Sell Magazine Articles, by Richard Gehman (Harper)
Another out-of-print little masterpiece, by a man who was the most prolific and successful magazine writer of his time (roughly, the 1940s, 1950s and 1960s). Gehman not only tells how he became a writer, but reprints fourteen of his best articles and tells how he researched and wrote them.

The Art of Writing Nonfiction, by Andre Fontaine and William A. Glavin, Jr. (Syracuse University Press)
Not only how to write and sell articles in general, but how to write such specific types as descriptive essays, profiles and dramatic narratives.

Writing With a Word Processor, by William Zinsser (Harper Colophon Books)
I'll have to admit being one of the few writers who still uses a manual typewriter, but I've read this book and know it offers valuable encouragement and advice for writers who may still be having problems with the new technology.

As I said, this list is far from complete, and I'm sure there are dozens of excellent books I haven't included. These are the ones

I refer to regularly, the ones that have sustained me in the various aspects of my profession.

Books to Enjoy and Learn From

The Essays of E.B. White, by E.B. White (HarperCollins)
The best work of one of the masters of American nonfiction writing.

The John McPhee Reader, by John McPhee (Farrar, Straus and Giroux)
And excellent introduction to one of the best and most prolific writers of our time.

Up in the Old Hotel, by Joseph Mitchell (Pantheon)
Ask any good contemporary writer who he learned the most from, and the answer is likely to be Joe Mitchell. This is the first complete collection of the marvelous stories he wrote for *The New Yorker* over a period of more than forty years. Some of his colleagues think he was the best they ever had.

My Life and Hard Times, by James Thurber (HarperCollins)
An autobiography, of sorts, by America's finest humorist and one of its finest writers. Also read *The Thurber Album* (Simon and Schuster) or almost anything else he ever wrote.

The Most of A.J. Liebling (Simon and Schuster)
Another one of the reporters who made the old *New Yorker* the greatest magazine we've ever had. This collection will make you want to find more of this writer's work.

Slouching Towards Bethlehem (Farrar, Straus and Giroux) and *The White Album* (Farrar, Straus and Giroux), by Joan Didion
Superb articles and essays by a writer who many consider the best writer now at work.

The Orwell Reader: Fiction, Essays and Reportage, by George Orwell (Harcourt Brace Jovanovich)
A brilliant collection from the author of *Animal Farm* and *1984*.

With All Disrespects, by Calvin Trillin (Penguin)
Not only a wonderfully funny writer, but a man many (includ-

ing Bill Zinsser) consider one of the best reporters and writers of our time.

Southerners, by Marshall Frady (Meridian)
A rich assortment of essays and profiles from another modern master.

The Literary Journalists, edited by Norman Sims (Ballantine)
The editor argues that much of contemporary journalism is literature, and this anthology goes a long way toward proving it.

The New Journalism, edited by Tom Wolfe (Harper and Row)
The 1960s brought a revolution in the style of writing nonfiction, and this anthology contains some of the best writers who emerged during that turbulent era. Their influence is still felt today.

A Treasury of Great Reporting, edited by Louis L. Snyder and Richard B. Morris (Simon and Schuster)
The best reporting from the sixteenth century to today, including work from Defoe, Dickens, Kipling, Hemingway and hundreds more.

The World of Jimmy Breslin (Viking)
One of the pioneers of the "new journalism."

Armies of the Night, by Norman Mailer (Signet)
The classic account of the march on the Pentagon, which many consider the best reporting Mailer ever did.

The Best of Plimpton, by George Plimpton (Atlantic Monthly Press)
Best known for participatory journalism (he played football to write *Paper Lion*, baseball to write *Out of My League*), he is also a fine writer of profiles and essays about all aspects of contemporary life.

The Best of Robert Benchley, by Robert Benchley (Avanel)
The finest humor writing of one of our best and most beloved writers.

More in Sorrow, by Wolcott Gibbe (Henry Holt)
If you've never encountered this great *New Yorker* critic, sati-

rist and humorist, see if you can track down this out-of-print classic.

Talking Woman, by Shana Alexander (Dell)
Brilliant reporting and commentary from one of the wittiest and wisest critics of our times.

The Mother Tongue: English and How It Got That Way, by Bill Bryson (Morrow)
A delightfully humorous and thorough account of the origins of the language we speak—and write.

The Autobiography of Mark Twain, edited by Charles Neider (HarperCollins)
Twain never actually wrote an autobiography, but this chronological collection of his best essays and reporting is the next best thing. Much of it reads as if it had been written yesterday.

Getting Even (Random House) and *Without Feathers* (Ballantine), by Woody Allen
Best known as a movie actor and director, he is also one of the cleverest writers of contemporary humor.

The Lives of a Cell: Notes of a Biology Watcher, by Lewis Thomas (Bantam)
If you want to write about science, this is the man to learn from.

Dispatches, by Michael Herr (Avon)
Not only the best book written about the Vietnam War, but one of the best accounts ever written about any war.

Reporting, by Lillian Ross (Dodd, Mead)
Another great *New Yorker* profiler and reporter, Ross includes her classic portrait of Hemingway.

Poison Penmanship: The Gentle Art of Muckraking, by Jessica Mitford (Vintage)
One of the very best contemporary investigative reporters reprints her major pieces and tells how she got them.

In Cold Blood, by Truman Capote (Random House)
The first, and probably the best, of the great true crime sagas.

This prize-winning book paved the way for hundreds to follow.

Fame and Obscurity, by Gay Talese (Ivy Books)
Early, and unsurpassed, articles from a master of modern journalism, author of such later bestsellers as *Honor Thy Father* and *Unto the Sons*.

The Years With Ross, by James Thurber (Amereon Limited)
Not only a chronicle of the early years at *The New Yorker* and a profile of its erratic but brilliant editor, but a book that tells much about being a writer.

Hiroshima, by John Hersey (Bantam)
An understated and searingly effective report on the horror of modern war. I may have overused the word "classic," but this one definitely is.

This list leaves out countless books that I have enjoyed and learned from, but these are the works that I will continue to read as long as I continue to write, and probably longer.

INDEX

More Great Books
For Magazine Writers!

Queries and Submissions—Looking for proven strategies for writing attention-grabbing query letters? This guide has an abundance of ideas, covering topics from formatting and targeting letters to deciding when a query letter is unnecessary. *#10426/$15.99/176 pages*

The Complete Guide to Magazine Article Writing—You'll write articles that are clear, focused, effective and best of all, salable, with the practical explanations and easy-to-follow instructions in this comprehensive guide. *#10369/$17.99/304 pages*

The 30-Minute Writer: How to Write and Sell Short Pieces—This guide shows you the best approach for writers who can't snatch more than a few minutes at a time. Includes the types of pieces best suited for "stop and go" writing. *#10350/$17.95/224 pages*

Writing Articles From the Heart: How to Write & Sell Your Life Experiences—Holmes gives you heartfelt advice and inspiration on how to get your personal essay onto the page. You'll discover how to craft a story to meet your needs, and those of your readers. *#10352/$16.99/176 pages*

Research and Writing Handbook—This all-in-one guide delivers great advice on everything from choosing a salable topic, to conducting quality research, to writing a knock-out piece. You'll also get the rundown on library research, copyright regulations and more. *#70091/$18.95/272 pages/paperback*

1996 Writer's Market—This edition brings you over 4,000 listings of buyers of freelance work—their names, addresses, submission requirements, contact persons and more! Plus, helpful articles and interviews with top professionals make this your most essential writing resource. *#10432/$27.99/1008 pages*

The Writer's Digest Handbook of Magazine Article Writing—This handbook is a valuable guide to every type of magazine article writing, featuring more than 35 chapters of writing amd marketing instruction. Practical instructions are included to guide you through the development, proposal and manuscript preparation process. *#10171/$12.95/248 pages/paperback*

How to Write Irresistible Query Letters—Don't shortchange your idea with a lukewarm query! Cool shows how to select a strong slant, hook an editor with a tantalizing lead, sell yourself as the expert for the job and more. *#10146/$10.95/136 pages/paperback*

Writing for Money—Discover where to look for writing opportunities—and how to make them pay off. You'll learn how to write for magazines, newspapers, radio and TV, newsletters, greeting cards and a dozen other hungry markets! *#10425/$17.99/256 pages*